REALISTIC RAILWAY MODELLING

Steam
Locomotives

To Bob Wills – 'Gentleman Bob' –
who made a realistic loco stud possible for a
generation of modellers.

Published in February 2013

British Library Cataloguing in Publication Data:
A catalogue record for this book is available
from the British Library

ISBN 978 1 84425 636 5

Library of Congress catalog card number 2012940366

Published by Haynes Publishing,
Sparkford, Yeovil, Somerset BA22 7JJ, UK
Tel: 01963 442030 Fax: 01963 440001
Int. tel: +44 1963 442030 Int. fax: +44 1963 440001
Email: sales@haynes.co.uk
Website: www.haynes.co.uk

Haynes North America Inc.
861 Lawrence Drive, Newbury Park, California 91320, USA

Printed in the USA by Odcombe Press LP,
1299 Bridgestone Parkway, La Vergne, TN 37086

Author's note on illustrations

With a few specifically identified exceptions, the
photographs used in this book were either taken by the
author or drawn from his extensive collection of railway
postcards and other photographs. Where the
provenance of these is known, it has been given, but a
very large number of the prints have been acquired
piecemeal over more than four decades, thus are devoid
of any particulars and are of unknown origin. These are
identified simply as being from the 'Author's collection'.
There's not a lot else one can do, really!

Acknowledgements

Thanks are due, as usual, to many people without
whose input this book would not have been possible. So
a big thank-you to Andy McCallum and Andrew Duncan
for allowing me to highjack their loco projects for my
own ends as well as for much practical help, and to
Simon de Souza, Terry Cole, Henry Tasker and Don
Leeper for the loan of models for photography. Bob
Wills gave me access to his archives and the fabled
Finecast Showcase, as well as providing much
background for my historical ramblings. Prototype
information was gleaned from Graham Warburton and
Alex Hodson, among others. Tim Shackleton provided
inspiration and ideas, and I must also acknowledge the
sound grounding in matters both prototypical and
practical the youthful Rice received from the late John
Edgson. The mistakes, on the other hand, are all my
own work…

Steam
Locomotives

Iain Rice

CONTENTS

INTRODUCTION

For most railway modellers, the locomotive lies at the heart of their interest in the hobby. Indeed, there are many enthusiasts – particularly those inclined towards the larger scales – whose interest extends no further. For them the acquisition or construction of a collection of miniatures of their favourite locomotives is the entire extent of their modelling involvement. They possess no trains for their engines to pull, no layout on which they could do so, and have no context for the choice of subject. They are quite content to let their mélange of prize exhibits sit, gleaming but immobile, in a display case – with maybe an occasional spin around the test-track at a club meeting from time-to-time by way of exercise. This is fine as the hobby has ever been a catholic and wide-ranging pastime. However, this book is not for the locomotive *collector*.

No, this is very much a work concerned with model locomotives as part of the convincing depiction of the overall railway scene in miniature. My concern here is the model locomotive *in context* – that is, on a layout, where the dictates of authenticity mean that it not only has to look the part, but also be able to act it as well. So this is a book about assembling a locomotive stud that is, above all, *realistic*. This is realistic as to context (the right loco for location, period and task), realistic as to performance and, of course, realistic in appearance, both as individual models and as a homogenous part of the overall model.

The ultimate source of realism in all railway modelling lies in fidelity to the prototype – in this case, the steam railway in its everyday working guise. This subject is now very much a matter of history, something that my generation of modellers (post-Second World War baby-boomers) were the last to know first-hand. There are many modellers today who, attracted by steam power as encountered on 'heritage'

lines and by the authenticity and sophistication of current RTR productions, set out to model the steam-era railway without the benefit of background familiarity with the prototype. While there are a plethora of books out there dealing in great detail with the minutiae of railway history and engineering, there seems to be a lack of basic background information on steam locomotion pertinent to the needs of the would-be steam-era modeller new to the topic. Therefore this book includes a 'potted' introduction to the functioning of the steam locomotive and its historical relationship with the traffic being worked.

This successful marrying-together of accurate model trains with their settings, with everything replicated to a high but consistent standard of detail and authenticity, has long been the 'trump card' of 4mm:1ft scale; a pragmatic virtue that has ensured its continued status as Britain's most popular modelling size. As such, it also offers by far the widest range of options for assembling a truly authentic loco stud (or fleet): RTR (ready-to-run) models, RTR rebuilds and hybrids, white metal, cast-resin, etched brass and composite kits, and scratch-built models – all are grist to the 4mm mill. That is why this book centres on this scale.

Obviously, detailed consideration of so wide a range of constructional possibilities lies beyond the scope of a single modest volume. Given the choice and quality of the RTR locomotives now available in 4mm scale, it is possible to base a stud for most layout themes around such models, rounded out maybe with a kit or two. But not all RTR models are equal, and not every locomotive type or variant is available. So addressing deficiencies (cosmetic or mechanical), together with the reworking of models to follow specific prototypes, forms much of the meat of this book. Finally, attention is paid the important business of blending models from different origins together so that they look 'of a piece'.

All of this, hopefully, will provide a reasonable recipe for creating a realistic loco stud without either taking a lifetime, or breaking the bank.

OPPOSITE If, as I do, you model the railways of North Cornwall, you won't get far without one of these – the indispensable Southern N class Mogul, which worked so much of the traffic. This is a mildly modified Bachmann model, reconfigured to match (almost!) a specific prototype engine appropriate to the chosen area.

Iain Rice
2012

1 THE MODEL LOCO STUD: A LOOK BACK

Part of the Little Western's extensive loco stud.

King James I hand-built Fourmillaid, super-detail, Triang motor, Beeson wheels.

Lord of the Isles, hand-built Fourmillaid, super-detail, Triang motor, Beeson wheels.

The Pirate (Atlantic), Fourmillaid, semi-detail, Pittman DC60.

Cory Hall, self-built, semi-detail, Hewitt & Gosden motor.

No 5200 2-8-0T, self-built, semi-detail, Hewitt & Gosden motor.

No 3576 0-4-2T, built by Hewitt & Gosden, semi-detail, Zenith Mark IV motor.

No 4600 4-4-2T, built by Hewitt & Gosden semi-detail, Hewitt & Gosden motor.

No 2846 2-8-0, built by Roche, semi-detail, Zenith 004 motor, Beeson wheels.

No 2408 0-6-0 Dean, built by Hewitt & Gosden re-motored with Triang.

No 4304 Mogul, hand-built by Fourmillaid.

Rebuilt Royal Scot *Border Regiment*, by Fourmillaid.

Midland 0-6-0T, cast body by K's on Hornby chassis.

Stroudley 'Terrier', by Messrs K's.

Collett '14xx' class, by Messrs K's.

LSWR P class 0-6-0T from Wills kit.

GER J69 from Wills kit.

Stanier 8F, rebuilt from Hornby to scale standards.

Fleischmann 0-6-0T converted to EM – a present from Germany!

Baldwin 0-6-0. American by Tenshodo converted to EM.

'Merchant Navy' *Royal Mail* rebuilt by owner from Graham Farish body with new chassis.

Hornby 2-6-4T, converted to EM.

Future plans include a 4-4-0 Armstrong 'Gooch'.

ABOVE *The loco list – in this case, a truly star-studded example, that for Jim Russell's EM-gauge 'Little Western' railway, an iconic layout of the 1960s. Many of these models were '200-pointers', built by the likes of Guy Williams. Taken from the pages of the* Railway Modeller *for July 1962.*

OPPOSITE *A scratch-built 'Lord Nelson' was just the sort of 'glamour' loco that most modellers of my generation aspired to place at the head of their loco list – even if their layout represented no more than some sleepy seaside branch line! This cracking 1960s-era EM model of No 853* Sir Richard Grenville *in 'Bulleid condition' – provenance unknown, unfortunately – forms the pride of my collection of vintage models.*

Time was – a mere half-century or so since, when spotty schoolboy Rice first embarked on this noble hobby – when a key component of every layout-description article that appeared in the popular model railway press was the 'List of Locos'. Usually placed at the end of the piece, the loco list was the key to status in the model railway world (and the bit of the article you always read first!). The length of the list was paramount, of course; we schoolboys were little in awe of lists a mere half-dozen locos long; a column was OK, half-a-page definitely impressive. Next in importance came the featured prototypes, where the ooh-gosh emphasis was definitely on glamour rather than utility. Lastly came the origins of the individual models, a provenance which earned most of the status points: out-of-the-box Triang, one point; custom-built by Beeson or scratch-built by Stubbs, a couple of hundred…

These lists were usually structured the same way: express passenger classes listed first, followed by lesser passenger and mixed traffic types, then passenger tank engines and (rare!) heavy goods engines, with general-purpose 0-6-0 tender or tank locos and shunting engines (if any) bringing up the rear. The more top-heavy the list, the more envy-points it earned among the denizens of form 4b! With provenance, too, there was a definite pecking-order, starting with those 'one-point' mass-produced efforts by Triang or Hornby-Dublo ('proprietary' models, they were called back then) and advancing through rarer, upmarket RTR products like Farish to 'scaled-up' proprietary models, and thence to the ranks of limited-production 'scale models' and locos built from kits.

Finally came hand-built models from the benches of the leading amateurs and those bespoke custom-built jobs by a top 'name' builder; the peak of the aspirational pile. On the way up, extra status points could be earned for such things as 'scale' wheels, 'super-detail' (whatever *that* was!), screw couplings, 'engraved' plates and a custom paint job. The vast majority of the locomotives thus classified were to 4mm scale for 00 gauge; only a few god-like creatures – stern, skilled and probably from Manchester – could append the hallowed letters 'EM' to their lists. 'TT3' and '2mm finescale' were little-known backwaters, while 'scale' 0 gauge was for Men of Means, late-middle-aged and invariably, it seemed, pipe-smoking. As for N gauge – well, that hadn't been invented yet!

ABOVE *Here's one of those fabled 'Little Western' locos as it exists today. No 5968* Cory Hall *was scratch-built by Jim Russell himself in 1946 and reworked in the mid-1960s. Charming – but nowhere near as good as today's RTR Bachmann model!*

Anatomy of a loco list

I'm a great believer in taking an occasional glance in the historical rear-view mirror of railway modelling to see where we've come from. I therefore thought it worth starting this essay with a quick look back at the development of the typical

ABOVE *Very much in the pre-war tradition of wild approximations were Trix, in spite of their upper-crust connection with Bassett-Lowke. This gruesome object was palmed off on an undiscriminating public as a replica of a Southern N class Mogul! Such crude toys had no value to the scale enthusiast of the day – which ultimately sealed Trix's fate.*

BELOW *The Hornby-Dublo N2 of 1937 epitomises the uneasy transition from out-and-out toy to semi-scale model that marked out the advent of mass-production British 00. Although, as seen here, things were still pretty laissez-faire: a change of décor and a token brass safety valve were deemed sufficient to transmute an LNER 0-6-2T into a GWR '56xx'!*

model loco stud. It is surprising how many echoes of tradition you find in the way people put together a collection today! Such a historical perspective also puts into context the state of the modern RTR art and the origins, status and value of the various non-RTR options.

The sources and subjects of the 4mm scale model locomotives available at this period (we're talking the later 1950s and the liberated '60s, for all those too young to remember) make a fascinating study – and a stark reminder of how well off for choice and refinement we are nowadays.

The first thing to make clear is that historically there was an enormous gulf in quality and realism between the mass-produced RTR 'proprietary' models and the best professional, or amateur-built 'scale' models. Most proprietary equipment of the day was conceived, manufactured and sold very much as a *toy*; this was, after all, the age when a train-set was a longed-for Christmas or birthday gift and most schoolboys had a model railway of some sort. It was also a time when railways loomed far larger in the national consciousness than they do today, and taking an interest in trains was a perfectly normal and natural thing to do, instead of a reason for calling in the psychiatrist.

This widespread interest led, in turn, to a true mass market for toy trains; production-run figures for many popular proprietary models of this period are mind-boggling by modern standards, often running to five or even six figures. The Hornby-Dublo N2 0-6-2T is generally reckoned to hold the model locomotive crown, with a total production in excess of a quarter of a million examples. That so many survive (just look on eBay!) is a testament to the toughness of this iconic toy, which even rates a passing mention in a John le Carré spy story (*The Secret Pilgrim*).

In the world of the toy-makers' product-planning departments, however, factors such as robustness, ease of manufacture, use and repair, a competitive first cost, and commonality of components came a long way before fidelity to prototype. It has long struck me as something of a miracle, therefore, that so many of these early 00 mass-produced models were as accurate to scale as they were – especially the original Hornby-Dublo locos, conceived in the late 1930s when scale models of any description or size were rarities. A Dublo A4 or 'Duchess' was, driving-wheel diameter aside, dimensionally pretty well on the nose as well as being faithful in outline and surprisingly well-detailed. Although their initial 'Princess' was a notable runt, Triang's 1951 'Jinty' was also surprisingly true to its subject – although some later stalwarts of their range were somewhat more approximate. Of the

ABOVE *The other iconic proprietary model tank loco of the pioneering RTR ranges: Triang's 'Jinty' of 1951 – which is about when this rather warped specimen dates. Again, quite recognisable and surprisingly close to scale, it formed the basis of many a 'scale' loco stud. At least it came in only one, authentic, livery: BR black!*

prototypical veracity of the products of 'Trix Twin', on the other hand, the less said the better!

The other great bugbears of these proprietary models so far as the serious or 'scale' enthusiast was concerned, were the

wheel and track standards used. These ranged from 'steamroller' (Trix Twin) through 'coarse' (Triang) to 'just about acceptable' (Hornby Dublo). None of them came anywhere near the putative BRMSB (British Railway Modelling Standards Bureau) 'Scale 00' profile, and none of them would thus run through turnouts – such as Peco 'Individulay' or ABC 'Chairway' – built to the then-current 'scale' track standards, using proper point-crossings with fixed wing-rails and functional check-rails.

Proprietary models were intended to run on proprietary track of the same brand as the trains; deliberate incompatibility was a foundation-plank of the 'big three' maker's marketing strategy. If you wanted to 'mix and match', it was either the banal compromise of 'universal' track (one size fits none…) or, infinitely preferable, re-wheeling to the common BRMSB 'scale' standard. Fortunately, it was perfectly possible to fit Romford or Hambling's 'scale' wheels to a Dublo or Triang chassis. (Trix was a complete lost cause in the scale stakes, at least until their 12V dc range appeared in the later 1950s.) Add a few extra details and your re-wheeled proprietary loco could merit the description 'scaled up'. Just such ameliorated RTR offerings were the foundation of many a 4mm scale loco stud of the era.

ABOVE *A typical scale layout loco of the 1960s – a worked-over Trix '56xx' with new, finer handrails, the odd bit of extra detail, and a passable repaint into post-1956 BR(W) unlined green. Still not very 'scale' with those clunky Trix wheels and, as was usual, everything all bright and shiny. The Peco couplings were the scale norm of the time.*

BELOW *The revolution; by the standards of 1958, when it appeared, the Hornby-Dublo 8F 2-8-0 was a full-blown scale model – accurate in dimensions and outline, well-detailed, and possessed of a powerful, smooth-running mechanism that was easy to re-wheel to BRMSB standards. The release of this model – together with the similarly endowed GW 'Castle' – as seen here – marked the dawn of the sophisticated RTR model and the death of the simple toy.*

ABOVE *The intrinsic rightness of the Hornby-Dublo 'Castle' is borne out by this EM conversion, which I carried out in the early 1980s. The Dublo body has had surprisingly little done to it; a Wills cast chassis with a prototypical bar-framed bogie and scale (Sharman) wheels help – but those are still the Dublo cylinders, albeit with lost-wax slidebars and crossheads. The rest is down to refinement of the body casting, new buffers, scale handrails and extra detail – all standard fare for the time. The tender was by Wills, from the 'Hall' kit – more due to the lack of a Dublo tender than any intrinsic defect in the latter.*

BELOW *A Stewart-Reidpath 0-6-0T. The standard six-coupled mechanism was surprisingly refined and had very nice BRMSB scale wheels. The body casting came in two variants: Belpaire, as here, or 'plain'. You added fittings and paint to choice, but the result – however you chose to describe it – was a long way from being a scale model of anything!*

ABOVE *Back in the 1950s, the Gaiety GWR '57xx' pannier tank was just about the only 'scale' 0-6-0T you could buy that bore any resemblance to a prototype – and then not over-much! This example has been fitted with a Jamieson turned-brass chimney, a popular upgrade. The slab-framed mechanism is the De Luxe Romford version, which came with a five-pole Phantom motor.*

BELOW *One of the best-detailed and most accurate of the proprietary cast loco bodies available in the 1950s was Kirdon's version of the evergreen N2 0-6-2T, which not only ticked all the dimensional boxes, but did a good job of catching the character of the prototype. The (factory?) paint job is also pretty nice!*

RIGHT *The cream of the scale cast-loco crop, and a great rarity: a Rowell kit for the Stanier 'Duchess' – a considerable notch up from the Dublo version in both scale accuracy and detailing. This complete specimen – started, but only to the tune of some rather poor paint – has Hamblings wheels (with alternate Romford drivers – quartering problems?), Romford motor and gears, and a set of Dublo cylinders and valve gear. Faced with the very basic DIY Walschaerts valve gear provided (the bits below the cast cylinders), this last ruse was a popular ploy with loco builders of the day.*

BELOW *The KMR LMS Compound was one of the better scale offerings of its day, even if it ran like a dog on the scent: nose down, tail high! However, leaving the outside cylinders off did not make a 2P of it!*

The 'scale' scene

It was not just the mass-produced proprietary toys that were a bit iffy in the fidelity department, either. Many models sold as 'scale' were at best approximate and often laughably inaccurate. 'Freelance' models (models following no actual prototype) were still alive and kicking in 1960, even if not as widespread as they had been in the 1930s and '40s. Stewart-Reidpath, for instance, had long peddled a 'generic' 0-6-0T – which gave you a bare and basic cast body which you then tricked-out with your own choice of boiler fittings to 'regionalise' it to the requirements of your layout. Stick on a brass safety valve, and bingo – you were a GWR modeller!

Even where a model did lay claim to a prototype, things were still pretty lax: KMR would sell you an LMS 'Compound' – a model that was basically in the ballpark dimensionally and quite recognisable as its subject, but they would equally-happily sell you the same thing minus the outside cylinders and claim it as a '2P' – to which it bore but a distant passing resemblance… Even such best-sellers as Gaiety's iconic cast-body GWR '57xx' pannier tank – pretty much the only 'scale' 0-6-0T you could buy off the peg – were not much to write home about in the fidelity or detail stakes.

In fact, the quality and sophistication of the sort of thing being sold at the economy end of the 'scale' market – the territory inhabited by the likes of KMR, Kirdon or Gaiety – was little better than Hornby-Dublo at best, and often nowhere as good. Loco bodies were usually relatively crude one or two-piece castings in Mazak (zinc-aluminium alloy, as used by Dublo) or, worse still, in 'type metal', a podgy lead-tin alloy whose chief virtue was its weight. These castings usually sat on mechanisms of traditional Ahern design: slab frames, the motor driving the centre axle by worm gear, and plain drilled rail for coupling and connecting rods. Such claim as these

models laid to the 'scale' description came by virtue of their Romford 'BRMSB' wheels – flangeless centre drivers on six-coupleds, nickel-tyred insulated wheels on one side only, plain Mazak on the other, and a solitary pair of wipers for pick-up. This was scarcely a recipe for either realism or refined running.

Not quite bespoke…

Even if you went up a notch from the cast-body models and looked at the batch-built off-the-peg offerings of the established 'trade' firms like Hambling's, Eames or W&H models, things were not a great deal better. True, the superstructures were assembled from stamped and formed sheet-metal parts and were usually dimensionally 'there or thereabouts' – but the mechanical fare was all-but identical to Gaiety *et al*. Neither were these models a great deal more authentic, due largely to the extensive use of standard 'one version fits all' components that were often somewhat approximate.

There were generic LMS and GW cylinder castings, LMS and 'the rest' smokebox fronts, a modest range of turned chimneys and buffers, and a basic stamped-out set of Walschaerts valve gear. The detailing and finish, however, were markedly superior to the cast jobs, with wire handrails and pipework, bent-metal steps and such niceties as buffer beam vacuum hoses. Paint-wise, the simplified liveries were nicely executed in spray-painted cellulose decorated with varnish-fix transfers. Such models were undoubtedly quite an investment, with prices typically four or five times an equivalent Hornby-Dublo model: say, £15–£20 apiece, when £12 was a week's wage for the likes of Rice.

The range of styles available off this particular peg was never that large either, and was almost inevitably biased somewhat towards the usual passenger classes and larger 'modern' prototypes; lesser engines hardly figured. As I recall, Hamblings' most popular offerings were the LMS rebuilt 'Royal Scot', the stalwart 'Black 5' and the evergreen SR 'Schools' class. Most *useful* were a bevy of mixed-traffic 2-6-4Ts, including the LMS Stanier and Fairburn types and the LNER Thompson L1 – the latter painted green, of course – and, praise be, the ubiquitous 4F and LNER J39. However, the majority of the subjects offered were Walschaerts-fitted engines; the wily Belgian's syncopated collection of rods and cranks has always fascinated modellers, but has long been reckoned a daunting subject to tackle. Hence, one supposes, the traditional readiness to pay someone else to do it for you!

If you wanted a less-obvious model locomotive at this sort of quality level – a workaday goods engine say, or something older and smaller – you could have it built to 'special order' by the same firms to a similar specification, at a cost running only a pound or two more than the off-the-peg offerings. But the possibilities in this direction were limited by the somewhat-

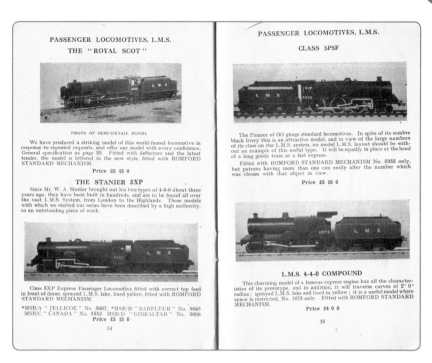

ABOVE *A page spread from the Hamblings catalogue for 1957, showing the inevitable selection of LMS types: £5 15s 0d may not seem much for a hand-built metal model, but it was all-but a week's wage at the time! Ten years later, when I worked (briefly!) at Cecil Court, these prices had more than doubled.*

restricted range of 'standard' fittings available; no custom turnings in *this* price bracket! This often led to such models having a 'not quite right' look about them. One recalls anomalies such as an otherwise-passable SR/LSWR M7 0-4-4T sporting an LMS 'Jinty' chimney, presumably the 'nearest available'. Nevertheless, both off-the-peg and custom-built models from these sources were rated pretty high on the status scale, decidedly superior to anything with a body in plastic or Mazak.

The kit-built option

Locos built from kits were a bit infra-dig in 1960. 'Serious' model railways were definitely seen as a preserve of the bowler-hat-and-rolled-umbrella brigade – not the sort of chap who would want to get his hands dirty wrestling with files, drills or soldering-irons while battling the somewhat-daunting contents of a Jamieson box. Far better to pop into Cecil Court or New Cavendish Street and see what the fellows at Hambling's or W&H had in their showcases…

No, kits were for bank clerks or tradesmen or engineering apprentices – and truth to tell, you *needed* a fair bit of engineering nous to make much headway with a Jamieson – a collection of very basic bent-metal stampings, the odd bit of strip and wire and a handful of cast or turned fittings, with two meaty slabs of brass and some drilled rail for a chassis. True, there were earnest pullover-toting young men out there who could, by some process akin to alchemy, transform such base metal into a Gold Medal at the Model Engineer exhibition. But for most modellers, such a feat was on a par

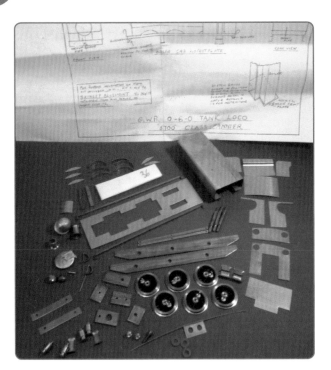

LEFT *Kits were for experts – and here's why! This is a Jamieson '57xx' – a somewhat-basic collection of stamped and formed sheet-metal parts, a pair of $^1/_{16}$th-inch slab brass frames, plain drilled rail for coupling rods, and a meagre handful of cast and turned fittings. Instructions were a single side of hand-scrawled sketch, and any surface detail was down to the builder. The set of Hamblings wheels shown were not included in the kit. Well-assembled, the model was an advance on a cast-body Gaiety '57', but not by much!*

BELOW *Take enough trouble over a Jamieson kit, and you could produce a pretty classy model. This taper-boiler 'Royal Scot' was very nicely built c1960 and well painted in LMS crimson lake. It is quite fully detailed – at least, above the footplate – and is powered by a Triang X04 motor. A loco like this scored high on the kudos point scale – 120 or so.*

BOTTOM *Inhabiting much the same part of the stratosphere as a good Jamieson were scratch-built models by competent amateurs, such as this racy-looking ex-GER B12/3 class 4-6-0, which I judge from the ingredients (early-pattern Romford wheels and gears, and a Romford standard motor with a lowish serial number) to date from the mid-1950s. Not quite top-hole, but full of charm!*

with a one-finger pianist sight-reading a Liszt Transcendental Study. Kits were for *experts*.

All that changed at the Model Railway Club's Easter Show in 1957, when K's introduced the hobby's first glue-it and screw-it together *white metal* model locomotive kit, the immortal GWR '14xx', which came complete with wheels, gears and motor, yet cost no more than a mid-sized Jamieson without the mechanicals. Not only that, but it could be assembled by the greenest novice in a couple of evenings on a tray in the parlour. Building the Jamieson took a proper workbench and toolkit – plus *months* of dedicated toil in celibate bed-sit, stoop-shouldered attic or Siberian shed. Wills joined the white metal-loco fray in the autumn of 1959 with the sophisticated but demanding GER J69 'Buckjumper'– then abruptly switched tack with their second introduction, the GWR '94xx' pannier body, which was designed to fit over an off-the-shelf Triang 'Jinty' chassis. Now that truly *was* a loco kit for everyman; so long as you could squeeze the nether regions of a tube of glue, you could – in theory – build it.

The pioneering Jamieson kit range – which had its origins in the late 1940s – had kicked off predictably enough with the usual express-passenger candidates, but soon branched out into secondary passenger power and mixed traffic types, followed by some truly useful general-purpose engines that included the LMS 'Jinty' and 4F, GWR '57xx' pannier and the LNER J39. When the white metal kit-makers got going a decade later, they were initially limited by the modest mould size of the early centrifugal casting machines – which meant that rather than rushing into large passenger classes, they concentrated on the smaller prototypes.

K's initial '14xx' was classic branch line power, the J72 that followed it was an archetypal shunting engine. The Wills 'Buck', by contrast, was a decidedly oddball choice; as offered, it was a pure pre-grouping GER suburban passenger engine. It all, apparently, came down to technical feasibility and the fact that Bob Wills rather liked the look of it! The '94xx' was GW and a modern general-purpose type although – being a 'red' engine with limited route availability – not the most useful of prototypes to pick, but people weren't that fussy in 1960! Anyway, within a few months it was joined by the GWR 2251 Collett goods – a

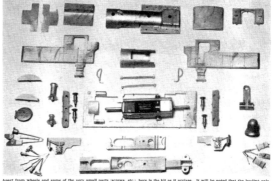

ABOVE Model Railway News – *ever the 'serious' modeller's magazine – regarded the introduction of the first white metal locomotive kit, the K's '14xx', as so significant that it took the unprecedented step of devoting a double-page spread in the June 1957 issue to reviewing it (enthusiastically!).*

BELOW *An early introduction in Wills highly successful range of body-only kits was the LBSCR E5 class 0-6-2T kit to fit the Hornby-Dublo R1 0-6-0 chassis. This is the original showcase model, dating from 1961. A pretty esoteric choice of prototype – but it just so happened that Bob Wills was living in Woldingham at the time!*

LEFT Both the Wills and K's ranges were a bit uneven as to quality and fidelity, but every now and then, either could produce a real corker of a kit, a cut above the run-of-the-mill. One such was K's '44xx', which was not only spot-on accurate, but surprisingly refined. Take a look at the tankside rivet detail and the fit and profile of the safety valve bonnet. This is Ken Northwood's '44' from the North Devonshire Railway. Ken's locos were never bulled-up in the popular fashion, but they all ran well. No 4400 has a whopping flywheel, visible in the cab.

LEFT The LNER J39 0-6-0, one of the stalwarts of the Wills range, and a very typical 'layout' loco of the 1960s and '70s. This one used the Triang 0-6-0 'Jinty' chassis, here fitted with Romford wheels of the correct size. No, the LNER never painted a J39 in full passenger livery – but a lot of modellers did!

true all-rounder – and the trio of mixed-traffic Moguls, the SR 'Woolwich', the LNER K3 and the LMS 'Crab'. K's completed the Mogul quartet with their GW '43xx'. They also added the '57xx' pannier, 'Dean Goods' and '44xx' 'small Prairie' to thoroughly sew up the burgeoning 'GWR branch line' market.

Savile Row

When it came to the top of the traditional tree, the choice of prototype was, of course, effectively limitless as you would either be skilled enough to build it yourself, or rich enough to have a top-flight professional do it for you. Although, that said, it is surprising how rarely these big-buck commissions strayed beyond the obvious ranks of the major modern passenger classes (the Stanier 'Duchess' seemed to be top-of-the-pops) or pre-grouping glamour queens.

It was the amateurs who devoted their skill and effort into making high-quality models of everyday goods or tank

engines and similar lesser subjects. I suppose if you were laying out the price of a modest family car on a top-end bespoke model locomotive from Beeson, Miller-Swan, Roche or Fourmillaid, it was only natural to choose a 'star' subject for its 'ooh-gosh' value – and, more prosaically, for ease of re-sale should the Stock Market take an unwelcome nose-dive!

At this level, the highest of quality was a given. Be you rich or skilled enough, you need brook no compromise; not for you the world of 'near enough' – even in such traditionally difficult areas as authentic wheels. Why accept Romford's approximations when effort or cash could sit your loco on hand-made scale wheels of impeachable appropriate diameter and conformity in matters of spoke numbers, rim profiles and crank configuration? And why compromise around an off-the-shelf motor (even a Pitman) when you could have a 'Manchester Can', complete with ball-race bearings and a balanced armature? As for boiler fittings – custom turned, exactly to scale and hand-seated to a fag-paper

LEFT Crème-de-la-crème: this exquisite EM gauge GWR Dean Single dating from the mid-1950s, is believed to be the work of F.J. Roche, very much one of the 'Savile Row' builders of the period. Wheels and fittings are Beeson, the mechanism by Zenith. This model probably cost the thick end of £50 when a new three-bedroom house was £2,500!

fit, naturally. Detail? Complete to the last rivet, bracket and lubricator-pipe. Paintwork? The work of a true artist, spray finished in the finest cellulose lacquers specially mixed to match the chosen livery, fully hand-lined and decked out with custom-engraved name and number plates.

These models were about as far removed from a one-point Triang model as a Bentley 'Continental' was from a side-valve Ford 'Pop'. They were quite without the experience of the vast majority of modellers, glimpsed – from a distance, with bated breath – at the Manchester or Westminster shows, or wondered at in the pages of the *Model Railway News*. With the tools, kits and components of the day, even a competent 'kitchen table' modeller couldn't hope to get within hailing distance of the standard exhibited by the cream of this particular crop. To do that, you needed a well-equipped engineering shop with a lathe and a pillar drill and preferably a milling machine as well; plus, of course, the skill and know-how to use them. Unsurprisingly, a lot of the leading 'amateur' practitioners of the loco-building art had formal engineering backgrounds; know-nothing schoolboys like Rice weren't in with a ghost of a chance of emulating their achievements.

The loco kit comes of age

The advent of the popular, accessible loco kit in the 1960s changed for ever the make-up and quality of the average loco list. Not only did the choice of subjects available burgeon, but loco kits as a breed rapidly evolved to become a great deal more sophisticated, user-friendly and far more authentic. Also, the range of components, tools and constructional aids available to help you build them expanded dramatically in scope and quality. Eventually, this process arrived at the point where a halfway competent modeller – armed with some decent hand tools and a precision instrument soldering-iron, and possessed of a top-flight kit, together with a set of proper scale wheels and a smooth-running 'can' motor – *could* produce a result to stand comparison with the paragons of that earlier era.

If production engineering is all about making for five bob (25p) what any darn' fool can make for a pound, model railway kit engineering is about coming up with a way of incorporating all the detail and refinement achieved by the best craftsmen in a form that Joe Average modeller, replete with five thumbs, can get to grips with. To a certain extent, the white metal kit achieved this – but the limitations of that particular manufacturing process meant that compromises had to be made on some matters of detail and in the form and size of the castings. In particular, the need for components to be robust enough for handling and to allow the metal to flow freely in the mould put a lower limit on the thickness of the cast parts, which led in many instances to cast-kit locos having a slightly 'chunky' look about them. Although the white metal casting process had good potential for incorporation of surface detail like rivets and beadings, the softness of the metal and the need to remove casting feeds and 'flash', clean up mould part lines, and fill joins made much of this detail vulnerable to damage during construction.

True, Bob Wills did address many of these problems with some of his later 'Hi-Fi kits' – most notably the SR 'Schools' class 4-4-0, the GWR 'Castle' and the lovely trio of SECR Wainwright engines – the D class 4-4-0, the C class 0-6-0 goods and the H class 0-4-4T. Not only were the patterns for these models of the

highest order for dimensional accuracy, authenticity and full detail, but the actual castings were far more refined. Taking advantage of experience gained with earlier kits, employing new grades of mould rubber, and using the best quality metal, it proved possible to produce components that were much more delicate, with thinned visible edges and very accurate joints. Careful quality control ensured an absolute minimum of flash, and the better closing fit of the new moulds reduced part lines. But good though these refined white metal models were, they still could not *quite* match the crispness, delicacy and realism of the best models built the traditional way from sheet metal. To achieve that look in a kit took a different manufacturing process: photo etching.

The etched revolution

The loco kit incorporating surface-etched detail actually has a far longer history than most people realise. The first such models appeared c1949 from the firm of Sayer-Chaplin of Ipswich, who employed printer's block-making techniques to manufacture sets of 'engraved' locomotive parts. These were fairly chunky brass sheets incorporating filigree detail such as rivets and beadings, together with component outlines and join lines. However, you still had to cut all these parts out the hard way with a piercing saw and files, and form them to shape as needed, just as for a scratch-built model. In the hands of the skilled, the results could be mighty impressive, especially in the matter of crisp, consistent, scale-sized, evenly spaced rivets; only the very best hand-builders could match Sayer-Chaplin's rivets!

BELOW An early encounter with an early etched kit. According to my albums, I built this 00 Mallard 'Barnum' in 1979 – pretty much when the kit first appeared. Some of the etched overlays were very thin, which is why No 3223 has a cockled smokebox wrapper; too much heat!

ABOVE The grand-daddy of all etched loco kits: Ken Northwood built Eaton Mascot Hall *using Sayer-Chaplin engraved plates; just look at the tender riveting to see what the fuss was all about! What with computer-designed etched kits and hi-fi plastic mouldings, we take this sort of detail for granted nowadays; in 1951, it was sensational. The model was the top prize-winner at the Model Railway Club's Easter show that year.* Ken Northwood

However, the quality of the rest of the job – especially the all-important boiler fittings and the small matter of a mechanism – was entirely down to you. Not a kit, then; more a starting-point for a fairly demanding constructional exercise, a decided notch more advanced even than a Jamieson.

The first true photo-etched loco kit arrived from Mallard Models circa 1978, in the aristocratic shape of the GER 'Claud Hamilton' 4-4-0 in original slotted-valence form, swiftly followed by a trio of classic GWR types: the double-framed duo of 'Duke' 4-4-0 and 'Barnum' 2-4-0 together with the long-lived (and truly useful) 517 class 0-4-2T, ancestor of the '14xx'. These early Mallard kits were not perfect; a lack of location aids, together with the use of over-complex assemblies and multiple half-etched overlays, made them quite tricky to build. The mechanical design was also a bit lacking and the hand-drawn artwork occasionally wavered a bit, but the combination of fold-up assembly of the main structure, full surface detail on the overlays, and with all the tricky cutting-out done for you it was a very substantial step forward. Add on nice detail castings in white metal or lost-wax brass, a high degree of accuracy to prototype, ready compatibility with fine scale standards and plenty of potential for additional refinement, and the merely 'good' could readily be elevated to the 'exceptional'.

Not all early etched kits went the sophisticated Mallard route, mind you. Many were far more basic, the etching process

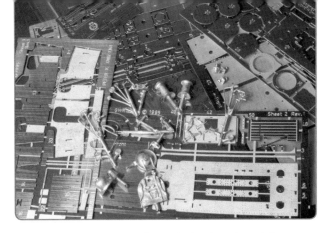

An example of a modern etched-and-cast brass fully detailed, 100 per cent-accurate fine scale 'super kit' – the GWR 1361 class 0-6-0ST from Peter K, now part of the Agenoria range. A kit like this is no sinecure to build, but it is capable of producing a model of the very highest quality.

ABOVE *A typical example of the sort of model that can be built from a modern mainstream etched or etched/composite kit: the LNWR Webb 2-4-0T radial tank or 'Chopper', from London Road Models. I originally designed this kit as part of my Riceworks range, which LRM now produce. It is not uncommon for such kits to 'change flags', which can make them confusing to track down sometimes! I built LNWR No 2251 a few years back, but Ian Rathbone did the lovely paint job.*

BELOW *Post-1975 it was 'Hornby Railways' and a move to much more authentic models and closer-to-scale wheels, with all the new tender locos using the Ringfield tender-drive mechanism. This called for a mighty coal load when it was concealed in a low-sided GWR 3,500-gallon tender! The rather toy-like 'bright and shiny' finish was also a characteristic of Hornby products of the era, but the basic body moulding of this '28xx' was fundamentally accurate, and it made a good basis for a scale model.*

being seen simply as a way of cutting the bits out rather than as a medium for adding detail. A lot of these lesser kits also fell down on fundamental accuracy, poor mechanical design and lack of proper use of fold-ups, alignment tabbing, and other tricks of the etching trade. There have been plenty of duff kits, both etched and cast, over the years! Eventually, the etching process started to cross-over into the white metal field, with firms like DJH going down the 'composite' route to produce kits using both manufacturing techniques: cast white metal for basic structure, boilers/fireboxes, cylinders and all the other 3-D bits, etchings for 'plate' components like cab and tender sides, footplate overlays, smoke deflectors and so on.

More recently, many of the makers of the contemporary high-end, uncompromised, fully detailed and fine scale-orientated 'super kits' have embraced this composite approach, using a combination of multi-layer etching, turned or lost-wax brass and cast white metal fittings with vacuum-assisted resin injection mouldings for things like boilers, to produce kits that have the potential to match – and maybe even possibly eclipse – the work of the very finest 'traditional' craftsman.

RTR: towards hi-fidelity

By the mid-1970s, the old order of 'proprietary' RTR models had withered and stagnated somewhat. Hornby-Dublo had keeled over in 1964, being bought out by rivals Triang – who promptly flogged the 'rival' Dublo two-rail range to Wrenn, who in turn kept on churning out the old stagers much as before, although with some jazzy livery alternatives. The Hornby *name*, however, was hi-jacked by Triang as a hyphenated appendix: Triang-Hornby.

The product range pedalled under this double-barrelled brand in the early-1970s was an odd mix, with the tired Triang old-timers from the 1950s jostling with newer (but still traditionally chunky-wheeled) models. The types offered encompassed some eclectic choices, such as the GWR 'Dean' single and Caledonian No 123. More down-to-earth were an LMS Ivatt Class 2 2-6-0, the GWR 'Hall', LNER B12 and SR 'King Arthur' 4-6-0s, an ex-LSWR M7 0-4-4T, a GWR '27xx' 0-6-0PT, and – of all things – an ex-NBR J83 0-6-0T. All of these models were somewhat approximate to varying degrees, and were still relatively unsophisticated both mechanically and in terms of realism and finish.

By 1975, things were changing – and for the better. The 'Triang' brand was quietly dropped and the newly revitalised Hornby Railways set off in a fresh direction with a 9F and a

ABOVE *Wrong-footed: Lima's unhappy entry into the British RTR steam loco market in the 1970s was out of step with the trend towards scale accuracy and refinement. This is their shot at the GW '45xx' 2-6-2T, which should have been a sure-fire winner, but not with a body badly distorted (much too high!) to accommodate a crude all-or-nothing 'pancake' motor, coarse-scale wheels, and that travesty of a chimney.*

'Mk 2' 'Britannia', the first of a range of far more authentic models powered by the new Ringfield tender-drive technology. Although these new models had wheel profiles that were still some way from anything that might be regarded as 'scale', they were a great deal more refined than the clunky Triang affairs of yore. And, for the first time, the

BELOW *One of the first really accurate and well-detailed RTR express passenger locos was Airfix's taper-boiler 'Rebuilt Scot', which set a new standard for detail and finish back in 1979, but all let down by the usual dire tender drive. This model still stacks up pretty well against Hornby's current version, which uses all-new tooling. More-refined handrails and finish, and a proper loco-powered chassis are the key improvements.*

Walschaerts was all there, while the body mouldings were pretty good – fundamentally accurate, reasonably well-detailed and generally quite refined, even if the paint finish was a bit 'in your face' bright-and-shiny. All-in-all, a considerable step in the 'scale model' direction and away from Triang's 'toy' roots, which was just as well, as dark competitive clouds were looming large on Hornby's horizon.

The storm duly broke in 1977, when three major players – Lima, Airfix and Palitoy – all waded into the fray with 'clean-sheet' ranges of 00 RTR models. Lima were wrong-footed, electing to sing off the same tired old hymn sheet as Triang-Hornby pre rebirth; their initial steam-outline offerings – a predictable 'King' and could-have-been-useful LNER J50 0-6-0T – were, if anything, even more lacklustre than traditional Margate fare.

By contrast, the Airfix and Palitoy offerings, produced in the new state-of-the-art plastic moulding facility set up by Kaders in Hong Kong, were very much *models* – and pretty good models at that! Airfix kicked off with a GW '61xx' 'large Prairie' and a BR Class 31 diesel, while Palitoy – sold under the Mainline brand – wowed the hobby with an absolutely delightful LNER J72 0-6-0T which was, by the standards of the day, a ready-to-run fine scale model. It came with correct-to-prototype all-flanged wheels conforming to the BRMSB norms, split-frame all-wheel pick-up and decent sectional coupling rods. The body moulding was also stunningly accurate and had neat, separately applied wire handrails and an exquisite paint finish. The only let-down was the cab-full of motor, a consequence of the complex mechanical design adopted by Palitoy. No matter; in all other respects, the Mainline J72 was simply leagues above the likes of a Hornby J83 or Lima J50.

The Hong Kong bonanza

Both the Airfix and Palitoy ranges expanded rapidly, with some delightful and iconic models appearing: Airfix gave us the N2 (again!) and, of course, the evergreen '14xx'. Their tender locos included a very presentable GWR 'Castle' and – at last – a realistic RTR version of the ubiquitous LMS 4F 0-6-0. Palitoy

produced a cracking LMS Stanier 'Jubilee', together with the GWR 2251 0-6-0 'Collett Goods' and '63xx' Churchward Mogul – both truly useful all-rounders.

Other prototypes which appeared included the rebuilt 'Royal Scot', the LNER B1 4-6-0, the GWR 'Dean Goods' and '57xx' pannier. About this time, 1979–80, the waters surrounding the Hong Kong production and UK marketing arrangements for many of these models started to get very muddy indeed. Disputes erupted as to who owned/had the rights to the various sets of tooling, while other brand names – Dapol and Replica Railways – appeared, selling exactly the same products.

At times, it was possible to buy an identical model from several different sources and in a variety of different packaging! I won't bore you with the ins-and-outs of all this complex commercial skulduggery, but eventually it all settled down when the American giant Bachmann (by then owned by Kaders, the actual manufacturer) stepped in and snapped up ailing Palitoy. This essentially meant that all of the former Mainline range ended up in the Bachmann stable, while the Airfix range migrated via Dapol to Hornby. Most of these models are still available in the current ranges of these makers, most with improved drivetrains, but a few are still in their original form.

Dodgy drivetrains

Unfortunately, those original drivetrains left something to be desired. Airfix's first tank locomotive offerings were conventional enough, with crude-but-chunky 5-pole motors and worm gear drive. With their tender locos, however, Airfix chose to go the tender-driven route, also then being pursued by Hornby – but with an all-plastic mechanism that was too feeble, too light and *much* too speedy. These flyweight tender mechs had all-plastic wheels with traction tyres – good for spreading dirt about the layout, if nothing else!

Electrical pick-up, however, was reliable enough, by wipers or plungers on the loco driving wheels, with a 'hard-wired' connection which meant the loco and tender were permanently coupled. Models equipped with this drive were usually fairly disappointing runners and could easily descend to the dire. The actual loco wheels had plastic centres – and not particularly authentic in matters of spokes, crank profiles and so on – with turned metal tyres to a profile which, while more refined than Hornby's, still wasn't to the BRMSB standards and so didn't really warrant the 'scale' description.

Palitoy, praise be, eschewed tender drive in favour of 'conventional' locomotive power for all their models – although of decidedly unconventional form. For reasons that are far from clear, they opted for a complex mechanical design that was, on the face of it, a far better bet than anything offered by Airfix or, come to that, Hornby. This was a split-frame set-up using two-part cast chassis blocks with cast-and-plated all-metal 'wheel-and-half-axle' assemblies, powered by a 'pancake' 3-pole motor driving through nylon spur gears. The actual wheels were decidedly superior – accurate representations of the prototype with correct cranks, spoke numbers and proper cast-in balance weights, and rims to BRMSB 'scale' dimensions.

This enticing chassis recipe – reminiscent of the highly rated Stewart-Reidpath products of the 1950s – proved, however, to have some rather undercooked ingredients and a

ABOVE AND BELOW *I have never quite made up my mind which of these two lack-lustre mechanism designs was the worst: Mainline's lumpy and under-cooked split-frame effort above, or Airfix's jack-rabbit tender drive below. Both suffered from rough-running 'pancake' motors and insufficient reduction in the all-spur gear-trains.*

Even with the cast ballast weight, Airfix's power tender only had 150g available for adhesion, against 200g for the loco-drive Collett goods – but traction tyres on three wheels gave it a slight edge in pulling power. Not that that is much to write home about; the Bachmann SR Mogul, with 300g and no traction tyres (but a Bühler can motor and decent gearing), will out-pull either by a factor of 50 per cent...

regrettable aftertaste. For a start, the actual motor was not all that good, lacking smoothness, torque and controllability, while the limited-reduction spur gear-train did it few favours. When Bachmann took over, they wasted no time in ditching this dodgy drivetrain in favour of a chunky can motor and worm-and-spur gearing. More seriously, the split frame pick-up system – which, on the face of it, should have been bombproof – in practice tended to deteriorate rapidly as the plating wore off the axle-muffs, leading to poor contact and intermittent pick-up as oil and dirt accumulated in the crude 'U-slot' bearings. That took a bit more curing, leading eventually to all-new chassis designs for most of these models.

The 'thin frame' loco chassis

The arrival of the etching process facilitated one other important development that is highly relevant to this book: the provision of much better and more user-friendly kit-built locomotive chassis. The traditional 4mm scale locomotive mechanism of yore – still very much current in the late 1970s when the first etched kits crawled out of the ferric chloride swamp – had been based on the ideas of John Ahern, as set out in his classic 1948 book *Miniature Locomotive Construction*.

Ahern's notion of a chassis was based on frames hewn from slabs of $^1/_{16}$in thick brass strip, with the axles running in plain drilled holes as bearings (never a good idea, as any engineer will tell you). Cosmetically, trying to cut an authentic frame profile from a solid sandwich of brass fully an eighth of an inch thick was a thankless task, roughly on a par with busting your way out of Parkhurst with a nail-file – so most such chassis bore little or no resemblance to their prototype. And that wasn't the end of the angst; the finished frames were intended to be soldered to solid brass spacers – an operation calling for the heat output of a small nuclear reactor. Little wonder that many modellers were deterred from even trying such manly blacksmithery!

As long ago as the mid-1950s, D.A. Williams, of 'Metropolitan Junction' fame, had questioned the need for this armour-plated approach, arguing that so long as you provided decent bearings then you could use much thinner metal for the actual frames, which could then readily be made to scale outline, complete with lightening-holes, spring-hangers and so on. Not only that, but you could easily solder on chassis details like brake gear and guard-irons – something that was all-but-impossible with traditional slab frames.

I adopted this doctrine when I started building my own locos in the late 1960s, basing the frames on $^1/_{32}$in steel packing-case binding strip (free from a skip near you!), mounted on L-section spacers and fitted with hefty size in phosphor-bronze bearings sold for slot-cars. This was a recipe I eventually described in a series of articles which appeared in *Model Railways* magazine c1980. Mallard perforce adopted this 'thin-frame' philosophy for their pioneering etched kits, using frames of accurate outline etched in 20thou nickel-silver and fitted with turned-brass 'top-hat' bearings – although they complicated the issue somewhat with a dummy inner chassis that carried the motor.

Etched chassis for RTR

Another pioneer of the etched thin-frame chassis was Bob Wills. When faced with the withdrawal of the original Triang 'Jinty' mechanism on which so many of his kits relied, Bob devised a simple-to-build replacement based on frames etched in 20thou nickel-plated brass. These were screw-mounted to turned brass spacers; bearings were the same top-hat brass turnings that had long been fitted to Wills's cast chassis blocks, and matching etched coupling-rods were provided. This simple chassis was intended to take the Triang X04 motor with Romford gears and wheels, and had a body-mounting system identical to the Triang original.

Apart from its primary role as a drive for the kits, this Wills chassis was thus also an instant scale upgrade for the faithful old Triang/Hornby 'Jinty' body moulding (by then in Mk. 3 iteration and not such a bad model). Mr Wills's pragmatic baby can thus lay claim to being the progenitor of the modern family of sophisticated etched chassis intended to be mated with RTR plastic superstructures.

It was Rod Neep, however, who saw the potential of the

ABOVE *With the demise of the long-running Triang 'Jinty' chassis around 1980, Bob Wills had to come up with a simple-to-build alternative for the many kits in his range designed around the use of this popular mechanism. The result was this pioneering, etched-frame chassis in nickel-plated brass, which had screw-assembly using turned-brass spacers and used a Triang X04 motor with Romford gears and wheels. This was very much the progenitor of the modern aftermarket kits designed to take RTR superstructures.*

etched chassis as an 'aftermarket upgrade' for the new generation of hi-fidelity plastic superstructures from Airfix *et al* – a market that was in part opened up by the drivetrain problems already described. But Rod went a few steps further with his innovative 'Perseverance' etched chassis kits. Not only did you get frames of accurate outline with a good level of detail including brake gear, but also a chassis incorporating a simple-but-effective suspension system designed along the 'Flexi-Chas' principles devised by Mike Sharman.

The Perseverance chassis – unlike almost all then-current kit chassis designs post-Jamieson – did not dictate the choice of motor, gearing or driven axle, but rather were configured to accept a wide range of drivetrain alternatives, some of which Perseverance went on to provide. Neither did the design of the chassis tie you to a particular gauge or standard, as it came with a range of alternative frame spacers, so was good for 00, EM or P4.

The first of these chassis was for the GWR '14xx' 0-4-2T, swiftly followed by the '57xx' pannier tank. Combining a 'Percy' chassis built to appropriate standards with the Airfix ('14xx') or Mainline ('57xx') body mouldings soon became the favoured *entrée* into fine-scale loco-modelling for EM and P4. It is still a popular route today. The original Perseverance suspension design used axle-slots etched direct into the frames, but that arrangement was soon superseded by the system based on a separate horn-guide locating into a cut-out in the frame. This is an arrangement that both facilitates simple but accurate setting-up of the chassis and allows a non-suspended 'rigid' variant. This basic design of chassis has since become the 'industry standard', not just for after-market replacements for RTR mechanisms, but also for the majority of

LEFT *An old stager. My model of '14xx' No 1434 was built in conjunction with Rod Neep and was described in issues 1 and 2 of the Model Railway Journal back in 1984. It used a worked-over Airfix body on the original design of Perseverance chassis and was built for EM gauge with a Portescap 1219 motor/gearbox, and Kean-Maygib wheels. Since then it has been reworked for P4 with Ultrascale wheels and gears, and a Sagami can motor. It is getting a bit dog-eared after nearly 30 years running, but still puts in the odd turn on 'Trerice'. Goodness knows how many such '14xx' conversions there are running about now!*

locomotive kits of almost any provenance. These etched chassis kits are a key resource for the modeller bent on assembling a prototypical stud of sweet-running locomotives.

Contemporary RTR

This brings us, at last, to the current scene. For once, Macmillan's famous polemic holds true: we *have* 'never had it so good'. The choice and quality of what the mass-produced branded ranges have to offer has improved dramatically since the first 'new-generation' RTR *model* (as opposed to ameliorated toy) locomotives appeared in the 1970s. In 1992, Kader relocated their manufacturing facility from Hong Kong to a brand-new state-of-the-art Chinese-government-sponsored factory at Dongguan in mainland China. Hornby followed suit in 1995 when they contracted manufacture of their range out to Chinese moulding specialist Sanda Kan, also based at Dongguan.

The move to Chinese manufacture brought huge benefits for both ranges: CAD/CNC design and tool-making techniques slashed tooling costs, new hi-tech moulding plant and finishing techniques gave a dramatic improvement in component quality. A deft and highly skilled, but 'economical' workforce, allowed a complex assembly process suited to the production of well-detailed models with a wide range of specific variations to suit individual prototypes. Drivetrains have also benefited from new, low-pressure die-casting techniques and the availability of cheap but high-quality miniature 'can' electric motors with a performance to better even the best of the traditional 'bespoke' model railway motors.

So, recent RTR models are pretty impressive. In fact, if you set out to write a bald description of the best of modern off-the-peg models you end up using the sort of superlatives I used earlier in this chapter when attempting to conjure-up a cream-of-the-crop custom-built paragon of yesteryear. Pretty much every attribute I ascribed to those handbuilt wonder-models could equally be ascribed to the likes of a Hornby 'T9' or Bachmann 'BR 4' 2-6-4T. Far from being at the bottom of the pile, much modern RTR sits pretty close to the pinnacle of the possible. Only a model built from a top-of-the-range sophisticated 'super kit' by a really competent craftsman and

painted by some wizard of the airbrush is going to be appreciably superior – and then, not by *that* much.

Of course, not every locomotive listed in the RTR current catalogues scales these heights of excellence. There are many models out there whose origins go back to pre-China days, while some of the older Chinese models fall some way short of the current standard. And – surprise, surprise – these older, less-satisfactory models are all too often the very types that are most fundamental to the creation of a realistically balanced locomotive stud. Several of the most fundamental types are represented by models that are throwbacks to the early days of Hong Kong manufacture. OK, but nowhere as near as good as the best of the contemporary crop.

However, taken overall, the RTR choice has never been wider and most of the basics of a loco stud suited to the Grouping – and BR eras are out there on the shelf – not to mention some pretty esoteric choices of rather more limited relevance. But before worrying about how we're going to produce the necessary models, it's a good idea to decide exactly what engines we need to reproduce. It's time to become better acquainted with the prototype.

BELOW *The mark that Lima missed by a mile back in the '70s was hit plumb in the bulls-eye by Bachmann thirty-odd years later. Their '45xx' exemplifies the contemporary RTR standard: 'scale' wheels on a refined mechanism with full chassis fittings under a body accurate in outline and dimensions, carrying plenty of fine detail, and a finish few modellers could equal. All it needs are a few refinements, the odd bit of detail, and the paintwork toning-down a tad.*

2 STEAM LOCOMOTIVES: MEET THE PROTOTYPE

Having poked a little fun at the unlikely loco lists of yesteryear, it is time to consider the situation today and to suggest a reasonable strategy for selecting and specifying a prototypical loco stud for an authentic, scale-orientated steam-era layout. I make this distinction because the post-steam modeller has it easy in this regard, in that the great majority of the twenty-or-so principal diesel locomotive designs running on pre-privatised BR, were general-purpose machines that were used extensively across the entire network for all classes of traffic. Livery and detail variations there are a-plenty, but the fundamental machinery remained constant, with very few locally specific or small, specialised classes.

For the steam man, however, things are far less straightforward. Not only does he have a far greater number of individual designs to get to grips with, but the situation is further complicated by matters of power class, traffic capability and route availability – not to mention the origins and peculiarities of the various pre-Group and Grouping 'families' of locomotive design. A loco with a firebox designed to steam freely on soft South Wales coal, for instance, would often be hard-put to boil an egg on a diet of South Yorkshire 'hard'.

Much also depended on the nature of the routes worked by a railway; the switchback GWR South Devon main line toiling up Hemerdon at 1 in 43 and Dainton at all, but 1 in 36 was a very different proposition to the LNER's race-track in the flat eastern counties, where they thought 1 in 150 was mountaineering! Just two reasons why a Churchward or Collett GWR engine is a very different animal to something LNER by Gresley… Then there were the variations in operating practice, which included some strong and sometimes-obdurate traditions. Cab layouts, for instance, varied widely; some lines put the driver on the left, some on the right, some had a foot in both camps. Braking was usually by vacuum but could be Westinghouse air or 'steam brake only' – or any combination of the three. And so on, and so on…

All engines are not equal…

All steam engines have a set of frames with driving and carrying wheels, a boiler, some cylinders with associated valve gear, and a set of connecting and coupling rods for power distribution. And there the similarity ends. There were huge variations in the resulting machinery and the way it was used. Many steam locomotives were designed for a specific purpose – and, very often, that was all they were good for. Generally speaking, a high-stepping express engine intended to whirl a relatively lightweight passenger train over a gently graded

ABOVE AND BELOW *Different lines call for different designs. The hilly GWR main line to the far west called for feats of hill-climbing unknown on the LNER's all-but-flat principal route to Scotland. Railways also bought their fuel from on-line sources – which meant that the GWR burnt soft coal from South Wales while the LNER had a choice of hard South Yorkshire, or softer coals from Nottinghamshire. A firebox designed for one fuel might not suit another… Both Author's collection*

main line at average speeds on the windy side of sixty, was no more capable of coping with a thousand slothful tons of minerals over an undulating and steeply graded route than it was of flying to the moon.

By the same token, the broad-shouldered eight-coupled that was unflustered by that 20mph uphill mineral drag was usually quite incapable of picking up its proverbial skirts for a mile-a-minute-plus sprint down the main line. A BR Class 47 diesel, by contrast, could routinely haul a 90mph express passenger working one day and a thousand-ton unit coal train the next. That adaptability – together with its turn-the-key availability, lower labour demand and relative kindness to the track – was the diesel locomotive's key advantage over steam.

The diversity in steam locomotive design reached its zenith at close of the 19th century and in the first decade of the 20th. In spite of the famed longevity of the steam engine, it is notable how short-lived many of the types of this era were – something particularly true of the express passenger classes,

OPPOSITE The essential machinery of the steam locomotive on full display on a 'modern' (relatively speaking!) express passenger type: boiler, cylinders with integral valve chests above, a crosshead and slidebar assembly with connecting rod to convert cylinder power to rotary traction, coupling rods to distribute this power among the driven wheels, and the 'gear' needed to activate the valves.

LMS 'Rebuilt Royal Scot' No 46162 Queen's Westminster Rifleman *wearing LMS post-war black livery, but with BR number, taking part in the 1948 Loco Exchange Trials. Author's collection*

ABOVE AND RIGHT *Horses for courses. In spite of many commonalities, the 1927 'Royal Scot' 4-6-0 and 1929 'LMS Big Goods' were designed for quite different and non-interchangeable roles and so used very different layouts. The 'Scot' was a high-speed machine with large (6ft 9in) driving wheels, a leading bogie for steady running and three cylinders for even power delivery and good balance.*

The two-cylinder 7F 0-8-0 had much smaller wheels (4ft 8½in) and, with no carrying axles, is an all-adhesion type with 60 tons spread over four driven axles. Although the 'Scot' – by dint of higher boiler pressure and greater cylinder volume – is nominally slightly the more powerful engine, it could not match the sustained low-speed tractive effort of the 0-8-0. Any attempt to run the latter at speed, on the other hand, would call for nerves of steel, and a steep downhill gradient! Both LMS Official postcard/Author's collection

where two important influences were at work. First, the period saw a whole raft of new technical developments – compounding, superheating and steam-sanding – which led to a flurry of experimental designs, quite a few of which were none-too-successful.

More significant, however, was the dramatic increase in the weight of passenger trains as new and much larger steel-underframe bogie stock replaced earlier wooden carriages, many of them four and six-wheelers. At the same time, public demand and inter-company competition was driving up train speeds; the old LNWR 'express' average speed of 40mph that had set the standard in Victorian times was no longer acceptable in the Edwardian era, where 55mph start-to-stop was the new 'express' benchmark.

Great Northern Express

It was this rapid increase in passenger train weights and speeds that saw so many classic express designs flit ephemerally though the railway firmament. Top-link power went from single-driver to six-coupled in a dozen hectic years. The classic 'Dean Singles' and large-wheeled double-frame 4-4-0s of the GWR, the various 'Spinners' and elegant Johnson 4-4-0s on the Midland, Adams high-stepping 7ft 4-4-0s on the LSWR and the whole unhappy family of Webb compounds on the LNWR, all came and went in little more than a couple of decades. On the other hand, a general-purpose 0-6-0 of the same vintage might soldier on for half a century or more.

Some of these passenger types – such as the Adams 4-4-0s – lingered on

ABOVE AND RIGHT *A sea change on the rails at the turn of the century. According to a handwritten note on the back of the postcard, the first of these views dates from 1896, and shows the down 'Flying Scotsman' passing Hadley Wood. This was based on a picture taken by fabled photographer Dr Tice Budden.*

The second card is dated by postmark to 1905 and depicts the same train 'near Hatfield'. Stirling elegance in tandem (which Stirling himself would never have allowed!) on a mixed string of four and six-wheeled stock has given way to Ivatt Atlantic power and heavyweight East Coast Joint Stock bogie coaches, in less than a decade. Both Author's collection

ABOVE *Ephemeral engines: few main-line express types were shorter-lived than the ten GER P43 class 'Holden seven-foot singles'. Built as late as 1898, the first of these elegant engines was scrapped as early as 1907 and the last in 1910. An expensive mistake? This is GER No 13, the last survivor, on what is hopefully – (in view of the stock!) – an excursion working.* Author's collection

ABOVE *If Holden's GER singles were a throwback design in 1898, the notable 'Claud Hamilton' 4-4-0s that appeared from Stratford only two years later were very much the way forward. With their 7ft drivers, large (4ft 9in diameter) boilers, 19in cylinders and 180lb/sq in working pressure, they were a far cry from the P43s, being one of the largest and most powerful express passenger classes of their day.* Author's collection

working lighter or secondary expresses, while lines like Midland – which never acquired any engine larger than the 4-4-0 'Compound', and which worked much of its traffic by hanging a brace of locomotives on the front, could always use a 'Beatrice' or a 'Spinner' on pilot duties. Elsewhere, though – even on the thrifty GWR – CMEs could find little use for obsolete, underpowered express engines (no matter how refined their pedigree or lofty their names), and so despatched them unceremoniously to the scrapyard.

But express passenger working was ever the froth on the top of the railway's bedrock operations: it was the bulk mineral, general and express goods traffic, perishables, mail and parcels that accounted for the bulk of the black ink on the balance sheet. (Or did until the motor lorry started to make inroads on the most profitable segments of this business.) It was the working of this core traffic that formed the majority of the traffic department's motive power requirement. Meeting that requirement was the *raison d'être* of the whole motive power department – in which context, you can forget the glossy racehorses of the express scene; it was the pit-ponies and carthorses that were the real wage-earners.

Power and speed

I ought perhaps at this juncture to touch upon those limitations of steam locomotive design that made a given type more suited to one role rather than another – something which came down, essentially, to the power output and sustained running speeds of which it was capable. The principal factors affecting the power output of a steam engine were all to do with how readily it could boil water and how effectively it could use the resulting steam. The first part of this equation was largely determined by boiler size and efficiency, coupled to the size of the fire that could be maintained, which, ultimately, came down to how much coal the hapless fireman could shovel, how quickly, how accurately, and for how long. The second part of the power equation was far more complex and subtle as it depended on the interaction of numerous factors, starting with the working pressure and steam temperature and going on to include the cylinder size and proportions, the type and setting of the valve gear and

the design of the associated ports and steam passages, exhaust blastpipe and chimney arrangements.

Speed potential, on the other hand, came down to just three basic factors – leaving aside the state of the track, the strength of the driver's nerve and the brake power he had available. These limiting factors were, first, the linear piston speed, followed by the efficacy of the bearing arrangements – more specifically, the bearing areas and lubrication system – and, finally – the balancing of the reciprocating machinery.

Of these three, piston speed was the ultimate arbiter as it determined the velocity of the valve events and hence the time available to get steam in and out of the cylinders. Try to run at too high a piston speed and the engine would 'choke'; the spent steam couldn't be exhausted fast enough and high back-pressures built up in the front-end of the locomotive, greatly impeding the steam flow. This led to a drastic reduction in the power developed and hence the ability to

BELOW *Ultimate power lies in the boiler – and few types had a bigger boiler relative to their wheel arrangement than the GER's hulking D81 class 0-6-0s of 1920 (LNER/BR Class J20). These massive machines, as long in the wheelbase as many an 0-8-0, had 20in cylinders and superheating to make them the world's most powerful 0-6-0 until the Bulleid Q1 of 1942 (using a much higher boiler pressure) eclipsed them by a few pounds of tractive effort.* Author's collection

ABOVE *Limiting factor: piston speed and the linked rate of valve events and steam flows, were the chief determinant of the ultimate speed potential of a steam locomotive. A typical 'Big Four' express passenger type like the LMS's three-cylinder 'Jubilee' of 1934 would be flat-out in the 90–100mph range. For a 'Jubilee', 95mph represented a piston speed of 1,710ft/minute. Only a handful of refined three and four-cylinder engines were appreciably faster. To set the 126mph record, Gresley Pacific* Mallard *achieved (fleetingly!) an ultimate piston speed of just over 2,300ft/minute.* BR Official/Author's collection

sustain speed and develop tractive effort. For many years, before the advent of truly accurate valve gears, large-diameter piston valves, 'streamlined' steam-passages and sophisticated multiple-blastpipe exhaust arrangements, practicable maximum piston speeds remained at much the same level, typically around 1,500ft per minute. Only the final generation of steam power would admit of substantially higher rates.

A handful of specialist types aside, steam locomotives are 'direct drive' – that is, they do without any form of clutch or reduction gearing. This means that the piston speed is directly

BELOW *Mechanical lubrication of cylinders and main bearings reduced wear, and allowed higher rotational rates. Here are multi-*

point gravity-feed (on the tank front) and Wakefield mechanical lubricators (on the footplate, driven from the inside motion), in this case fitted to a suburban tank engine in the cause of improved reliability and faster preparation. Author's collection

determined by driving wheel rotation rate. Thus, the only way of regulating piston speed is by adjusting the driving wheel diameter to keep rotation rates within bounds at the speeds the engine is required to maintain in service. This rotation rate also has a direct effect on the locomotive's various bearings: the axleboxes, the big and small-ends of the connecting rods, the coupling rods, and valve gear pivots.

With a few modern roller-fitted exceptions, these bearings were all plain white metal-lined affairs, quite heavily loaded and very dependent on adequate lubrication. Such bearings are very prone to overheating and eventual seizure if run at sustained high speed. Once again, it was only the final generation of steam locomotives, benefiting from better bearing materials and lubricants together with force-fed mechanical lubrication, that could withstand continuous high rotational speeds without doing themselves damage.

Even if the valve events and bearings could cope with high rotational speeds, there was still the vital matter of balance to take into account. The machinery of a steam locomotive is all about converting the fore-and-aft linear motion of the pistons into rotary motion of the wheels. It is a reciprocating engine, involving reversals of thrust and having many substantial components in angular movement. As the forces involved are very high, all this machinery has traditionally been pretty massive.

Unfortunately, many of the components making up the transmission and the associated valve gear of a normal two-cylinder steam engine are asymmetrical both in form and movement, with the result that the basic machinery is fundamentally unbalanced. The net effect of all this out-of-kilter ironmongery flailing about at high speed is to set up some pretty violent oscillations and vertical shock-loadings that can knock seven bells out of the permanent way, as well as giving a rough ride and impeding track holding and traction. Three and four-cylinder engines are inherently much better-balanced, one of the main justifications for their adoption in the face of higher first cost and maintenance requirements.

Balance weights added to the cranks and/or driving wheel rims of steam locomotives can go some way to cancelling out these out-of-balance forces, but all engines delivered a 'hammer blow' loading to the track that was directly related to the rotational speed of the wheels – yet another reason to keep that revolution rate down. Again, modern designs like the BR Standards – which benefited from lightweight rods and valve gear and far more accurate dynamic and static balancing – could run at substantially higher rates of wheel rotation while keeping 'hammer' within acceptable limits. Good balance was also one reason why the final generation of express steam power managed to go far faster on wheels of only 6ft or a little over, than had older express passenger engines which had very much larger wheel diameters – up to a ponderous 8ft 6in on some famous old 'flyers'.

The tractive influence of wheel diameter

Driving wheel diameter is thus an important factor in determining the suitability of a locomotive type for the different classes of duty and associated line speeds. In fact, wheel size actually affects a lot of other aspects of locomotive design apart from speed capacity; it is also fundamental to the critical parameter of tractive effort. In this context, the *smaller* the driving wheels, the *greater* the effective 'reduction gearing' of the locomotive's transmission system and the resulting magnification of the piston thrust in terms of rotational torque exerted at the rail head. This thrust is expressed as a linear pull quoted in lb – the 'tractive effort' of the locomotive. Tractive effort is what moves trains and hence loads; ultimate power only determines how fast you can go once you are rolling.

What this means is that a boiler and cylinders of a given power rating fitted to a smaller-wheeled eight-coupled freight locomotive will be capable of starting and pulling a much heavier train than an equivalent power plant fitted to a large-wheeled express passenger class – but only at a much lower speed. The famous Gresley P1 class 2-8-2s, built to haul 1,600-ton coal trains up to London, had the same boiler and cylinder arrangements as the 100mph A1 class Pacifics – but with 5ft 2in rather than 6ft 8in drivers. The P1's tractive effort (even without the auxiliary 'booster' engine on the rear truck) was 38,500lb, compared with 29,835lb for the Pacific, but its speed capability was decidedly more limited. Striking the right balance between wheel diameter, cylinder proportions and boiler power is a critical design factor in producing the right locomotive for a given role.

Given that the wheel diameter generally used for shunting engines was 4ft or a tad under, and the largest for express types was 6ft 6in, or a bit more, then the mid-point of the range falls at about 5ft 3in or so – for many years, the most common wheel diameter for the

ABOVE *Substantial balance weights, together with lightweight alloy valve gear, enabled this post-war Thompson L1 class mixed-traffic 2-6-4T to run at service speeds of 70+mph on 5ft 9in wheels without excessive damage to the track. Well, that was the theory, anyway!* Author's collection

BELOW *The Gresley A1/A3 4-6-2 and the P1 class heavy 2-8-2 shared identical boilers and cylinder arrangements, but to very different ends. The Pacific, with 6ft 8in drivers, was a fleet-footed express passenger design, probably the first such class to have genuine 100mph capability. The 5ft 2in-wheeled Mikado was intended for heavy main line mineral traffic, i.e., moving 1,600-ton coal trains down to London as smartly as possible.* Both LNER PRO/ Author's collection

ABOVE *The Gresley J38 0-6-0 of 1926 was a pure freight design, intended for heavy mineral traffic in the Scottish coalfields. With 4ft 8in wheels, 20 x 26in cylinders, piston valves, and a large boiler with superheat and 180lb/sq in pressure, it was not far behind the J20 in size and power. Although fitted with vacuum brake, the class was never intended or used for passenger work, having no steam-heat.* Author's collection

BELOW *The J39 general-purpose 0-6-0 was 'spun off' from the J38, with a very slightly smaller boiler, but with the same cylinder and valve arrangements. The big difference was a six-inch increase in wheel diameter, to 5ft 2in, together with steam-heating, as well as vacuum brakes. Many earlier J39s were also Westinghouse brake fitted, as with GE-section No 64799 seen here. The change of wheel-size dropped the tractive effort from 28,415lb to 25,664lb, but gave 65mph+ speed potential for passenger working.* Author's collection

general-purpose 0-6-0 tender engine, the railway's true 'maid of all work'. Goods-only and mineral classes typically hovered around the 4ft 7in mark, passenger tank locomotives normally spanned the middle ground from 5ft 3in up to 5ft 8in, and mixed traffic went from there to about 6ft 2in. Some locomotive designs – like the SR 'Woolwich Moguls' – existed in variants having different wheel diameters, while several well-known classes of mixed-traffic 4-6-0 were created by fitting an express-passenger design having 6ft 6in or larger wheels with smaller-diameter drivers in the 5ft 6in–6ft range. Generally speaking, therefore, the driving wheel size is a pretty good guide to an engine's intent.

Adhesion

No matter what the wheel size – or that of the cylinders and boiler, or any other of the myriad bits affecting the power output of a steam engine – all counted for naught if the engine lacked sufficient grip on the rails to exert the tractive force of which it was otherwise capable, especially when starting from rest. Adhesion was the critical factor – and had been since the day the first 'iron horse' challenged the sure grip of a quartet of equine hooves. It was still a problem right at the end of the steam era – as witnessed by the wilder wheel-spinning antics of Mr Bulleid's high-powered 'light Pacifics' when attempting to get under way on a damp rail.

Maintaining an adequate purchase at the railhead has thus always been a prime consideration in the design of all railway locomotives – steam, diesel or electric. It is a factor of an importance equal to all the aspects concerned with power production and overall efficiency. In which regard, effective sanding gear can ultimately be seen as one of the most critical components of any engine!

The adhesion potential of a steam locomotive is made up basically of two factors: the frictional grip of the wheel-tyres on the railhead – the 'coefficient of friction' between the

materials of which they are made – multiplied by the number of axles transmitting the thrust developed by the cylinders. More driven axles = greater overall grip, which is why locomotives required to develop high sustained pulling power tend to have more driven axles.

Powered wheelsets on a steam engine are classified either as 'driving axles' – those driven directly by the connecting rods – and 'coupled axles', receiving drive indirectly by means of the coupling rods. The level of frictional grip provided by each wheelset is itself determined by a number of further factors – principally, the composition and state of wear of the wheel-tyres and railheads, the weight carried by the axle, and the presence – or otherwise – of lubricants (oil, water, wet leaves) and – most importantly – abrasives (sand), in the wheel-rail interface. The former is a hindrance and the latter a considerable boon. In fact, sand is more than a boon – it is an absolute necessity in many situations! The normal coefficient of friction of a steel wheel on steel rail in clean, dry conditions stands at a value of around 0.25–0.3. Add a little water/oil emulsion to the railheads, however, and it can easily plummet to less than 0.05! Dry sand effectively applied to the rail-head immediately ahead of the wheel brings the value back up to 'dry' levels; without it, the engine will be highly prone to slip.

The frictional grip of wheels on rails was also affected by the ability of the locomotive's suspension system to follow exactly the undulations of the rail-heads, especially at speed – which is why some express passenger locomotives used more-responsive helical coil springs on their driving axles rather than slower-acting self-damping leaf springs. Generally speaking, however, the more coupled axles there are, the greater the weight on each and the more effective the sanding gear, the greater the power that can be transmitted. Which is why those engines needing to produce ultimate tractive effort tended to be more massive and possessed of more driving wheels serviced by more sand-pipes (preferably steam-assisted) than engines designed for lighter duties involving no great feats of traction.

As with most things in the locomotive world, there are, however, direct trade-offs and several inviolable limitations in the matter of the grip obtainable at the coupled wheels, such

ABOVE *The unmistakeable underpinnings of a Bulleid Q1, ultimately the most powerful 0-6-0 on the planet, showing the vital sanding arrangements: three good-sized sandboxes a side with steam-jet assistance to the feed-pipes placing the sand on the railhead just ahead of the wheel.* Author's collection

as the match of tyre profile to rail-head, the maximum permissible axle-load and – most critically – the need for high speed and consequent requirement for larger driving wheel diameters. Apart from all other considerations, there's only so much room under a given size of locomotive boiler for the driving wheels – so the bigger they are, the fewer you can fit in. Ditto with the all-important sanders; big wheels necessarily spaced close together don't leave much room for sanding gear between them, making it much more difficult to deliver sand effectively where it does most good – precisely onto the area of the railhead immediately in front of the wheels.

BELOW *More coupled wheelsets = more grip and greater effective (as opposed to nominal) tractive effort. But there are limits on wheel size if the wheelbase is to be kept reasonable. The GWR 47xx 2-8-0 with 5ft 8in wheels was Britain's only true mixed-traffic 2-8-0, equally at home with heavy fast freight or on summer Saturday peak holiday traffic. The only British eight-coupled engines with larger coupled wheels were Gresley's massive P2 'Cock o' the North' 2-8-2s.* Author's collection

ABOVE *A high-speed engine, Victorian style. Specifically designed for running fast but relatively lightweight express trains on an 'easy' road, the GNR Stirling '8-footer' of 1870 was a pioneering bogie single that proved capable of 85mph and more. This is No 550, built in 1878 and fitted with the Smith simple (non-automatic) vacuum brake; the pipe on the smokebox is the ejector. There is no front brake hose or screw coupling as double-heading was forbidden.* Author's collection

BELOW *A truly ancient 0-6-0, one of the first of the breed to be built. Elephant was one of four Gooch 'heavy goods engines' constructed by the LSWR in 1844, seen here as re-boilered by Beattie c1865. Adjustable brasses to the coupling-rod bearings allowed for adjustment to set up the rods to match the axle centres by basically, trial and error.* Author's collection

The coupled dilemma

Finding room enough for coupled axles was not the only factor accounting for the long popularity of the large-wheeled, single-driver express locomotive in Britain – a predilection that persisted long after the rest of the world had 'gone coupled'. There were good reasons for this; for a start, very few foreign railways of the Victorian era went in for anything like the sort of speeds that were customary back here in 'Blighty'. The old GNR raceway from London, north through the flat eastern counties towards York was generally held to be the fastest stretch of railway in the world for many a long year and, indeed, was to see the ultimate in steam-powered speed. Before 1900, true high speed was normally seen as the province of the pure 'uncoupled' flyer; to many a Victorian railway engineer, the sure route to a fast, free-running engine was that single driven axle and its large-diameter wheels. Coupled engines were perceived – not without reason – as having limitations due to the smaller wheel-sizes possible and the greater friction inherent in the necessary coupling rods and cranks.

That this friction was considerable in earlier coupled locomotive designs was hardly surprising, given the relatively crude methods of manufacture available and the consequent difficulty in producing coupling-rods matched exactly to the coupled wheelbase of the engine – not to mention the maintaining of this correlation in the face of wear in service. Anyone who has ever tried to build a model of a steam locomotive (however powered) will be well aware of just how fundamental this matching is to the free-running of the chassis; an error of a few thou is enough to rob it of any smoothness. Most early coupled locomotives did not even try for such exactitude; the coupling-rods were simply made with 'adjustable brasses', allowing an adequate match to be made and maintained by trial-and-error – which was good enough for a lowly goods engine lumbering along at 20mph.

There was also the matter of the effect on the coupling rods of undulations in the track. As the driving wheels rose and fell on the springs, the net result was to lengthen the effective axle centre distances slightly due to the angular deflection of the longitudinal axle centreline from its 'mean' position. The accompanying variations in the coupling rod centres were allowed for by not making the actual rods too rigid, permitting them to flex slightly. It was also usual to allow a relatively generous running fit on the crankpins – accompanied, doubtless, by a resounding 'clank' and a regular 'thumping' as the slack was taken up twice each revolution. That was OK in a slow-running goods engine of modest power, but not so clever in the context of a fast-moving passenger express type. It was only with the advent of much more precise machine tools and 'elastic' steels in the 1870s, coupled with flatter permanent way resulting from the use of longer steel rails and better ballasting, that it became possible to produce a fast, free-running four-coupled express engine, as exemplified by Webb's immortal 2-4-0 'Jumbos' of 1874.

When it came to goods engines, such things were less critical and the need for brute tractive effort was generally greater. Six-coupled goods engines had arrived in the late 1840s and got steadily larger until the heavy eight-coupled goods engine made its debut on the LNWR in 1892. In the early 1900s 0-8-0s and 2-8-0s proliferated on many railways while the first British ten-coupled – in the brutish shape of the GER's experimental maximum-traction 'Decapod' – arrived in 1903, followed in 1913 by the Midland's monumental 0-10-0 banking engine for the Lickey incline. Otherwise, ten-coupled engines never cut any ice in Britain before the Second World War and the WD 'Austerity' 2-10-0s. It is perhaps not generally realised that these were actually little more powerful

ABOVE *When LNWR Webb 'Jumbo' 2-4-0 No 790* Hardwicke *averaged 67mph from Crewe to Carlisle during the 1895 'Race to the North' – a feat requiring speeds of 80mph and more in places – it finally laid to rest the myth that a coupled engine could not run freely and fast. Here is sister engine* Merrie Carlisle *in early LMS days.* Author's Collection

than the eight-coupled 'Austerities', the extra axle being more about obtaining an ultra-low (13½-ton) axle-load for running on lightweight PW and over temporary bridges, than in a quest for substantially increased tractive effort. Only with the advent of the magnificent BR 9F class 2-10-0 in 1954 did Britain possess a true ten-coupled 'super power' freight engine.

Power classes

Before the 'Grouping' in 1923, each railway had its own system of classifying locomotives. On many of the smaller lines, engines were built to work a specific route – as with the Highland Railway's 'Skye Bogies' or the LSWR's 'Ilfracombe Goods'; they were thus described by the duty for which they were intended. Larger railways used more general descriptions: the LNWR went on cylinder diameter and usage – as in '17-inch coal engine' or '18-inch standard goods'.

BELOW *An engine built for a specific section of line, in this case, the steeply-graded Ilfracombe branch of the LSWR in North Devon. Beyer, Peacock supplied a compact but powerful 0-6-0, the long-lived 'Ilfracombe Goods'.* BP works photo/Author's collection

ABOVE *Power class markings '2P' on the cabside of LMS Standard Class 2 4-4-0 No 692, which is seen when brand-new at Derby in 1929. LMS Official/Author's collection*

The Midland adopted the same usage descriptions as the LNWR, but allocated a numerical power rating initially based on firegrate area, describing an engine as a 'Class 2 Passenger' or 'Class 3 Goods'. The GWR in 1920 adopted an alphabetical scheme of power classification based on nominal tractive effort, starting from 'A' at 16,500–18,500lb and going up to 'E' at 33,000–38,000lb. But overall, there was no unified or generic method of denoting an engine's suitability for a specific duty; it all relied on the motive power foreman's knowledge of the capabilities of the engines at his disposal.

With the formation of the 'Big Four' grouped companies, with their much larger but far more variegated inherited locomotive studs, it became imperative to devise some comparative classification system so that the traffic and operating departments could accurately assess and allocate locomotive types with which they were unfamiliar. It was on the LMS – the largest and most diverse of the grouped companies – that this problem was most acute; and it was the

LMS which devised the most useful classification system, based on the Midland idea of numerical power classes. Every locomotive type was allocated a rating based on its boiler power and haulage capability. Classifications ran from '0' – engines suited only to light shunting or branch line work – up to '8' – the largest and strongest classes suited to heavy express passenger or freight workings.

However, power alone is not the measure of a locomotive's suitability for a given role, so the LMS added a simple suffix to indicate the purposes for which an engine could best be used. This classification took into account wheel size and speed capability as well as tractive characteristics. The basic suffixes were simply 'P' for passenger and 'F' for freight: a 'Royal Scot' was 6P, a Stanier eight-coupled goods an 8F and a 'Jinty' 0-6-0T 3F. But that wasn't the end of the story; where a locomotive was deemed capable of fulfilling both basic roles, then a double classification was applied – varied if necessary to reflect the suitability in each application. Thus, a Hughes-Fowler 'Crab' 2-6-0 was originally classified 5P/4F, whereas a Stanier mixed-traffic 4-6-0 was 5P/5F.

These power class codes appeared in small characters on the upper cabside of the loco. British Railways generally adopted this LMS system after 1948 – the exception being, of course, the Western Region, which stuck with the GWR power class letters. Otherwise, it was applied to all locomotives, including the new BR Standard designs. BR also added a further suffix: 'MT', for mixed traffic engines – defined as types having a common power rating for both basic roles. Most BR Standards were classified as mixed traffic, even the 'Britannia' Pacifics (7MT). With the arrival of the BR Standard 2-10-0s, the LMS power classifications were extended upwards to give a class '9', occupied in solitary state by the 9F.

Route availability

These power/use classifications only took account of a locomotive's tractive and traffic capabilities. Of equal importance to the operating department was its Route Availability – a measure of the nature and extent of the routes over which the locomotive could work. All locomotives impose

BELOW *This is what interested the civil engineer – the Weights Diagram for a locomotive class; a maximum axle load of 19 tons 13cwt put the J39 into category RA6 under the LNER scheme.*

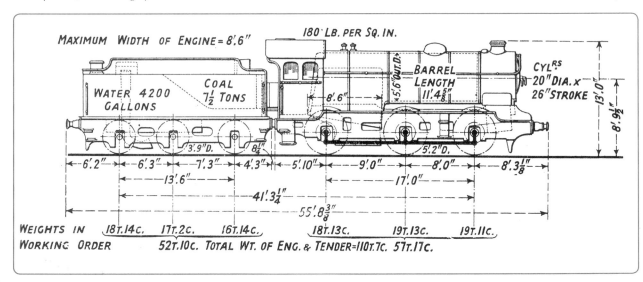

a loading on the track, primarily made up of two components: the static weight, particularly the maximum load on a single axle, and the completeness and effectiveness of the balancing. A heavy engine or one with poor balancing could exert a severe shock loading on the track – the 'hammer blow' already mentioned. Such an engine obviously could not be used over lightly laid track or on routes with weak bridges or less-stable earthworks. The Civil Engineer's department therefore determined the acceptable loadings for each stretch of line, values enshrined in book form as 'Route Registers'. This is information vital to the Operating Department, who need to relate the acceptable load figures to the characteristics of the locomotive types available, to decide what could (or, more importantly, could *not*) be used over a particular route. The resulting restrictions were published as Working Notices and listed in Working Timetables, the railway's fundamental operating documents.

This was a somewhat ponderous system, calling for frequent reference to the paperwork and the issuing of extra notices and revisions every time a new or modified locomotive type entered service or a PW improvement was made. This led two of the 'Group' railways, the GWR and the LNER, to devise coding systems for denoting the track-loading characteristics of their locomotives and the corresponding capacities of the different stretches of track. The GWR used a simple colour-code; the various lines in the maps and plans included in the route registers were coloured differently: the lightest-laid routes were 'uncoloured', being shown by a pair of fine black lines with white between. The next classification up had a yellow centre between the lines, then blue and finally red, for the heaviest main lines.

Locomotives displayed matching colour codes by means of small coloured discs on the cabsides above the numberplate; no disc was an 'uncoloured' engine and could go anywhere, red was 'main line only'. The categories went on static maximum axle load: under 14 tons for 'uncoloured', 14–16 tons for yellow, 16–17tons 12cwt for blue, over 17 tons 12cwt for red. When the 'King' class came out in 1927 with an axle-load of 22½ tons, it was put into a special 'double red' category which restricted it to certain nominated routes. The power class code letter was superimposed on these route availability discs.

The LNER system – still in use by Network Rail today – was based on a numerical code that ran from RA–RA9, with the higher numbers denoting the heavier engines and hence more restricted route availability. As with the GWR system, the classifications went on static axle loadings, but with far smaller, 25cwt, increments between the 'steps' – a reflection not just of the variety of the motive power to be classified (the LNER had more distinct locomotive classes than any of the other 'Grouped' companies), but also on the dubious load-bearing characteristics of the many odd, old and lightly laid secondary and branch lines the company had inherited, especially in East Anglia. In order to maximise utilisation of so varied a locomotive stud on such restricted routes, a relatively precise classification system was needed. 'RA1' corresponded to the GWR 'uncoloured' at less than 14 tons, while 'RA9', at 21 tons 5cwt, was equivalent to a 'double red'. These codes

ABOVE Route availability markings: on the left, the GWR coloured disc (yellow in this case), with power class 'C' superimposed on a '57xx' pannier tank. Right, LNER/BR RA code RA5 on a Gresley K3 2–6–0. Author's collection

were displayed in small letters, usually low down on the cabsides of the engines.

Locomotive usage

The potential uses to which a given design of steam locomotive could be put were thus hedged-about with a lot of restrictions and provisos – factors that were ultimately responsible for the wonderful diversity that characterised British motive power throughout the era of the traditional steam railway, and which persisted into the age of the diesels. Choosing an apt stud of locomotives for a realistic model railway also calls for consideration of these prototype factors, allied to an understanding of the jobs the railway had to do and the types of locomotive best suited to the various types of traffic. This is the aspect of the motive power equation we consider next.

BELOW Not for common use: the GER/LNER N7 0-6-2T was designed for a very specific set of conditions – heavy, high-intensity suburban traffic with frequent stops and tight schedules. The result was a very powerful but relatively small-wheeled engine giving rapid acceleration, and equipped with Westinghouse air braking for brisk station stops. Condensing gear was fitted for running through on to the underground network. The RA was 5 for a tractive effort of 20,500lb. LNER Official/Author's collection

3 'TO WORK THE TRAFFIC OFFERING...'

The original purpose of the common-carrier public railway was to make money for its shareholders, by moving all the traffic it could legitimately lay hands on as efficiently (that is, cheaply!) as possible. The furtherance of this basic aim was the sole purpose of the motive power department. Locomotives were almost invariably bought-in or built in response to an established need; only very rarely was a 'speculative' design postulated in an attempt to develop an entirely new class of traffic. Indeed, with hindsight, it is possible to argue that quite early on in the development of the British railway network, it would have been possible to evolve a relative handful of 'standard' types that could have answered all motive power needs, much as was done in Germany. Fortunately for that intrepid species, *Homo Enthusiastes Britannicus*, virtually every one of the 40-odd pre-Grouping main line railways here had their own ideas on the subject – with the result that nowhere else on the planet did such a diversity of motive power rule the rails.

In seeking to choose the right engine for the right job in the context of a model railway based on a more-or-less-fictional subject (as the majority still are) it is useful to have a good understanding of the various prototype roles, and which locomotive types the real railways used to fill them. So it seemed a sound idea to identify the various tasks the railways had to accomplish in working their traffic and to look at what sort of engines, and in what numbers, were needed for each role or division of traffic – starting at the base of the whole operational pyramid: goods workings.

Goods working

In his classic *Great Northern Steam*, that most erudite of railway authors Dr W.A. Tuplin wrote: 'Railways were originally made as a means of transporting minerals, goods and merchandise economically, which meant not specially fast, and over the history of steam as the tractive agent on railways it was the non-passenger trains that brought in the bulk of the revenue.' In the case of some lines – such as many of the South Wales railways – such traffic made up more than 95 per cent of the receipts. Goods working was the bedrock of the balance sheet for all but a few predominantly suburban railways – the Metropolitan and London, Tilbury & Southend spring to mind as the obvious examples. Even the passenger-orientated lines running between London and the South Coast still earned the better part of half their money in the freight business.

Goods working essentially came in four categories: mineral traffic, general merchandise working and shunting, latterly joined by express goods. Each of these categories called for locomotives with specific characteristics and abilities – and usually in substantial numbers, at least as far as 'road' locomotives were concerned. It is noteworthy that the two most numerous designs

OPPOSITE Glamorous and glorious though they were, it is doubtful whether the GCR's London–Sheffield–Manchester expresses ever earned a penny for the long-suffering shareholders. As popular wit had it, when the Manchester, Sheffield & Lincolnshire became the Great Central in 1899, 'Money Sunk & Lost' was then 'Gone Completely'! F. Moore postcard/Author's collection

ABOVE *Bringing home the dividend; even the passenger-orientated London, Brighton & South Coast Railway earned all but half of its total receipts in the freight business. A Billinton 'Vulcan' 0-6-0 trundles a mixed 'ordinary goods' train for Hastings down the Brighton main line at the customary 25mph or so behind a typically complex LBSCR headcode.* Author's collection

BELOW *The two main classes of goods traffic: minerals – the GNR moving coal to London, in this case – and general merchandise, here being worked by the Midland Railway in South Wales. The locomotives are two Victorian classics of the goods engine genre: Patrick Stirling's powerful 1874 GNR design with 17½in cylinders, built as needed down to 1896 with only minor variations, and Kirtley's Midland 'curved double-frame' type that first appeared in 1863. These were constructed in very large numbers over the next decade, with a few destined to survive into the BR era.* Dr T.F. Budden

of British locomotive – the 943-strong LNWR 'DX' 0-6-0 and the 935 'Austerity' 2-8-0s – were both designed for goods working. Throughout the history of the traditional common-carrier railway, on the vast majority of lines goods engines outnumbered pure-passenger types by a considerable factor.

The goods locomotive – a brief history

Dedicated goods locomotives have existed as a distinct type since the very earliest days of the railway; the first such had four hooves and were fuelled with hay. All the pioneering steam locomotive designs were conceived for goods – specifically, mineral-working and only with the coming of the 'common-carrier' Liverpool & Manchester Railway in 1829 did passengers figure as anything other than the merest casual afterthought.

Right from the start of the common carriage arrangement – which required a railway to convey *all* the classes of traffic offering – goods engines were a breed apart from their passenger siblings. For a start, they were almost-invariably 'coupled', the first series-produced design probably being the haycock-firebox bar-framed inside-cylinder 'Bury' 0-4-0 engines of the L&M and Grand Junction railways. These were succeeded on those pioneering lines by the Buddicom-inspired outside-cylindered 2-4-0 'Crewe Goods' family, which first appeared in 1846.

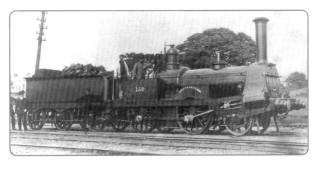

ABOVE *The earliest goods engines were 0-4-0s, so the 2-4-0 LNWR 'Crewe Goods' of 1845 was a useful advance in boiler power and general size. The outside cylinders avoided the need for a crank axle. This is No 159* Adjutant. *Author's collection*

BELOW *Stephenson's 'long boiler' 0-6-0 goods, the first of which was built in 1843 for the York & North Midland Railway, a constituent of the NER – which railway adopted the type extensively. NER No 85 dates from c1860 and is seen here in 'Fletcher' condition, in the mid-1870s. Author's collection*

However, three years before that, George Stephenson had introduced – in the form of a pair of 'long boiler' engines built for the York & North Midland Railway – the first examples of what soon became the standard British goods locomotive: the inside-cylindered 0-6-0. The third such engine constructed went to the Midland Railway proper, which thought it such a wonderful 'piece of kit' that thereafter they never worked a goods train with anything else!

The six-coupled goods engine with wheels of from 4ft 6in to 5ft diameter and 15in or 16in cylinders, proliferated throughout the 1840s and '50s. They were slow and ponderous, but they could pull a decent load – 150 tons or so – at speeds of up to 20mph, which is all anyone asked back then. A typical single-driver passenger engine of the period would typically manage no more than half that tonnage, although it might hit the dizzy heights of 45mph; quite fast enough, given the negligible braking power then available!

The inside-cylinder 0-6-0 remained the primary British goods type until well into the 20th century, but gradually separated into two sub-species: the dedicated 'heavy slow goods' mineral engines with wheels of 4ft 6in–4ft 10in diameter, and a more versatile general-purpose machine with 5ft 0in or 5ft 3in wheels for ordinary mixed-goods and merchandise traffic. The 'heavies' were the real cart-horses of the railway, slogging along at 20mph or less with loose-coupled negligibly braked trains of several hundred tons, their ranks including some truly extensive classes, such as the LNWR '17-inch coal engines', of which Crewe turned out no fewer than 500 examples.

As wagons got slightly larger in size and considerably heavier in payload, the heavy mineral engine also grew in size; the 0-8-0 arriving on the LNWR in 1892 and the 2-8-0 bowed in on the GWR in 1903. By the 1923 Grouping, all the principal mineral-carrying lines except the Midland and the GER boasted eight-coupled mineral power. But while the GER possessed a monstrous 0-6-0 – the D81 class (LNER J20) – that was as big and powerful (having a tractive effort of no less than 29,000lb), as many an eight-coupled, the Midland made do with a vast fleet of relatively puny 0-6-0s, usually toiling along in pairs.

BELOW *A slogger: the pure heavy goods/mineral engine, small-wheeled and unbraked, rarely straying much above 25mph. The LNWR built 500 of these '17in coal engines' to work its colossal mineral traffic. The first cousin to a DX, but nowhere near as versatile. Author's collection*

Initially, the larger-wheeled 'general goods' engines normally worked the slightly less-slothful (25mph!) main line 'ordinary mixed' goods trains, still loose-coupled, together with local trip, branch line and pick-up workings. Later in the 19th century, the role of such engines expanded to take in much faster vacuum-braked 'express' goods (speeds up to about 45mph) and, increasingly, passenger-rated traffic including milk and perishables, parcels and some true passenger trains, most notably excursion traffic.

Indeed, some railways – notably the LNWR and the Lancashire & Yorkshire Railway (LYR) – had a long tradition of using essentially 'goods' engines for some classes of passenger working, and many such locomotives were built or retro-fitted with vacuum brakes for this purpose. Although still usually described as 'goods', they thus became, effectively, 'general-purpose' engines – of which more anon.

Goods shunting

This fundamental, extensive and demanding 24/7 non-stop aspect of steam railway operation was the province of three distinct families of locomotive: those designed specifically for the job; goods and general-purpose types that included suitability for shunting in their range of abilities, and engines designed for other purposes but which had been cascaded-down into the shunting role – often in spite of dubious suitability.

Purpose-designed shunters were actually pretty rare beasts on most main line railways in steam days and only during the Second World War did the rapid proliferation of the WD 'Austerity' Hunslet 16in 0-6-0ST see a common-use shunter design appear in really substantial numbers. Specialised shunters were universally tank locomotives of compact size and modest weight, usually outside-cylindered and riding on small (4ft or less) driving wheels on an abbreviated wheelbase. This recipe was good for tractive effort and acceleration, as well as for inching around tight curves, but it made for poor riding qualities and frenetic activity at any sort of speed. Boilers were often small in relation to the cylinder size – fine for short bursts of 'maximum effort' but unsuited to sustained power output. Lever reversing facilitated frequent and rapid changes of

BELOW Not all that many pre-Grouping railways built specialised shunters in any sort of numbers, but the Midland was one that did. Samuel Johnson turned out successive versions and batches of this small inside-cylindered 0-4-0ST design, 13 of which survived into the BR era. S. Dewsbury/Author's collection

ABOVE *Heavy metal: with the increasing weight and length of goods train permitted by more powerful 'road' locomotives and the growth of marshalling yards in the later 1890s, the job of shunting became far more demanding. Several railways acquired powerful dedicated locomotives for this work; LNER J88 class 0-6-0T No 9846 was built by the North British Railway in 1905.* Author's collection

direction while a good powerful steam brake permitted briskness of movement in tight spaces. Maximum speed, however, was never much to write home about, most true shunters being flat-out at 20mph or so – while limited coal and water capacities restricted their operating range. Such a shunting engine, ideal in tight industrial or dockside locations, was an absolute liability when let loose on the main line…

Relatively few pre-Grouping railways had many such locomotives. This was because in many areas the majority of the shunting work was carried out, not by the railways themselves, but by their customers. Time was when any rail-connected mining or industrial concern of consequence would have provided their own shunting motive power, usually in the shape of one or more of an absolute plethora of off-the-peg, small 0-4-0 and 0-6-0 'industrial' tank locomotives – of which the '16-inch Hunslet' adopted by the War Department in 1943, was a late but typical example. In the pre-Grouping period, therefore, many of the main line railway companies were able to get away with a relative handful of dedicated shunting engines – and such as they did possess – were often older 'road' engines pensioned-off from running-line work and put out to grass in some goods yard or other. How well and efficiently these old-stagers coped was of little significance in the general scheme of things in those relatively undemanding days.

The goods tank engine

As goods and mineral traffic increased dramatically in volume in the last decades of the 19th century however, these old *laissez-faire* arrangements could no longer cope. Goods depots, works and collieries were now being linked to a network of district classification and larger regional marshalling yards, while over-the-line goods trains were getting much longer as more powerful 'road' goods engines became available. These longer trains took more assembling and breaking down, while the rapid forwarding of loads and swift return of empties became essential to avoid wagon shortages. Efficient and speedy main line yard shunting

ABOVE *The epitome of the goods tank engine: an ex-LYR 23 class 0-6-0ST Rebuilt in 1891–1900 by Aspinall from standard Barton Wright 'Ironclad' 0-6-0 goods tender engines, to the tune of no fewer than 230 examples, of which 95 survived into the BR period. These robust engines handled the bulk of the L&Y's extensive yard shunting and trip working.* Author's collection

coupled with brisk goods short-trip working assumed a high importance – work somewhat beyond the capabilities of the dedicated shunter, with its lack of speed and range. CMEs had thus to address the provision of suitable locomotives.

The type that appeared to meet this need was a compact, six-coupled tank locomotive with wheels of 4ft–4ft 10in diameter on a moderate wheelbase and possessed of a larger boiler more suited to sustained steaming. The provision of reasonable coal and water capacity allowed a combination of

BELOW *A seminal design: the Webb 'Special DX' (SDX), an 1881 re-boilering of the 1858 original – of which 943 were built in the period 1858–1872. That's the equivalent of one new DX every five days for nearly 14 years!*

shunting capability with reasonable over-the-road performance and range. Thus was born the goods 0-6-0T – a type that was soon found to be invaluable for a far wider range of duties than those for which it was originally conceived.

The success of these versatile engines in the general shunting role largely did away with the need for specialised shunting locomotives outside docks and industrial locations with ultra-sharp curves of below about 4 chains radius. Only with the advent of large 'hump' marshalling yards in the early 1900s did a need for further dedicated shunting designs arise – in the hulking broad-shouldered shapes of a handful of massive and very powerful eight-coupled tank locomotives built specifically to heave heavy rakes of wagons over the steep hump gradients.

The general-purpose 0-6-0

At the heart of the traditional railway's traffic operations lay a large number of what might be called 'everyday workings' – pick-up and local freight trains, 'ordinary' goods trains on main lines, some perishable or less-demanding 'express' goods traffic, local, cross-country and branch line passenger workings. These were all duties calling for no great endurance or prodigies of tractive power or speed – and which thus might well be handled by a medium-sized tender engine with modestly proportioned cylinders and boiler sitting on driving wheels of a median diameter – 5ft 3in or thereabouts.

On Britain's railways in the age of steam, these 'bedrock' duties were largely handled by the ubiquitous 'goods' 0-6-0. To quote Tuplin again: 'For the large part, six-coupled six-wheeled engines did the work; it may well be that they were the only engines that earned more than they cost.' Be that as it may, it is a fact that 0-6-0 tender engines made up a very substantial proportion of the locomotive studs of three of the

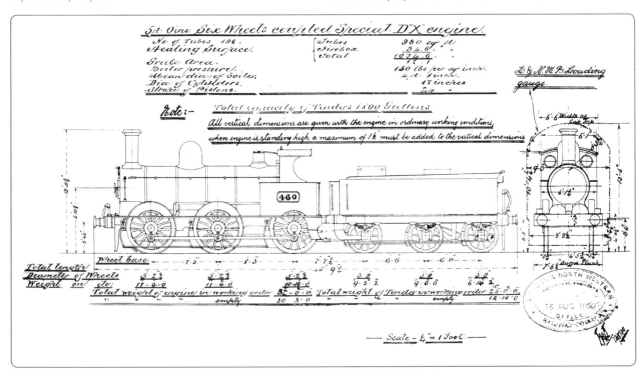

'Big Four' grouped railways; only on the passenger-orientated Southern were they in a relative minority.

The 0-6-0 'general purpose' tender engine that came to be the predominant British locomotive type for the thick end of a century can be pinned very precisely to a particular prototype – John Ramsbottom's LNWR 'DX Goods' of 1858. Like many seminal designs, the DX broke little new ground; rather, it brought together the best features of a range of existing types to establish the layout, general dimensions and proportions of the whole prolific breed of classic British 0-6-0s. This was an inside-cylindered, inside-framed engine on a modest wheelbase of 7ft 3in + 8ft 3in, with the firebox lying between the second and third axles (rather than hanging out at the back in Stephenson 'long-boiler' style). The engine had simple (but very robust) plate frames and rolled on driving wheels of 5ft 2in diameter. The inside cylinders were 17 x 24in, the boiler pressure was a modest 120lb, and valve gear was Stephenson's. The only real innovation was that the DX was the first engine to have screw, as opposed to lever, reverse.

They were also an outstanding success – not only on the goods traffic for which they had been intended, but proving quite speedy and steady-riding enough for many lesser passenger duties as well. The DX rapidly became the LNWR's most useful locomotive type – so useful, in fact, that no fewer than 943 of them were built, including 86 for the 'Lanky'. They thus formed the most numerous single design of British steam locomotive.

Webb produced a 'souped-up' rebuild – the 'Special DX' – in the 1870s. This had a bigger boiler with a bit more 'oomph' (150lb/sq in) and many were fitted with the vacuum brake and steam-heat for passenger working, thus becoming true general-purpose machines. The SDX was also arguably one of the best-proportioned and most comely of all Victorian-era British locomotives, very much a case of 'what looks right…' The basic DX formula was widely copied by most of the major English and Scottish pre-Grouping railways and resulted in some very large 'families' of 0-6-0 tender engines; only the Great North of Scotland knew it not. In 1913, out of a total British main line motive power stock of 23,664 locomotives, no fewer than 7,387 were 0-6-0 tender engines; all-but one-

third of the total. In earlier times, the proportion was probably even greater.

Post-Grouping 0-6-0s

The general-purpose 0-6-0 continued to proliferate after the Grouping, with the LMSR, LNER and GWR all building substantial numbers of the type. The Derby-dominated LMS administration unsurprisingly chose to perpetuate (in huge numbers) the 1911-vintage Midland 4F 'Big Goods' design – staid, reliable and workmanlike, but more than a trifle old-hat by 1924. By contrast with such LMS conservatism, Gresley on the LNER went in for a much more advanced 0-6-0 design in the form of the powerful and speedy J39 class of 1926, the very model of a modern general-purpose engine with 5ft 2in wheels, nice big 8in piston valves, and a large superheated boiler working at 180lb/sq in pressure. This was an engine well able to gallop along at a mile-a-minute or more when called upon, while sheltering its crew in a comfortable and commodious side-window cab.

By contrast, the last substantial series of traditional general-purpose 0-6-0 tender engines built – the GWR 2251 class

ABOVE *The odd mix of old and new that was the GWR Collett Goods of 1930: an 1883 Dean Goods as to chassis and machinery, but with a large, high-pressure taper boiler and superheating. The last of these did not emerge from Swindon until 1948.* Author's collection

introduced in 1930 and built thence down to 1948 – mixed the new with the decidedly old, being essentially an 1883 'Dean Goods' as to frames, cylinders and valve gear, but fitted with a modern Swindon No 10 Belpaire taper boiler pressed to 200lb/sq in and modestly superheated. It is worth remarking that the 2251s had all-but identical layout and dimensions to Ramsbottom's 1858 original: 17½ x 24in cylinders, 7ft 3in + 8ft 3in wheelbase, inside plate frames, 5ft 2½in driving wheels, and Stephenson valve gear with slide valves and screw reverse.

The last two classes of 0-6-0 built – the Southern Q and Q1 classes of 1938 and 1942 respectively – although conforming to the 'general-purpose' type in terms of capability – were in practice almost exclusively used on goods traffic, especially during the Second World War. The Southern had no shortage of passenger power, but was woefully deficient when it came to powerful goods locomotives. The Q was an odd throwback,

BELOW *A throwback? The SR Q class of 1938 was the last-but-one 0-6-0 to be designed. Odd, then, that it should essentially use the basic layout and dimensions of a 1911 machine, the Midland Class 4 'big goods', and a boiler intended for a 1926 rebuild of a 1914-vintage 4-4-0. The whole thing has the air of a stop-gap – which is more-or-less what it was! Handsome, though…* Author's collection

a sort of latter-day copy of that old stager, the MR/LMS 4F in general proportions and dimensions, although using the relatively modern boiler of the Maunsell L1 class 4-4-0. This gave it a bit more tractive effort, and as it was fitted for steam-heat it was thus suitable for passenger work if required.

The Q1, of course, resembled nothing else seen before or since on any railway anywhere on the planet. With a tractive effort of over 30,000lb it was the only 0-6-0 to develop more pulling power than the massive ex-GER/LNER Class J20. It was much the same size and weight as the older engine but had a shorter wheelbase, better route availability and substantially more boiler power, with a pressure of 230lb/sq in and high superheat. It was a resounding final chapter to the 100-year history of the British 0-6-0 goods engine.

Of these latter-day 0-6-0 types, the 4F was by far the most ubiquitous; after all, there were 772 of them! Apart from their home territory in the English Midlands and North West, you could just as well see a 4F in the Home Counties and London, down on the South Coast at Bournemouth, all over Scotland, just about anywhere in Wales, and in the more northerly nooks of East Anglia as far east as the North Norfolk coast. They were used on virtually every type of duty including, on occasion, express passenger workings. However, they were also heartily disliked by many footplatemen (notably those from LMS-constituent companies *other* than the Midland!) for their often-slothful performance, rough riding, suspect bearings and, particularly, for their uncomfortable cabs – skimpy, cramped, draughty and prone to invasion by the contents of the ashpan. Nevertheless, they were truly the epitome of the general-purpose engine and probably form one of the most useful of prototypes for post-Grouping modellers of most geographical bents.

Six-coupled general-purpose tank engines

As already noted, the six-coupled tank engine appeared as a significant breed in the mid-1870s to answer the need for a goods engine that was compact, powerful and handy enough for shunting work, yet that could run far and fast enough on the main line to undertake local trip workings. Such a design of engine was soon found to be useful for a far wider range of duties – including station pilot work, carriage shunting, general minor local traffic and, when provided with the vacuum brake, branch line or suburban passenger working.

The general-purpose vacuum-fitted six-coupled tank engine rapidly became a stalwart of the British railway scene and was proliferated in very large numbers over many designs. Once again, going on those 1913 motive power figures, 0-6-0Ts were the second biggest group of engines at some 3,700 units. Some railways went in for the type in a really big way – most notably the GWR which, by 1918, possessed no fewer than 1,100 of the things out of a total stud of 3,119 locomotives.

ABOVE *A very long-lived general-purpose 0-6-0T was the 25-strong SER Stirling R class of 1888, rebuilt by Wainwright as class R1 in 1910–15. Many of these useful engines survived well into the BR era, the last until 1960. Hornby-Dublo memorably chose it as the prototype for their first two-rail loco – a very good model in its day.* Author's collection

These ubiquitous engines came in three basic sizes: small and medium 0-6-0Ts and somewhat larger 0-6-2Ts with the odd 'heavy' 0-6-0. The 'small' 0-6-0T engines generally had wheels of 4ft diameter or a trifle more, were of compact overall dimensions and weighed in at 35–40 tons all-up. Typically, they had room for 600–1,000 gallons of water and a ton or so of coal, giving them a modest range. Well-known examples included the Brighton 'Terriers', GER 'Buckjumpers', NER E and E1 classes, and the GWR 850 and 2021 series of saddle (later pannier) tanks.

The next step up was the predominant 'medium' 0-6-0T, tipping the scales at 45–50 tons and having wheels of 4½ft or so. Tank capacity was typically 1,200 gallons with bunker space sufficient for 2–3 tons of the black stuff, giving them reasonable range and a fair turn of speed when needed. The assorted hoards of GW 4ft 7½ in saddle and pannier tanks

BELOW AND RIGHT *The plebian duo: the 412 LMS 'Jinties' and no fewer than 842 GWR '57xx' pannier tanks were all built for the general-purpose role. The two classes were comparable in basic dimensions and power output, with the '57xx' having a slight edge in tractive effort and coal capacity.* Courtesy Graham Warburton/ Author's collection

(including all 842 members of the '57xx' class) came into this category, as did the variegated multitude of Johnson MR 0-6-0Ts and their latter-day LMS descendants, the 412-strong army of 'Jinties'.

For anything needing greater range and/or power, the usual answer was an 0-6-2T with similar-sized drivers and a radial axle under the bunker. These are not to be confused with the legions of suburban passenger 0-6-2Ts, which generally had 5ft 3in or larger wheels and sacrificed tractive effort for a bit more speed. The greater length and additional carrying axle of the general-purpose 0-6-2T engines permitted a larger boiler or increased coal and water capacity. The first true example (designed as such rather than being a rebuilt 0-6-0) was the LNWR 'Coal Tank' of 1881, but the type really proliferated in South Wales, culminating in the powerful 62-ton GWR '56xx', which many folk don't realise was a red-coded 'main line only' engine.

The other great user of general-purpose 0-6-2Ts was the Great Central, which built themselves 186 of the breed in the shape of the 9A/9C classes (LNER N4/N5); like the '56xxs', these were 62-ton heavyweights, albeit somewhat bigger in the driving wheel at 5ft 1in. As for 'large' (over 50 tons) 0-6-0Ts, there were only ever a couple of such classes: the goods-only 57-ton/1,500-gallon Gresley J50 GNR/LNER of 1922, and the 55-ton GWR red-coded Hawksworth '94xx' series of taper-boiler 'super panniers' of 1947.

Suburban passenger

The 'suburb' as an entity requiring rail service, arrived in the last quarter of the 19th century. Indeed, it was the very availability of rail transport that made many suburbs possible in the first place, while in the early 20th century many enterprising railways – most famously the Metropolitan, north of London, became actively engaged in suburban development with the aim of providing themselves with important and profitable new traffic. To railway companies serving any conurbation (which was most of them, somewhere on their system), suburban passenger traffic soon became an important item in the balance sheet. Only truly provincial railways like the Highland and the Cambrian had no significant suburban workings.

Suburban passenger working – high-density and tightly

ABOVE *The ultimate in beefy six-coupled general-purpose tank engines: the GWR '56xx' of 1924, a 68-ton heavyweight with a 'red' route-availability code, and nearly 26,000lb of tractive effort. This one is hardly being overworked!* Author's collection

timed, with heavy ladings on short headways, frequent stops and the need for a swift turn-around at terminal points – was probably the most demanding form of railway working there was in the traditional railway era. Indeed, it still is today! While a few railways muddled by working such traffic with conventional passenger or general-purpose tender locomotives, it very soon became apparent that such a specialised traffic called for specialised motive power – and the suburban passenger tank engine was born. Chief among the attributes of the breed was the ability to run at the required line speed (which could be surprisingly brisk) in either direction, while frequent stopping and starting called for plenty of brake and boiler power, and lusty lungs. They also needed sufficient coal and water capacity to manage the distances involved, with both requisites being quick and easy

BELOW *The London, Brighton & South Coast Railway was early in the suburban passenger business and had a dense network of both short-distance 'inner suburban' lines together with lengthier runs to 'outer suburban' and 'retreat' destinations on or near the South Coast. Here is a Billinton D3 class 0-4-4T on an outer-suburban run c1900. The 0-4-4T type was widely favoured for suburban work in the 1890s.* Author's collection

to replenish, and were often equipped with condensing gear to 'consume their own smoke and steam' when working in city-centre tunnels and terminals.

This is a traffic role that spawned some famous families of locomotives: the 4-4-0T Beyer-Peacock 'Met Tanks' and Adams 'North London Passenger' engines, the GWR's 2-4-0T 'Metros' and 0-4-2T '517 class', the LSWR Beattie 2-4-0 'Well-tanks' and later 4-4-2T 'Adams' Radials', Stroudley's tenacious 'Terrier' and 'D Tank' 0-4-2Ts on the Brighton, F.W. Webb's 2-4-0 and 2-4-2 LNWR 'radial tanks', the many Johnson 0-4-4T types on the Midland, the North Eastern's 0-4-4WT BTP ('Bogie Tank, Passenger'), the GER's radial-trucked 2-4-2T 'Gobblers' and 0-6-0T 'Buckjumpers', the legion of 4-4-2 'Tilbury Tanks', the smart-but-sombre LYR 2-4-2T 'Large' and 'Small' radials… The list could go on and on!

Four-coupled designs initially predominated on most lines – 2-4-0, 0-4-2 or 4-4-0 tanks, soon joined by the radial truck-at-either-end 2-4-2T invented by Webb and subsequently taken up by several other lines (the L&Y, GER, NER and GCR) as it truly did ride equally well in either direction. The 0-4-4 'bogie passenger tank' was also widely favoured, particularly by Stroudley on the LBSCR, Drummond on the Caley and then LSWR, Stirling on the GNR, James Stirling and Wainwright on the SER/SECR and, of course, by Kirtley and Johnson on the Midland.

Suburban super-power

The widespread advent of fashionable and wealthier 'outer suburbs' in the late 19th and early 20th century led to longer suburban routes and a consequent demand for more speed and greater range from the motive power. This requirement – together with the introduction of heavier, more luxurious stock – soon led to bigger and more powerful suburban types: larger 2-4-2T types on the LNWR and LYR, followed by powerful new 4-4-2Ts on the Tilbury, GNR, GCR, GWR, LNWR, NBR, CR and Brighton. Mr Webb wheeled out a big-wheeled 0-6-2T for the LNWR's heavy Watford services in 1898, and six-coupled suburban power soon caught on elsewhere: 'radial' 0-6-2Ts on the GNR and GER, 2-6-2Ts on the L&Y and Churchward's GWR. By 1912, Robinson on the GCR and Bowen-Cooke on the LNWR had both unveiled large and very powerful superheated 4-6-2Ts for heavy outer-suburban working. Even the small-minded Midland expanded their traditional suburban 0-4-4T into the beefy-but-suspect 'Flatiron' 0-6-4T.

Towards the end of the pre-Grouping period, the demands of premium long-distance suburban working produced some of the largest tank locomotives ever to run in this country – in the shape of a handful of powerful, 4-6-4 'Baltic' tanks. This was a trend started by Whitelegg on the Tilbury and perpetuated by him on the G&SWR in 1922 with some truly massive (if somewhat-eccentric) engines. Most successful and most durable of the breed were the septet of Billinton LBSCR locomotives, used as effectively, express passenger power for fast runs from London down to the fashionable residential areas of the South Coast.

The most technically advanced were the Hughes-designed L&Y engines, actually built by the LMS in 1923. These magnificent superheated four-cylinder engines were swift and

ABOVE *The large 4-4-2 'Atlantic Tank' for heavy, fast long-distance suburban traffic was more-or-less invented by the London, Tilbury & Southend Railway back in 1879. This is No 80* Thundersley, *of the final and largest 'Tilbury' series of 1909. The LMS built a further nine engines to the same general design after the Grouping in 1923. No 80 is, happily, preserved.* Author's collection

ABOVE *The first of what soon became the most numerous type of suburban fast passenger tank locomotive, the large 2-6-4T with outside cylinders and Walschaerts valve gear. The original 1927 Fowler 4P was followed by Stanier and Fairburn versions, and culminated in the outstanding BR Standard Class 4MT.* LMS PRO/ Author's collection

powerful; far swifter and more puissant, in fact, than the traffic demanded. As with the Whitelegg G&SW tanks, they were short-lived under the Derby-biased LMS management of the 1920s.

Latter-day suburban steam

In the immediate post-Grouping period, things carried on much as before; the 'Grouped' railways either soldiered on with existing power or – as on the GNR and GER sections of the LNER – introduced modern superheated derivatives of the existing types: the N2 and N7. On the GWR, Collett was content to continue development of the Churchward '31xx' 2-6-2T into larger, more powerful superheated versions. It was not until the later 1920s that all-new designs were produced for suburban traffic.

Surprisingly, perhaps, the most significant such type appeared on the conservative pre-Stanier LMS, when the racy Derby-designed Fowler 2-6-4T made its debut at the end of 1927 – an engine with no obvious antecedents. Stanier was quick to seize upon this layout, producing his own taper-boiler derivative in two and three-cylinder variants, the latter specific to the demands of the Tilbury line. On the LNER, Gresley produced the handsome V1/V3 design of three-cylinder 2-6-2T in 1930 for faster and longer distance work in Scotland and on Tyneside, otherwise leaving the existing pre-Grouping designs to get on with it.

The Southern also made do with in essence, pre-Grouping power, while pressing ahead with its extensive and far-sighted programme of suburban electrification – a truly apposite solution to the particular demands of the traffic that had first appeared in the early 1900s. Ultimately, of course, virtually all suburban traffic throughout Britain was to acquire the live rail or go beneath the wires.

It was only right at the end of the 'Grouped' period – in 1945 – that more modern 2-6-4Ts were introduced, the Fairburn on the LMS and the Thompson L1 on the LNER. Although widely used on suburban duties, both these classes were actually intended for a far wider general-purpose/mixed traffic role, as were the smaller Class 2 Ivatt 'Mickey Mouse'

2-6-2Ts that appeared on the LMS in 1946. Both the Fairburn and Ivatt LMS designs were perpetuated in ameliorated form within the BR Standard range as the type 2MT 2-6-2T and the highly successful 4MT 2-6-4T – a type which saw much suburban working through to final electrification.

That suburban tank engines have historically been such a mixed bunch is indicative of the widely differing conditions pertaining on the various suburban networks. The LBSCR and GER in London, faced with short but densely trafficked lines with many stations close together, opted for powerful, small-wheeled six-coupled tanks for rapid acceleration, allied to the strong and swift-acting Westinghouse air brake to facilitate speedy station stops – a virtue which also found favour in Scotland and in the North East.

The LNWR's convoluted and hilly routes around Manchester and in West Yorkshire called for powerful, small-wheeled radial tanks, whereas the GNR, scudding out to Welwyn or Hatfield on the main line, needed larger-wheeled engines with a pretty fair turn of speed – and so on. There never has been a truly 'universal' design of suburban passenger tank engine, although I suppose if anything can lay claim to such a crown it must be the BR Standard Class 4 2-6-4T, which is fitting, really, as it was the 'last word' before all such traffic fell to the lot of the multiple unit.

Branch line passenger power

The dedicated branch line passenger engine has never been a very significant category of locomotive, for the good and sufficient reason that such generally undemanding work fell within the capabilities of either older main line passenger or suburban tank engines bumped off of their primary role by newer arrivals, or general-purpose 0-6-0s of one sort or another.

Not many British branch lines were long enough to demand the services of tender locomotives although some railways used them anyway, mostly because they had them available – as on the GER, where the ubiquitous J15 0-6-0s put in a prodigious amount of branch line mileage. Lack of turntables at branch line termini meant that a lot of this mileage was tender first; small wonder, then, at the prevalence of improvised tender weatherboards sported by engines so engaged! By and large, though, tank engines of one sort or another were used on branches, but only a few of them were *designed* for the role.

Leaving aside a handful of engines built to work a specific line, such as the 'Killin Pug' on the Caley, it was the Churchward-era GWR that first went in for dedicated and purpose-built 'standardised' branch line motive power, starting in 1904 with the 'Small Prairie'. Up until then, the GWR's branches had largely relied – like everybody else's – on a mix of small general-purpose engines like the 850 class 0-6-0STs and lesser/older suburban designs, notably the 517 class 0-4-2Ts, plus a handful of one-offs for lines with particular requirements. But with traffic getting heavier – especially on lines made holiday-popular by the efforts of the Paddington PR machine – something with a little more power and 'zip' was required.

The answer was a dapper lightweight 2-6-2T with pony trucks both ends, two decent-sized outside cylinders and wheels 4ft 1½in or 4ft 7½in in diameter. These engines were a great success; the larger-wheeled variant was good for a mile-a-minute, while their powers of acceleration stirred many a sluggish rural liver! There wasn't anything remotely like them anywhere else on the British railway network; or was there destined to be for a further four decades, until the LMS Ivatt 2MT 'Mickey Mouse' 2-6-2T and its BR Standard clone appeared.

The GWR went on to build several other notable classes of branch line engine, of which the best-known (especially among modellers) is the '48xx' (post-1946, '14xx') 0-4-2Ts introduced in 1932. They were built specifically to replace worn-out engines of the 517 and 'Small Metro' classes and were actually far more modern in detail and performance than their traditional outline might suggest. Also in the same mould were the family of 'Wolverhampton wheelbase' 0-6-0PTs built to take over from the 850, 2021 and 1854 classes; the big-wheeled (5ft 2½in) auto-fitted '54xx' passenger pannier tank, the 4ft 7½in '64/74xx' general-purpose engines, and the 4ft 1½in '16xx' 'lightweight pannier' that didn't actually see the light of day until after BR had taken over.

BELOW Dedicated branch line power: the GWR '44xx' of 1906, as modified with a bigger bunker by Collett. These 'small Prairie' engines, with pony trucks fore and aft, rode well on indifferent track and through tight curves. The ten '44xx' engines had driving wheels of 4ft 1½in diameter; those of the far-more-numerous '45xx' series were 4ft 7½in. Author's collection

Railmotors and auto-trains

As the 20th century sprinted off the starting blocks, the railways started to face their first real competition in the rapid-transit passenger business, courtesy of the electric tramcar and, subsequently, the motor omnibus. A search for economy and operating efficiency was soon under way and the steam railmotor and the push-pull 'auto train' were two attempts to address a traffic need that was not decisively answered until the diesel railcar and multiple unit arrived in the mid-1950s. Steam railmotors – essentially, a coach with a small, built-in 0-4-0 steam locomotive – became all the rage in the pre-1910 era, with many railways dipping a toe in the water. Only the GWR and LNWR held their corporate noses and jumped into the deep end, commissioning substantial fleets of the things which they used for both short-haul rapid-interval suburban and quieter rural branch line workings.

The drawbacks – which soon became apparent – were, first, lack of flexibility in accommodation and capacity (most railmotors were not powerful enough to manage much in the way of tail traffic) and secondly, availability – where a fault in either loco or coach put the whole outfit out of commission. It is notable that the most successful and longest-lived of railmotors were the LYR's articulated design, where the loco unit (which was anyway decidedly larger and more powerful than most) could readily be detached from the coach portion when required and replaced with a 'spare'. The ensemble could also manage a decent-sized trailer car to double the seating capacity if needed.

The push-pull or auto-train was another take on the same basic idea, but used a conventional stand-alone steam locomotive fitted with motor control gear which allowed it to be driven from a special compartment from the appropriate end of the train. This cut out the need to run-around at terminals. Although not restricted as to length by lack of power, most auto-trains were still quite short with one or two coaches being the norm. Again, the GWR was an enthusiastic user of the concept, building special trailer cars for the work; most other railways making do with normal – usually older – passenger stock, suitably modified. Ironically, a lot of the GWR's later trailer cars were rebuilt from redundant railmotors. While an 0-4-2T and trailer car is often seen as the archetypal GW branch line passenger train, the concept also saw considerable use in a suburban context, where Swindon used motor-fitted 0-6-0PTs sandwiched between a pair (or even quartet) of trailers.

Mixed Traffic arrives

At the turn of the century, several developments took place which had a fundamental effect on the demands made on motive power. In the previous chapter, we noted the swift and dramatic increase in passenger train weights and speeds at the end of the 19th century. Something similar occurred in the freight side of the business, with the advent of larger-capacity wagons on steel underframes fitted with better bearings and – most significantly – power brakes.

The traditional Victorian loose-coupled ordinary goods train was limited to its lowly maximum of 25mph by a combination of built-up iron wheels – prone to disintegration at high rotational rates – with grease axleboxes which ran hot at any

RIGHT *The GWR famously favoured auto-trains for branch line service, but they were not alone. The Southern also adopted the principle widely, using their own compressed-air-operated control gear, mostly fitted to former SECR and LSWR 0-4-4Ts. Here is the Hawkhurst branch auto in 'push' mode behind H class No 31533, about to leave Cranbrook in Kent. Note the tail-lamp on the engine's smokebox lamp iron.* Author's collection

sort of speed, and a lack of effective braking. With new wagons boasting screw-couplings, solid cast-steel wheels, oil-lubricated axle bearings and powerful automatic vacuum brakes, far higher speeds – 45mph or more – were readily attainable; the 'express goods train' was born. The only snag was that there were precious few suitable engines to pull them! The majority of existing dedicated goods engines lacked boilers with a capacity adequate for the sustained output required, being designed only to provide sufficient steam to trundle along in the twenties. Most such engines also lacked adequate lubrication for higher speeds and had no vacuum brake gear to control these racy new wagons. Only the better, larger-wheeled and more modern of the vacuum-fitted 0-6-0 general-purpose types had a brisk enough turn of speed and sufficient boiler power to cope with the new role, but something better-fitted to the purpose was soon being considered.

The initial response to this need for an express goods engine was a large vacuum-fitted traditional 0-6-0 type with enhanced boiler and cylinder power riding on 5ft 3in or even 5ft 8in wheels. Such high-stepping 0-6-0s proved, however, still to be short of boiler power and often rather rough riders at speed – so the next step was to add a leading bogie to permit an even bigger boiler and to give steadier fast running. The result was an entirely new breed of express goods engine, once again

pioneered by Webb on the LNWR just before he retired in 1903. This was the 'Bill Bailey', an ungainly four-cylinder 4-6-0 fitted with the 5ft 2½in-diameter driving wheels of the general-purpose LNWR '18-inch' 0-6-0 (aka the 'Cauliflower').

Although unsuccessful, these engines led directly to the Whale '19-inch Goods' of 1906 – essentially, an 'Experiment' class two-cylinder express-passenger engine fitted with the small-diameter driving wheels. It very soon became apparent that such a locomotive, as well as being well suited to the express goods role for which it had been conceived, made a very useful second-rank semi-fast passenger engine – especially valuable in working the then-popular but highly demanding excursion traffic. Thus, the idea of the true mixed traffic type was born and soon assumed an important place in the motive power strategies of the more progressive railway companies.

The mixed traffic locomotive

If I had to nominate the first true modern mixed traffic engine (that is, designed for the dual role from the outset), it would have to be Churchward's iconic GWR '43xx' 2-6-0 of 1911.

BELOW *Mixed-traffic dawn: a 1903 LNWR 'Bill Bailey' Webb four-cylinder 4-6-0 express goods engine. These were resounding duds, but gave rise to the 1906 Whale '19in Goods', often cited as the first true modern mixed-traffic engine – even if it was not designed as such!* Author's collection

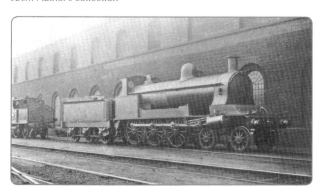

BELOW *An early and outstanding example of the modern mixed-traffic engine was the 1917 Maunsell Mogul for the SECR, which had several variants. This is a larger (6ft) wheeled two-cylinder U class, No 31793, working a typical secondary passenger duty – a cross-country Southampton–Bournemouth train.* Author's collection

ABOVE *The other side of mixed traffic – and the aspect many modellers neglect: ordinary freight workings. Here is a very sad and run-down ex-GWR 'Hall' right at the end of steam, minus name and cabside plates and carrying only an (illegible) chalked number. It is working a partially fitted (not less than one-third vacuum-braked) 'express' goods. Very different to the sort of summer-holiday express working most people associate with this class.* Author's collection

The LNWR engines had been conceived as a goods locomotives and hence had coupled wheels only 5ft 2½in in diameter, which limited ultimate speed potential somewhat, to around 60mph. Churchward went for 5ft 8in drivers for his Mogul, as did Gresley for his similarly sized K1 class 2-6-0 of 1912 – a size which made for a much more fleet-footed engine. The Churchward Mogul was intended from the outset as a genuine mixed-traffic locomotive, with blue route-availability, 70+mph speed potential, plenty of boiler power, large-ejector vacuum brakes and steam-heat for passenger working. The Gresley engine, although conceived initially for fast freight and perishables working, soon proved to be equally versatile. The outstandingly successful SECR Maunsell N class 2-6-0 of 1917 was also cooked to this new multi-role recipe from the outset.

Between the wars, the mixed traffic engine really came into its own, growing in size and power in the process. The LNWR's '19-inch Goods' of 1906 had been confected by the simple dodge of turning out a version of an existing express passenger type with smaller wheels. Urie pulled the same trick on the LSWR in 1921 when he introduced the H15 and S15 classes of mixed-traffic 4-6-0s, effectively a 6ft 7in-wheeled N15 'King Arthur' but with 6ft or 5ft 7in wheels respectively. The GWR went a similar – but more literal – route in 1924 to create the seminal mixed traffic 'Hall' class, the prototype of which was simply a 6ft 8in 'Saint' class 4-6-0 retro-fitted with 6ft driving wheels. Collett intended it as 'a 43xx, but more so' – an aim more nearly realised when the 'Grange' class appeared in 1936. This was effectively a 'Hall' fitted with '43xx' 5ft 8in drivers – literally, in this case, as the wheels came

from withdrawn Moguls. A further class of similarly endowed but lightweight 'blue disc' 5ft 8in mixed traffic engines appeared in 1938, in the shape of the 'Manor' 4-6-0s.

Over on the LMS, mixed traffic design kicked off with the highly capable Hughes-Fowler 'Crab' of 1926, a large-boilered 5ft 6in-wheeled 2-6-0 of pure L & Y design, which was followed by the slightly more powerful but similarly dimensioned Stanier Mogul design of 1933. But when the real doyen of the mixed traffic breed – the Stanier 'Black 5' – appeared in 1935, it was a 4-6-0 with 6ft wheels in the mould of the GW 'Hall'. This was an outstanding design, destined to be proliferated in huge numbers (over 800) by the LMS and perpetuated in slightly modernised 'Standard' form by BR.

The last LMS mixed traffic design was the utilitarian Ivatt Class 4 2-6-0, also perpetuated by BR. On the LNER, Gresley took a different course when he sought to go one-up on the original K1/K2 class 5ft 8in 2-6-0s, producing first the ultra-big-boiler three-cylinder K3 variant in 1920, then in 1936, unveiling the racy three-cylinder V2 class 2-6-2 with 6ft 3in drivers and a Pacific-style wide-firebox boiler. These engines were a notable success, proving exceptionally capable in express passenger working. The V2s were joined in 1942 by the austere Thompson B1 class 4-6-0s, which had 6ft 2in drivers but only two cylinders. The LMS and LNER also produced modern 2-6-4T mixed traffic designs, in the shape of the Fairburn Class 4 and Thompson L1 already noted.

By the time the Railway Executive's Motive Power Committee came to plan the Standard range of post-war steam locomotive designs, the mixed traffic role was so predominant that virtually all the BR Standard classes were specified to fill it and accordingly classified 'MT'. The only exceptions were the solitary three-cylinder 8P Pacific *Duke of Gloucester* and the iconic 9F 2-10-0 which formed the swansong of the British steam locomotive. In practice, the later double-chimney 9Fs could well have been classified MT as well as they proved remarkably successful when pressed into passenger service, famously proving capable of speeds in the 90mph bracket on their 5ft-diameter drivers – a testament to the sophistication of

the front-end design and the quality of the lubrication, balancing and bearing arrangements.

Express passenger

We now come at last to the familiar froth on the top of the whole heady broth – the express passenger locomotives, the ones everybody knows about. The first thing to point out is that, in comparison with the more utilitarian types, there were never that many of them. Even in the late 'Grouped' era and under BR, an overall total of little more than 1,200 or so such machines was spread between the Big Four companies, or across the BR regions – less than 6 per cent of the total stock. 'Twas ever thus, even in pre-Grouping days, when many 'express' engines were built in penny numbers. Some railways, like the South Wales coal lines, never had any at all, while lines like the Cambrian, Furness or Highland rostered only a handful apiece.

A lot of express classes led somewhat ephemeral lives, especially in the two decades from 1895 to 1915 when, as already noted, passenger train weights shot up dramatically at the same time as journey times were being drastically pruned. This called for much brisker point-to-point timings and a corresponding quantum leap in power and tractive effort. A sub-200-ton train running to a 40mph average in 1890 was a very different proposition to 350+ tons at 60mph in 1910, usually calling for all but double the drawbar-horsepower.

On the GWR, crack power went from a Dean Single in 1892 to the prototype Churchward two-cylinder 4-6-0 No 98 in 1904, and the production 'Saint' class by 1908; startling progress indeed! Similarly, on the GNR, the Stirling 8ft singles – still premium power in the mid-1890s – had given way to the big-boilered, wide-firebox Ivatt 'Large Atlantic' by 1902. The story was the same elsewhere. Many of the intermediate express designs of this period – such as the Dean/Churchward double-framed 4-4-0s on the GWR and the Webb

ABOVE The most glamorous and probably the swiftest of the principal mixed-traffic designs to appear in the 1930s – the Gresley three-cylinder V2 2-6-2 – a sort of pint-sized version of his classic Pacific design. They saw widespread use on express passenger duties, as here, where No 60936 is hurrying north on the main line through Hatfield. During the Second World War the V2s performed prodigious feats of heavy haulage. Author's collection

four-cylinder compounds – had very short lives indeed as front-line express passenger motive power. By 1910, big-boiler 4-4-2 Atlantics and 4-6-0s had taken over all the important workings on all the principal railways – except, of course, on the Midland, where a 4-4-0 three-cylinder Compound was as big as motive power ever got.

BELOW The express passenger 4-4-0 had a very brief reign on the GWR. The first – the small-wheeled hill-climbing 'Duke' – appeared in 1894 and the last – the Churchward two-cylinder 'County' – in 1904. From then on, all 'standard' primary express engines were six-coupled. Here, a straight-frame 'County' hurries a Weymouth express down the main line c1910. The class became extinct in 1933. Author's collection

ABOVE *The first of the 'new breed' of post-Grouping premium express locomotives was the Southern's 1926 'Lord Nelson' 4-6-0, the first of which, No 850, is here seen at Southampton when brand-new running trials on the heaviest boat trains. Based on their 33,500lb of nominal tractive effort, the 'Lord Nelsons' briefly held the 'most powerful express engine' crown before being deposed by the GWR 'King' of 1927.* SR Official/Author's collection

ABOVE *The ultimate 'premium' express engine? This well-known 1935 LNER publicity shot of the first Gresley A4 Pacific at the head of its matching streamlined train underlines the public relations value of such prestigious types as image-setters for the whole railway. At this date, a lot of LNER trains made do with far more prosaic motive power!* LNER postcard/Author's collection

Premium power

Express passenger steam engines essentially came in three varieties: premium, primary and secondary. The first category was an exclusive club, with membership restricted to the biggest, fastest, most powerful, most glamorous, and least numerous engines of their day. Sometimes, such locomotives were seemingly built almost as much for PR purposes as for merely pulling trains. By no means all pre-Grouping railways went in for such rarefied thoroughbreds, many preferring to work all their express traffic with prosaic studs of more utilitarian machinery. But throughout railway history, there have been a succession of 'star' locomotive types, engines that achieved a fame and status well above their numbers and operational significance. They impinged on the public consciousness in a way the more run-of-the-mill types never did; Ferraris rather than Fords, to borrow an automotive analogy.

Such 'premium' engine classes have ever been a rare breed; most of the famous Victorian examples numbered 30 locomotives or less apiece. There were just 26 8ft Stirling singles on the GNR, ten each of the larger series of Webb compounds on the LNWR, and 24 broad gauge 'Rovers' on the GWR, succeeded by the 30 Dean singles of the 'Achilles' class. In the Edwardian era, there were just five of the Caledonian's mighty 903 class 'Cardean' inside-cylinder 4-6-0s and, of course, the solitary 'Super Star' 4-6-2 *The Great Bear* on the GWR – only later joined by a pair each of prototype Pacifics on the GNR and NER.

The premium breed re-emerged in the later 1920s, starting on the Southern with Maunsell's 16 four-cylinder 'Lord Nelson' 4-6-0s in 1926, closely followed by the 30 GWR four-cylinder 'Kings' of 1927 – the first British express passenger class to breach the 40,000lb mark for nominal tractive effort, and hence the subject of extravagant 'most powerful' claims from the GWR's ever-sharp PR department.

The similarly puissant Stanier four-cylinder 'Princess Royal'

Pacifics on the LMSR were introduced from 1933, a dozen engines edging the 'King' to second place in the TE stakes by a few pounds. They in turn were comprehensively eclipsed by Gresley's mighty P2 class 2-8-2 *Cock o'the North* of 1934 – in terms of nominal tractive effort, the most powerful design of British express passenger locomotive ever built, although LNER No 10000, the so-called 'Hush-Hush' – the solitary experimental water-tube-boiler 4-6-4 – ran it very close after rebuilding with a conventional boiler in 1937.

Not content with the power crown, the LNER comprehensively stole the 'Glamour' and 'Speed' categories with the introduction of the dramatically streamlined three-cylinder A4 Pacifics in 1935, engines that soon proved readily capable of velocities in excess of 110mph. Eventually, 35 A4s were built, one being lost to bombing in the Second World War.

The LMS responded in 1938 with the four-cylinder 'Princess Coronation' Pacifics, the largest and heaviest of British 4-6-2 classes; 25 of the 38 engines were built as streamliners – mainly, apparently, for publicity purposes. Stanier is reported to have referred to the non-streamlined engines as 'the proper ones'. Having kicked-off the rebirth of the 'premium' breed, the Southern also had the last word, in the unmistakeable shape of Bulleid's unconventional but super-powerful 'Merchant Navy' Pacific, 30 three-cylinder 'air-smoothed' engines introduced from 1941.

Post-Nationalisation, British Railways added but a solitary specimen, the three-cylinder Caprotti 4-6-2 No 71000 *Duke of Gloucester*. Do the sums and you come up with a total of just about 160 such 'premium' engines, out of a total locomotive stock a whisker in excess of 20,000 in 1948; considerably less than 1 per cent.

Primary and secondary power

'Premium' locomotives handled only the heaviest, fastest and most important express passenger workings. Secondary express types or mixed traffic engines worked the lesser and slower trains on the principal main lines and general express traffic on less-important routes. All other main line fast passenger workings – that is, the vast majority – fell to the lot of the 'primary' express passenger classes, which thus formed the most numerous group of such engines.

The GWR got by exclusively with a fleet of 6ft 8in-wheeled 4-6-0s – 77 two-cylinder 'Saints', 61 four-cylinder 'Stars' and (eventually) 169 of the four-cylinder 'Castle' class, the latter total including many engines built as replacements for, or as 'renewals' of, the earlier types. At any one time, Swindon had around 250 4-6-0 primary passenger engines in service.

The LMS also favoured the 4-6-0 for such work, with a trio of 6ft 9in-wheeled three-cylinder classes available: 71 'Royal Scots', 52 'Patriots' and, equivalent to the GWR 'Castle', 191 Stanier 5XP 'Jubilee' 4-6-0s. The LNER favoured 6ft 8in three-cylinder Pacifics and 4-6-0s, with 78 Gresley A1/A3s and 73 'Sandringhams' forming the core provision, augmented after the war, by a further 90 modern Thompson/Peppercorn Pacifics of classes A1 and A2.

On the Southern, the 75 two-cylinder 6ft 7in 'King Arthur' 4-6-0s were the backbone of the primary provision, joined after the war by the 110 Bulleid three-cylinder 6ft 2in 'light Pacifics', although strictly, the latter were categorised as 'mixed traffic'. The same was true of the 55 BR 'Britannia' 6ft 2in-wheel two-cylinder Pacifics, although, like the Bulleids, they worked much primary express traffic in their day.

Secondary express passenger working was often left to older 'primary' types bumped off the top links by newer arrivals. In the earlier years of the Grouping period, the Midland-derived three-cylinder 'Compound' and Class 2/3 4-4-0s, LNWR 'Prince of Wales' 4-6-0s and 'Precursor' 4-4-0s, served the LMS in this role, with the Ivatt GNR 'Large Atlantics', Robinson GCR 4-4-2 and 'Director' 4-4-0s together with ex-GER 1500 class 4-6-0s and 'Claud Hamilton' 4-4-0s on the LNER and various Drummond LSWR and Wainwright/ Maunsell ex-SECR 4-4-0s on the Southern.

Some new secondary power was built during this period and the LMS kept on churning out 'standard' Compounds throughout the 1920s, and Gresley introduced the 'Hunt' and 'Shire' class three-cylinder 6ft 8in 4-4-0s in 1927, using the existing J39-type boiler. In 1930, Maunsell on the Southern topped all the others by introducing the big, powerful three-cylinder 'Schools' class 4-4-0s, true state-of-the-art machines to work the fast Kent coast traffic and lighter trains on the Southampton/Bournemouth main lines.

With the arrival of powerful and speedy 6ft-wheeled mixed traffic locomotives from 1920 or so onwards,

ABOVE *It was the less-glamorous but far more numerous primary classes that worked the bulk of the express passenger traffic. The LMS 'Patriot' was a power class 5 middleweight, effectively, a small-boilered 'Royal Scot'. Here is No 5916* E. Tootal Broadhurst *brand-new in 1933, which was renumbered 5525 the following year.* Author's collection

the need for secondary express engines as a separate breed largely evaporated, and many of the older pre-Grouping designs were phased out during the 1930s. By the outbreak of war, the vast majority of lesser express workings were being handled by the likes of the GW 'Halls', the LMS 'Black Fives' and the LNER's V2s. Only on the Southern, which had relatively few mixed traffic engines and kept those that were available busy with express goods and perishables workings, did the secondary express traffic keep classic pre-Grouping designs like the Drummond T9 and Wainwright D and E class 4-4-0s at work until well into the BR era.

After 1948, BR policy favoured the mixed traffic engine at all sizes and power ratings and these were the engines that saw off the pre-Grouping survivors, only to be eclipsed by the diesels a few short years later.

BELOW *Secondary express passenger power was often an older, front-line type 'bumped down' by newer arrivals. The 40 Smith-Deeley three-cylinder Compounds of 1906 were top-end power on the Midland up to the 1923 Grouping. After this, the LMS built another 155 of them for second-rank express duties across the system.* LMS Official/Author's collection

4 SOURCING A REALISTIC LOCO STUD

In my book, to be deemed 'realistic' a model loco stud needs to be convincing on three levels. First, it needs to embrace an appropriate selection of prototypes in harmony with the subject of the layout – a choice which will hopefully have been facilitated by my attempts to analyse what the real railways got up to in matters of motive power. Secondly, the individual models which go to make up the stud should not only be realistic in their own right, but realistic in *context*; that is, they should be to a common standard of detail and finish – a standard, moreover, that tallies with that of the rolling stock they will haul and the layout on which they will haul it. Thirdly, each model in the stud needs to *function* as realistically as possible – not just in absolute terms, but in the context of the job it has to do. A mechanical specification that suits a lowly shunter won't necessarily do a general-purpose 0-6-0 any favours and certainly won't help a high-stepping Pacific.

To these basic requirements, I would add a fourth aspiration: that the model locomotives making up the stud possess individuality and character. Rather than settling for a generic model of a given class of locomotive, my aim is always to produce a 'portrait' of a particular engine as it existed at an appropriate point in its history – complete with any little quirks and imperfections, variations in detail or state of finish. Rather than settling for a 'Hornby T9' or a 'Bachmann Small Prairie', I'm all about producing a replica of No 30717 as it was when shedded at Okehampton in 1960, or No 4561 in its late-1950s state when allocated to Laira.

The Hornby and Bachmann models are thus regarded as mere starting-points. Along the way, I'll do whatever I have to do to them to achieve an authentic portrait. Quite apart from the gain in realism that always comes from such applied observation, I find that a model worked on in this way acquires a personality of its own, an individuality that sets it apart from the hordes of basically similar replicas that also arrived on the not-so-slow boat from China.

The realistic choice

Deciding which particular locomotives you actually need to work a given layout calls for a bit of research and perhaps a spot of 'creative extrapolation'. The object of the exercise is, ideally, to arrive at a list of *exactly* which engines you need to render your layout truly authentic. Not just general types, but – in the cause of ultimate historical veracity and realism – the individual examples that would have been most likely to have

ABOVE *Individuality and character – the twin virtues of the portrait model. This is not just any old 'Buckjumper', but a replica of J69/2 No 64899 c1959 that incorporates the exact combination of features (which, on a class as extensive and long-lived as the 'Bucks', were extremely variable), of that particular engine – right down to the chalked nickname! The model was rebuilt in 1984 from the remains of my original Wills J69, which dated back to 1964. Waste not…*

worked the trains you're replicating. This is an exercise that is straightforward enough for a layout based on an actual prototype location; fictional subjects, on the other hand, call for a little more imagination and a spot of creativity in the accounting! But whatever the subject of the layout, arriving at an appropriate loco list forms a fascinating exercise in prototype research, with the main sources of information being photographs and published motive power allocation lists – of which, more anon.

Much will depend on the nature of the layout. If you're modelling a stretch of busy main line, then the choice of engines that could, potentially, have passed your chosen spot is obviously pretty wide – although not infinite. A BR 'Clan' Pacific

BELOW *The GWR '45xx', a real general-purpose type if ever there was one, is just the sort of loco many modellers will look to as a key element of their studs. Bachmann's RTR model is a sound basis to work on; it is fundamentally accurate, well-detailed and finished, and generally a good runner. All it needs, as seen here, is to be brought up to the benchmark specification for detail and finish and to be individualised to a suitable prototype. Not too daunting a task.*

OPPOSITE *Not so many years ago, a model of a T9 as accurate, detailed and well-finished as this would have been an object of remark and admiration. Now it is (yawn!) 'just another Hornby' – in this case, converted to EM and skilfully weathered by Philip Hall. The challenge nowadays lies in bringing all the other locos on the layout up to this standard.*

LEFT *The locomotives here are commonplace enough – but there was only one place they could have been seen in tandem like this: the Somerset & Dorset. A BR-period Somerset & Dorset layout can actually accommodate an amazingly wide selection of locomotive types, from pre-Grouping 4-4-0s to the final batch of double-chimney 9F 2-10-0s. Note the headlamp code – the original S&D code for a passenger train, which persisted to the end. Everywhere else this code referred to a non-fitted express freight!* Author's collection

on the GWR or a Bulleid Q1 on the Cambrian Coast is somewhat on the far side unlikely, at least in the pre-preservation 'steam special' era… But it won't take much study of line-side photographs and a quick peek at a shed allocation listing to come up with a nice long list of possibilities – probably far more engines than you could ever hope to buy or build. A layout as ambitious (but authentic) as Roy Jackson's 'Retford' could accommodate any of several hundred different prototype locomotives without stretching credulity a millimetre. In the face of such a wide potential choice, Roy has been careful to base his stud upon 'regulars' – engines known to have been rostered to work the various trains on a regular basis.

Rostering

This is an important aspect of prototype operating practice which effectively determined what locomotive did which job. All time-tabled workings were normally assigned to a given

BELOW *Standing outside the running shed of its home depot, 31B March, ex-GER D16/1 class 4-4-0 No 62589 was a member of the 'Ordinary Passenger' link at this very large depot. As such, it would have been seen on secondary passenger or stock (parcels and perishables) workings to Ely and Cambridge, and onward to London via the Cambridge Line. Alternatively, on trains up to King's Lynn and Hunstanton, all turns rostered to this link; it would have been most unlikely, however, for it to have turned up on the East Suffolk Line that I model.* R. Blencowe/Author's collection

'link' at the motive power depot (MPD) responsible for providing the requisite power for that train. These 'links' consisted of groups of appropriate engines together with their crews. They ranged from the 'Top Link' – a handful of premium or primary express passenger engines in peak condition, crewed by the most senior and experienced men at the depot – down to the 'Extra' or 'Spare' Link'. This last was usually a largish but somewhat rag-tag and bobtail collection of motive power manned by whoever was available, and was intended to cover any shortfalls, extra workings, breakdowns and routine 'works' visits, odd jobs or pilot duties, and to provide assisting engines where needed.

In between these extremes would lie lesser links: Second, third and so on passenger links – responsible for working ordinary main line, secondary, suburban and branch line passenger trains – together with one or more 'Goods Links' to handle mineral traffic, main line freights, local-pick-up, 'trip' and branch line goods trains. Shunting would usually lie in the province of either the 'goods' or 'extra' links, unless there was enough of it to justify a separate dedicated 'Shunting Link'.

Of course, it was only the principal MPDs which boasted a full range of links; lesser establishments would only possess such links and locomotives as befitted their place in the overall scheme of things. Few sheds not on a main line or at a major traffic centre, for instance, boasted a 'top link' of express passenger locomotives. Smaller provincial depots might possess only two basic links: 'goods' and 'passenger', perhaps plus a 'spare'. The exact establishment would reflect the traffic for which a depot was responsible, which, in turn, meant that this traffic would be exclusively in the hands of the locomotives stationed there. This is why the same engine (or one of a small group of engines) would turn up day after day on a given working, narrowing things down nicely – at least when you can lay hands on the relevant information! It's only where workings lie in the province of a principal MPD that strict authenticity demands that you perm an engine from a link of thirty or forty – which does pose a somewhat greater demand for hardware!

RIGHT *A Divisional (principal) depot on the GWR: Worcester, which in 1934 had an allocation of 66 locos and administered a Motive Power District embracing two main depots (Hereford and Gloucester), one other depot (Kidderminster), and 15 sub-sheds and outposts. By the time this wartime view was taken, the allocation had grown substantially and included locomotives on loan from other railways – hence the LNER J25 0-6-0 at the bottom left.* J. Peden/ Author's collection

Motive power districts

Motive power allocations went by a sort of 'family tree', whereby principal MPDs normally lay at the heart of a Motive Power District, with the other sheds in that district being subservient to it as sub-sheds. Such sub-sheds could range from substantial establishments boasting 40 or 50 allocated engines to modest affairs calling themselves home to a mere dozen or so. These sub-sheds themselves had sub-sub-sheds, or outposts with the most basic motive power facilities, such as those located at branch line termini. These had no locomotives allocated to them as such, being simply stabling points. They were regarded as being a part of the parent depot and housed locomotives from that depot's allocation, which were then described as 'out-posted engines'. These engines would return to their home depots for boiler wash-outs and any other regular maintenance above the daily routine of preparation.

Sub-sheds and their outposts were administered and serviced by the principal depot, which normally had enhanced repair facilities and a pool of spare locomotives not allocated to any link; engines which could be loaned-out to sub-sheds to cover the duties of locomotives 'in works'. In the BR era, all loco depots were identified by a code consisting of a one or two-digit number followed by a letter suffix, with the allocation of a loco displayed by means of a small cast oval plate on the smokebox door. The number identified the district, and the letter code the particular shed within it, with the principal depot taking the 'A' suffix. Thus, '32' was the Norwich district, with Norwich (Thorpe) as '32A', ranging down in order of importance to '32E' Yarmouth (Vauxhall), home to a mere five engines.

Location, location . . .

What has all this got to do with choosing the appropriate engines for a model railway, you may ask? Well, if you're interested in authenticity, then it is helpful to appreciate the

LEFT *In BR days the shed to which a loco was allocated was indicated by an oval cast plate on the smokebox door, bearing the depot code – in this case, 73C (Hither Green).* Author's collection

BELOW *A sub-sub-shed, not even graced with a discrete shed code. This is Callington, an outpost of 83H, Plymouth Friary. The locomotives using it as a stabling point. Ivatt 2-6-2Ts, came from the 83H allocation and carried shed plates to that effect.* P.J. Kelley/ Author's collection

extent of the pool from which you can make your selection. The underlying rule is that a possible locomotive for a given working will have to come from within the appropriate district allocation, and is most likely to come from the allocation of the sub-shed covering the workings being represented on the layout. The further out along the branches of the 'allocation tree' you can go, the more precise you can be about what you should be modelling. Get down to an outpost, and you can usually pin-point a particular locomotive.

As the above will have made apparent, modellers favouring the main line will need deep pockets or long lives, as their authentic shopping list will be long indeed. Fortunately for most of us – modelling some lesser location – the motive power focus will be drawn a great deal tighter. At the extreme, if you're sticking to a given timeframe and modelling an actual minor country branch line prototype that was worked by an out-posted engine, then it will be easy enough to determine with precision which particular engine you should be modelling – leaving you with a build or shopping list of one! Economical, but not too exciting... Often, however, this out-posted engine would only be responsible for the branch passenger train, with goods workings being the responsibility of the appropriate link at the parent MPD – which does offer a little more scope for motive power variety. Of course, even the assigned branch engine would have had to spend time away for regular boiler wash-outs at the parent MPD and occasional spells 'in works' for overhaul. The former absence would have been covered by an engine from the MPD's extra link, the latter by a substitute locomotive on temporary allocation from the 'District Pool'. Either eventuality is valid justification for a little more variety in motive power.

Powering a fiction

As already remarked, things become somewhat more fluid when the subject of your layout is fictional. Well, how *do* you decide which engines would have run over a railway that never actually existed? If you're going to be truly pedantic about it, any choice is the wrong choice as on any given day, whichever prototype engine you chose to model would actually have been somewhere else! My own answer to this conundrum has always been to step back a little and go on the 'geography' of the fiction, basing my selection on those engines known to have worked in the relevant area at the period in question. How difficult this approach is rather depends on just *how* far-fetched your fiction is: a completely imaginary railway in an equally imaginary and geographically indeterminate setting casts one adrift on a foggy sea of possibilities; the 'Hogwarts Express', perhaps?

Such rootless layouts rarely qualify for the 'realistic' tag around which this book is predicated. Much more on the mark is what I like to term 'factional' railway modelling: the insertion of a believable railway fiction into an actual and defined historical and geographic setting. In this instance, the fiction is composed of plenty of carefully researched *fact*, both with regard to the normal practices of the particular railway company that supposedly built the line, as well as to the landscape and setting. Such a model will readily lend itself to a similar blend of actuality and possibility when it comes to choosing apt motive power. For once you know where you are, so to speak, it is easy enough to determine which motive power depot or depots would have been responsible for powering trains in that area, what engines they had available, and even the identities of likely candidates.

This is exactly the situation I have always found myself in with my own BR-period East Anglian endeavours. Although neither the East Suffolk Light Railway nor the Lowestoft Direct line (my own pet fictions) existed in reality, they both 'connect' with the East Suffolk main line, the ex-GER route north of Ipswich to Beccles and Yarmouth. And that connection gives me a firm starting point in selecting appropriate motive power,

BELOW *A one-engine wonder – the out-posted branch locomotive. This GWR 517 class 0-4-2T, No 1473* Fair Rosamund *(the only officially named member of this extensive class), famously worked the Woodstock branch in Oxfordshire for over 30 years, overhauls excepted. If you're modelling Woodstock, this is the one loco you must have!* N.R. Miller/ Author's collection

BELOW *The other regular one-locomotive duty that often gets overlooked is that of pilot engine – an assignment that was far more widespread than many modellers realise. It was not only major stations and main yards that called for the presence of an on-call shunting/trip working locomotive. This is Radstock on the Somerset & Dorset section, with 'Jinty' No 47316 (appropriately, one of the batch built for the S&DJR in 1929) doing the honours. It is displaying the pilot lamp-code of a red and a white light over the buffers at each end. The 0-6-0T was allocated to 82F, Bath Green Park and sub-shedded at Radstock.* Author's collection

ABOVE *I chose No 65454 as the subject for my J15 class 0-6-0, primarily because it was a long-time resident of 32B, Ipswich – the depot most likely to have provided motive power to the location of my fictions, both branches off the East Suffolk main line. The fact that it had a stovepipe chimney (fitted during the Second World War), was a bonus. This is another portrait model; the faded wartime 'NE' showing through the tender paint and the dent in the tender side were features of the real No 65454.*

as it is relatively easy to identify where the locomotives needed to run my fictions are likely to have come from.

The East Suffolk Light is (allegedly!) a rambling affair that straggles circuitously from Orford northward to Debenham (Cade's Green), crossing the East Suffolk main line at Melton, a dozen or so miles north of Ipswich. The ESL sheds at Orford Haven and Cade's Green would thus have been outposts of 32B Ipswich. The 'Lowestoft Direct', by contrast, is a convenient reordering of railway history that adds an alternative route to that bustling fishing port, leaving the main East Suffolk route at Darsham and heading out towards the coast via Blythburgh and Kessingland to approach Lowestoft from the south, thus 'closing the triangle' and avoiding the hike round via Beccles. Such a route places it neatly within the purview of two prototype depots: 32B Ipswich to the south, and 32C Lowestoft to the north. With Ipswich as a common factor, therefore, engines from that depot have long formed the basis of my East Anglian stud, as they could reasonably figure on local workings over both lines – with Lowestoft getting in on the act in providing some power for the 'Direct'.

Next in order of probability as provider of locomotives running on either line, would be that great-grand-daddy of all MPDs, Stratford (30A). With a running shed allocation of more than 400 locomotives, as well as a being a principal locomotive works, Stratford was Britain's largest single MPD. Unsurprisingly, it completely dominated motive power affairs on the GE section, providing the engines for a large number of through workings to all manner of East Anglia destinations originating in the London area as well as for 'circular' duties. These last involved locomotives being rostered to work a whole succession of trains over routes covering pretty much the whole GE Section – workings that would ultimately bring them in a full circle and hence 'back home'. Serving a full-blown locomotive works, Stratford running shed also maintained a large fleet of pool engines that were loaned out to other depots to cover locomotives in works for major overhaul – quite a usual practice. Swindon did the same on

the GWR, and doubtless other MPDs associated with major works did likewise. In GE-section terms, what this means is that a Stratford-allocated engine could turn up just about anywhere! Very handy…

'Ghost' engines

A last ploy in coming up with believable motive power for a line which did not actually exist is to argue that *had* it been built, then the motive power department would have *had* to provide the engines to work it. This might, at the extreme, have led to extra engines of actual classes being built, adding a few extra numbers to the tail of the class tally: what one might term the *Tornado* solution… Rather more likely, at least on railways enjoying a relatively generous overall provision of motive power, is to suppose that our 'altered' traffic requirements would have led to appropriate engines being reallocated to bolster availability at the relevant depot.

Where such 'slack' in availability did not exist, then I think it is quite plausible to argue that locomotives which in reality were withdrawn as being surplus to requirements would have been retained in traffic to meet the 'need' we have so conveniently created. This is a scenario that has plenty of prototypical veracity, with many recorded examples of just such scrap-road reprieves; certainly, it is a jolly handy way of squaring the historical circle! It's the dodge I used to provide an out-posted engine for Blythburgh, prolonging the service life of Stratford-allocated ex-GER F5 class 2-4-2T No 67217 – in actuality 'laid aside' in November 1955 – by one more heavy general overhaul that, says I kept her in service until the last few surviving ex-GER F5/F6 2-4-2Ts were swept away en masse in the spring of 1958.

While I was at it, I re-allocated No 67217 to Lowestoft, to join the two F6s surviving there. In engineering this sort of scenario, it is worth bearing in mind that MPDs rarely had single specimens of a single type, usual policy being to group examples of a given class (particularly survivors of an old and

BELOW *A 'ghost' engine. In reality, ex-GER F5 class 2-4-2T No 67217 went for scrap in November 1955. I have given her an extra couple of years, until May 1958, when all the remaining members of the class were withdrawn en masse. Here, she is at Cade's Green; the station building has just been repainted, so closure can't be far off!*

declining class) at certain depots, to simplify spares and maintenance. Which is why I 'moved' my F5 to Lowestoft – which still had that allocation of 2-4-2Ts at my 1957/8 period – rather than to Ipswich, from which the last such engine had disappeared at the end of 1955.

Sources of information

You may well ask how I can be so specific as to where these particular engines were, and when. Well, for a start, I'm lucky enough – in this context – to be old enough to have a certain amount of first-hand information to hand, in the smudged and scrawled forms of my own schoolboy lists and well-thumbed Ian Allan *ABC*s. Many of the engines I'm now modelling are those with which I had personal familiarity half a century ago. But my main source has always been photographs – in many ways the most authoritative and informative fount of wisdom, as they show not just which engines were working which trains where and when, but also exactly what they looked like at the time. In this context, it is amazing just how often certain engines turned up in front of the lens, and just how fugitive other examples of the same class at the same period and in the same area could be. A case in point relates to two of the eight or so J15s resident at Ipswich in the mid-1950s. It seems quite an achievement to find a picture which *doesn't* feature 'film star' engine No 65447 – I've found nearly 50 portraits of her to date! But only three of sister-engine No 65454, which must have worked many of the same duties… Why? You tell me!

The other important source of locomotive allocation data is published listings. These are available from a number of sources, the most detailed being the *Railway Observer*, the monthly journal of the Railway Correspondence and Travel Society (founded 1928). This chronicles, month-by-month, all manner of developments on the railways, including changes in locomotive allocations, withdrawals or additions, modifications and works visits. Extracting the information relevant to a specific location and date does take rather a lot of ploughing through, however. More accessible are the classic Ian Allan 'Locoshed books', which used to be published annually alongside the *ABC* listings. The 'Locoshed' books gave the current allocation of each individual engine in the list at the time of publication.

Even more relevant and detailed are the specialist books published by the likes of Wild Swan or Irwell Press covering locomotive allocations for a particular locomotive class, railway or geographic area at a given date or period. These usually well-illustrated volumes contain exactly the information we need to draw up our shortlists of likely candidates. More modest were Peter Hand's Defiant Publications booklets in the *BR Steam Shed Allocations* series, self-published back in the mid-1980s, they consisted of little more than basic typewritten lists for each loco depot – taken on a geographical and regional basis – leavened with a few grainy photographs. However, those painstakingly compiled lists contain allocation and transfer/withdrawal dates from the beginning of 1957 until the closure or end of steam of each depot, telling you *to the month* what engines were where. As an information source for a BR-period modeller, they're worth their weight in uncut diamonds… Nowadays, these booklets have been superseded by the far glossier and even more informative *Shed by Shed* series of locomotive allocation books produced by Tony Walmsley, which cover the period 1950–1968 (details in the Bibliography).

Sourcing the models

So after a spot of detective work we've got a credible list of prototypical classes and – hopefully – even some individual candidates for the loco stud of our model railway, whatever its subject or timeframe. All we have to do now is turn this collection of Good Intentions into a matching collection of realistic, individual, smooth-running models. In this age of widely available, affordable, high-quality RTR locomotives and sophisticated kits – no problem, surely? Well, yes and no.

Leaving aside for a moment the questions of available budget and whether you prefer to buy your models ready to go or would rather go build 'em yourself, a lot hinges on the period and subject of the layout. If your interest and modelling intent lies with the later years of the 'Big Four' or the BR pre-diesel era, then much (but not all) of what you need by way of locos will be available RTR. The further back you go in time, however, the less you will be able to depend on the Dongguan paragons and the more you will be thrown back on to kits. That is also true of some geographical areas of the British Isles. If your fancy lies north of the border, say, or in North East England, East Anglia or rural Kent and Sussex, you will look in vain for key locomotive types that will be

BELOW Locomotive allocation listings are available from a number of sources and provide a sound basis for selecting engines to model for a given layout.

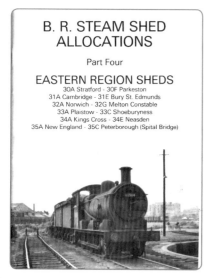

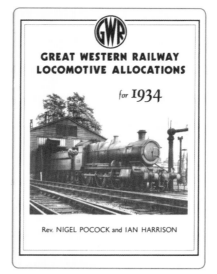

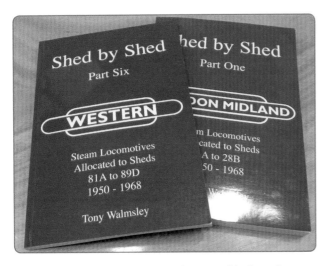

ABOVE *The most recent (and comprehensive) of the loco-allocation books are the* Shed by Shed *series compiled by Tony Walmsley and produced to a high standard; an invaluable reference!*

ABOVE *If your modelling interests bend to the historical – particularly to the pre-Grouping period before 1923 – then the RTR makers have very little to offer you and most locomotives and stock will need to be sourced from kits. Here is Simon de Souza's Highland Railway 'Yankee Tank', built from an etched-brass kit by Alan Gibson. Not much chance of Bachmann ever obliging with this one!*

needed to populate your rails authentically. In particular, you will find a dearth of the older and smaller pre-Grouping types that in reality, worked much of the railway's traffic in these areas, in many cases right up to the end of steam.

It has long been an eternal irony of the model railway business that the degree of choice and quality in the range of model steam locomotives available in ready-built form, seems perversely to be in inverse ratio to their usefulness to the guy building a typical modest-sized home layout with pretensions to realism. I'll be the first to accede that we have 'never had it so good' in the choice of RTR motive power, but the bias towards glamorous express passenger or large impressive freight power that goes back to Hornby-Dublo days is still evident, albeit with a much better selection of medium-sized mixed-traffic engines to back up the heavy metal. That's not to mention a surprising number of 'oddballs' like the S&DJR 2-8-0 and Beattie well tank; tiny classes of engines that only ever ran on certain short stretches of secondary railway! This, on the face of it illogical situation perhaps underlines the 'collecting' nature of a large part of the modern-day hobby, where demand is driven by the preserved engines people get to know on rail tours and heritage railways. It is quite probable that you and I – the guy trying to build a realistic and authentic home layout – are actually a small and insignificant minority!

The precise nature of a typical 'realistic home layout' is, of course, all but impossible to nail down – but surely only a relative minority that can be sweeping depictions of the principal main lines? Unfortunately, it was just such main lines which, in reality, were the *sole* stamping grounds of all those glamorous express passenger types; the country branch line terminus with the through carriages from London arriving behind a 'Duchess' or 'King' is a hoary old railway modelling chestnut that achieves an instant maximum deflection on the Scale of Improbability.

No branch layout that is not based on Kingswear can actually offer a believable role to such a premium heavyweight! Even a primary express passenger class is well on the far side of unlikely at most secondary locations,

including those where through working from the Capital was in force. Almost invariably, route-availability restrictions would see to that! Second-rank express or heavier mixed-traffic power is somewhat more plausible, particularly on workings to popular branch-served holiday locations like Windermere, Newquay, Padstow, Ilfracombe, Scarborough or Hunstanton, where permitted axle-loads were up to the relevant main line standards. A lighter mixed-traffic type is even more likely and could take in many 'restricted' routes like the Minehead line or the Cambrian Coast to Pwllheli and Aberystwyth.

General-purpose power off-the-peg

As even a cursory glance at a few prototype photos will reveal, at almost any location in Britain at any time from 1860 to 1960, the likelihood of a general-purpose 0-6-0 of some sort

BELOW *The engine most likely to turn up… Back in the previous chapter I nominated the LMS 4F 0-6-0 as the most ubiquitous and widespread of British locomotives, likely to be found almost anywhere on any type of train. Here is 4F No 4560 on a typical passenger duty at Bournemouth, on the South Coast! It is a through high-season holiday train to the north of England via the S&D line. No 4560 was formerly S&DJR No 60, and the train once again carries the unique S&D passenger headcode.* Author's collection

turning up on such through passenger workings – as well as on any of a wide range of other duties – was a virtual racing certainty. Yup; unless you're modelling the Great North of Scotland Railway, the MET in London or one of those South Wales coal lines, the appropriate general-purpose 0-6-0 engine is almost invariably going to be the bedrock of your loco stud, the most useful engine, the type you really cannot do without.

Such a key locomotive thus needs to be a really good model in every respect – but especially in terms of performance and reliability, as it is going to be doing so much of the work. The irony is, of course, that this is the very group of engines so steadfastly ignored by the big RTR makers, at least until very recently. However, a couple of all-new state-of-the-art models of just such types – the LMS/BR(M) ex-MR Deeley 3F and SR/BR(S) ex-SECR Wainwright C – form part of Bachmann's current (2011/12) programme and very welcome they are.

There are also good third-generation models of two post-Grouping 'modern' 0-6-0s, Bachmann's workmanlike version of the 1926-vintage LNER Gresley J39 and Hornby's truly impressive rendition of Bulleid's 1942 SR Q1 or 'Charlie'. The former is a useful all-rounder, but the Q1 was essentially a heavy, powerful main line goods engine. Bachmann's ex-Mainline GWR 'Collett Goods' has also been much improved of late (although still a little lacking in the chimney department) and now comes with a choice of tenders. Both the other RTR 0-6-0s listed in the current catalogues are warmed-up leftovers from a previous era: the LMS 4F and GW 'Dean Goods' by Hornby out of Airfix. The 4F has a new drive under the original body (complete with oversize splashers but otherwise very good), but still has rather coarse wheels and clunky handrails. The sorely needed 'Dean' is currently in limbo, which may just be a hopeful sign!

Which leaves a goodly list of widespread and long-lived prototype 0-6-0s designs out in the cold. I commend to the House of Hornby the BR/SR ex-LSWR 700 class, for which they already have the six-wheel Drummond tender, courtesy of the

BELOW *RTR general-purpose 0-6-0s have never been that plentiful. Here are the three stalwarts of the Hong Kong-made second-generation ranges: Mainline's GW Collett Goods and the GW Dean Goods, and the LMS 4F from Airfix. Although fundamentally accurate and, in the case of the Airfix models, very well-detailed, none of these 1980s-vintage offerings ran very well. They are prime candidates for a new chassis and a make-over, along the lines to be described.*

T9. Bachmann could likewise do worse than consider the handsome BR/LNER ex-GCR Robinson J11 'Pom-Pom', which could make use of the tender from their excellent model of the same designer's O4 2-8-0.

Other 0-6-0 candidates crying out for notice include the BR/LMS ex-L&Y Aspinall A class, the ex-NER J25 and ex-MR lightweight 2F, not to mention that long-needed modern version of the GWR 'Dean Goods'. Any of these additions would facilitate a whole range of layout-prototype possibilities. Given that the RTR trade has now worked its way through most of the more glamorous/obvious subjects (and indulged in quite a few surprising obscurities!) they might *just* get around to a few such Truly Useful Engines…

Until they do, the quest for most older general-purpose 0-6-0s has usually been a case of reaching down the files and soldering iron or of saving up several hundred pounds for a custom kit-built model from a decent maker. However, there is now a 'middle path' between these extremes, in the shape of limited-production batch-built RTR 00 models from the likes of 00 Works, which come with a price ticket roughly twice what you would expect to pay for a similar prototype from Bachmann/Hornby. These 'bespoke/off-the-peg' models occupy much the same niche as the productions of Hambling's or Eames described in Chapter 1 – although the current crop are to a considerably better standard, being generally of commendably accurate outline and basically well-made and finished.

These models have solid and straightforward 00 mechanisms fitted with Romford/Markits RP25 wheels – chassis that run well enough without scaling the heights of refinement. However, detailing – while neatly applied and to scale – is limited, especially below the footplate, but with a bit of extra work, such models can readily be brought up to the contemporary par. The 00 Works range has included some useful general-purpose 0-6-0 types including the SECR C class, the LSWR 700 class and the LMS ex-MR 2F. The chief drawback is lack of availability; you need to get your order in at the appropriate time because if you miss the production run your chances of acquiring such a model second-hand are close to zero.

Branch line power

The steam-era country branch line has long been a popular choice of subject for British railway modellers, and in this case, there is a reasonable selection of apposite motive power available off the shelf, even allowing for the fact that quite a high proportion of branch line traffic was handled by just the sort of pre-Grouping 0-6-0 general-purpose engines just noted. More modern all-rounders like the GWR '57xx' pannier tanks and LMS 'Jinties' also saw plenty of branch line use, working alongside ex-suburban passenger power and purpose-built branch line engines like the GWR '44/45xx' 'Small Prairies', '48xx/58xx/14xx' 0-4-2Ts, '54xx' big-wheeled 'Passenger Panniers' and the 'lightweight' LMS Ivatt 'Mickey Mouse' Class 2 2-6-2T of 1946.

Of the GWR 'custom jobs', the '45xx' and 0-4-2Ts are available, although the Hornby (née Airfix) version of the latter is one of the oldest RTR models still around – and looks it. Coarse wheels and clunky handrails, a totally erroneous smokebox door and a chimney that has only a vague

RIGHT *Custom-built branch line power – the Ivatt Class 2 'Mickey Mouse' 2-6-2T, modern lightweight locomotives built by the LMS after the Second World War, and used all over BR. Sprinting through Somerset on his 'New Mere' layout is Chris Longley's P4 version, which uses a Bachmann body over a Comet chassis – a thoroughly satisfactory 'layout' loco that lives happily alongside kit-built engines.*

resemblance to the prototype, mean that a lot of work is needed to bring this model up to par. The 2-6-2T is a relatively recent Bachmann model and a thoroughly nice job that catches the character of the prototype very well. It is one of the most useful of recent RTR offerings, alongside the same maker's 'Mickey Mouse' – a very geographically widespread type seen on minor lines of all types in BR days. A notch up is Bachmann's BR Standard 3MT class 2-6-2T, a far less numerous type which also saw considerable branch line service in the 1950s.

As usual, it is the older types that are largely absent – although Hornby's M7 class 0-4-4T is an absolute peach in the ex-suburban tank division. But branch line stalwarts like the LMS ex-MR Johnson 0-4-4Ts, GW veterans like the 2-4-0 'Metro tanks' and 517 class 0-4-2Ts, and the many and various 2-4-2T's of the LNWR, LYR, GCR, GER and NER are all totally absent from the RTR ranks. The same goes for the larger 4-4-2Ts of the LNWR, GCR, GNR, Caley and North British. As for down-graded main line power, Hornby offer their cracking T9 – a 4-4-0 class that saw quite a bit of branch line service, notably in the Far West. There is also the LMS 'Standard' 2P 4-4-0, another workmanlike candidate for branch line honours that I fancy used to lurk somewhere in the old Mainline stable, but has now re-emerged in updated form wearing Hornby colours. Otherwise, as with the older suburban types, it is time for a spot of travail at the workbench.

Suburban passenger power

With the exception of the older pre-Grouping designs already noted above, suburban passenger power is now exceptionally well represented in the RTR listings, with virtually all the significant Grouping/BR types available. This is odd really, when you see how few suburban-themed layouts there are about! With the exception of the Stanier three-cylinder engines (restricted, anyway, to the LT&SR section), all the LMS 2-6-4Ts and their BR derivative are out there, along with the Ivatt Class 2 2-6-2T and BR Standard 3MT already noted.

The LNER does not fare *quite* so well: The Gresley N2 superheated 0-6-2T and three-cylinder V1/V3 2-6-2Ts are to be had, as is the 1945 Thompson L1 2-6-4T. The glaring omission is the Hill/Gresley N7 class 0-6-2T, a 130 of which worked the extensive ex-GE suburban network to the north and east of London into the early 1960s. I went to school behind an N7!

The GWR had essentially one large, modern suburban tank locomotive design, the Collett '51/61xx' 'Large Prairie' derived from the original Churchward '31xx' design of 1905. This formed the subject of Airfix's first RTR steam offering way back in 1977 – a model that was dimensionally reasonably accurate, but rather lacking in detail and possessed of a rather basic drivetrain. This veteran still figures in the Hornby catalogue – somewhat improved, but still a country mile short of the modern RTR mark. It *can* be worked on and turned into a very presentable affair – but the type (more or less the only 'missing link' in modern GWR motive power) must be well overdue for a 21st century rework in model form, surely? Over on the Southern, new suburban power came in the form of electric multiple units and such little steam suburban working as remained did so in the hands of essentially pre-Grouping types like the M7. So not too much missing there – not even the EMUs!

Heavy goods, mixed-traffic and express passenger

I've lumped these three classes of motive power together because so far as RTR models go the story is much the same across the board: virtually all the main modern post-Grouping and BR-period engines are available – some in alternative versions from different makers. The vast majority of these

BELOW *The Airfix GWR '61xx' 'Large Prairie' was the first of the Hong Kong-made second-generation RTR models. Although crude by contemporary standards, it was a good step up from vintage Triang and Dublo fare, and lent itself to upgrading and conversion to finescale.*

ABOVE *An early addition to the Mainline range of the late 1970s was a passable rendition of the pioneering GWR mixed-traffic Mogul, the '43/63xx' class, which, with a better chimney and a little refining and detailing, had the makings of a convincing model. If, like Andrew Duncan, you go the extra mile and fit a decent chassis – Perseverance-built for fine scale 00 in this case – the result is a truly useful loco that catches the character of the prototype really well.*

ABOVE *The Airfix 'Castle' of 1979 was another of the Hong Kong 'new-breed' and, for its day, was a pretty good model, even if missing a fire-iron tunnel on the fireman's side. The Airfix models were over-produced and 'dumped' on the market at knock-down prices (£6.50 brand-new, I recall). This means that there are lots of them about for relative peanuts. Add a few details, a Comet chassis, some decent scale wheels and a Mashima motor with a gearbox, and you can make yourself a mighty fine 'Castle' for a bargain price.*

models are of modern pedigree and some of the most recent introductions are getting very hard to fault. Rather than wading through and commenting individually on the various offerings, I'll content myself with pointing out the most significant and problematic *omissions*.

Hornby have now reworked their GWR '28xx' and released the '42/52xx' 2-8-0T and its monstrous '72xx' 2-8-2T derivative, as well as producing the LNER O1, the heavy freight department is just about wrapped up. About the only other likely candidates are, I suppose, the O2 derivative of the O1 and the lack-lustre and lumbering LMS Fowler 7F 0-8-0 (the 'Austin Seven'), plus perhaps the big-boiler ex-NER engines of Classes Q5 and Q6; they'd certainly get my vote!

I also harbour a sneaking suspicion that someone, somewhere, will probably trot out an LMS 2-6-0 + 0-6-2T Beyer-Garratt ere long – just the job for the throng modelling the southern end of the Midland main line and 100-wagon Totton–Cricklewood coal trains, but no earthly use to anyone else! It would look good on the mantelpiece, though…

Mixed-traffic is exceptionally well-served, unsurprising, given that most of the locomotives meriting this description are relatively modern and embraced a relative handful of designs that were extensively multiplied to form some very well-populated classes. Oldest – in both prototype and model form – is the GWR '43xx' 2-6-0. Bachmann's model started out under the Mainline label and shows its age in several areas. It is no longer listed, so hopefully a new version is in the pipeline. The only glaring omissions that strike me are the Southern Maunsell S15 4-6-0 and the post-war LNER Thompson K1 2-6-0, but given how closely the latter is related to the L1 2-6-4T that Hornby already produce, its advent would not be a great surprise. Come to that, an S15 is even more closely related to the 'King Arthur' – a veritable star in the current Hornby range.

The only other notable gap in the modern mixed-traffic ranks is the GWR 'Manor' – a rather offhand version of which was another early introduction from Mainline. Bachmann withdrew it some while back, but a new version, fit to live

alongside their splendid 'Hall', would be a logical step. Likely to remain kit-fodder are the pre-Grouping types – of which one of the most attractive, widespread and long-lived is the ex-NER B16 4-6-0.

When it comes to modern express passenger locomotives the world is very much your oyster, with just about every significant type currently available in modern hi-fidelity RTR. Even such also-rans as the BR 'Clan' class 4-6-2 (a whole ten engines were built!) are now represented. Some classes – including, inevitably, the *Tornado*-powered A1 – are available in alternative versions from both main makers. As usual, what is really missing in third-generation form are the older and smaller pre-Grouping express types that lingered on into the BR era as secondary or branch line power, with the Hornby T9 and 2P the sole current RTR examples. (Bachmann's GWR '32xx' 'Dukedog' I don't really count as 'express', although useful it undoubtedly is.) Possible future RTR candidates in this category might include the ex-GCR Robinson 'Director', the SR Maunsell L1 and ex-GER 'Claud Hamilton' 4-4-0s – not to mention the same company's compact B12 4-6-0, which alongside the SR L1, was one of the more inspired prototype choices in the old Triang range.

Alternatives to 'off-the-shelf'

As I think the above whistle-stop survey will have made clear, good though the choice of contemporary high-fidelity RTR models is, there are (and likely to remain) significant gaps in provision of authentic motive power when viewed from the standpoint of a modeller seeking to equip a layout based around a great many prototype themes. From rural East Anglia to the Weald, throughout vast tracts of the industrial North and North East, and over much of Scotland, key locomotive types are not to be had. Only for 'mainstream' GWR lines and for certain odd corners of other railways – such as the Southern's 'Withered Arm' lines west of Exeter – can all the required locomotives come straight off the model-shop shelf in a nice blue Bachmann or bright red Hornby box. For most of us then, it will be

ABOVE *Alternative solutions: the kit-built engine. In this case, 'kit-mingled', in that the engine was built from an old MPD Deeley 3F kit, while the tender came from K's. The result was this long-serving portrait of Somerset & Dorset 'Bulldog' No 66 as running in 1928. The model is not so much artistically weathered as simply naturally aged. It has been running on Henry Tasker's large EM S&D layout for more than 30 years!*

ABOVE *There are some locomotives so obscure that even the most esoteric of kitmakers won't consider them a saleable proposition. In which case, you're on your own! I scratch-built this EM model of S&D Fox Walker 'banking tank' No 1 sometime back in the late 1970s for Henry Tasker's Bath–Midford layout. She's had a couple of refits in the intervening years and now boasts a Portescap motor-gearbox. A true layout loco, built to do a specific job.*

necessary to mix modern hi-fidelity RTR models with at least a few culled from other sources.

How you regard this situation depends upon your attitude to loco-building, as opposed to loco-buying. I have a good friend whose model motive power acquisition policy can be succinctly summed-up as 'sit tight and wait' – and I must concede that he has a point! Who other than the rashest of gambling men would have bet on the likes of an ex-LNWR 0-8-0 or a Beattie Well Tank as front runners in the mass-production RTR stakes even a year or two since? However, it is only comparatively recently that there has been any real choice in this question of 'to build, or not to build?'

Traditionally, most layout-builders reckoned to include a modicum of model loco construction in their modelling diet, while those modellers favouring wheel and track standards more accurate than the *de facto* 00 RTR norms have always had to reckon with a certain amount of spanner-work to adapt off-the-shelf models to their requirements. Ironically, the greater refinement and sophistication of current-generation RTR mechanisms has in many ways made such adaptations a rather trickier proposition than they used to be! So, for all the cornucopia of goodies available, there is no doubt that the current situation still throws up some interesting DIY loco-modelling challenges – even where mainstream standards are in use and the kernel of the stud can be drawn from the state-of-the-art RTR ranks. Time to consider the non-off-the-peg options…

Origins of the species

Basically, in the popular 4mm scale, around which this treatise is based, an authentic model locomotive can have one of five basic origins. It can be a modern RTR offering, hopefully suitably titivated and individualised but otherwise 'out-of-the-box'. Failing that, it might start life as an older and more basic RTR model 'reworked' to bring it up to the required standard. One stage further down that DIY road lies the 'hybrid' – a model concocted ('bashed', in the vernacular) using RTR, kit or aftermarket components from a variety of sources

combined and modified as necessary to achieve the desired result.

Next we encounter models built from kits – these days, a very variable bunch embracing cast white metal, moulded resin and plastics, all-etched or 'composite' construction. Lastly, we come to that true homew-brew, the 'scratch-built' model – strictly speaking, one hand-built entirely from raw materials, but nowadays taken as one that combines such Herculean toil with the use of specialist components (of which there is, I'm glad to report, no shortage available nowadays). Any or all of these approaches can be combined to provide the necessary motive power for any layout theme.

Of the listed options, it is the first three that most concern us in the context of this book; the nuts-and-bolts of loco kit construction and the scratch-building of model locomotives are both complex topics on which I (among many others) have

BELOW *A kit-bashed hybrid: Andrew Duncan and I cobbled together this GWR 1813 class 0-6-0PT out of an old Wills 1854 kit-built body bought second-hand, hacked about here and there, and fitted with a scratch-built bunker and cab and alternative cast chimney. The resulting hodgepodge was mounted on a slightly adapted Comet chassis kit for a '57xx' pannier, which has the same wheelbase. Marvellous what you can hide with a coat of paint!*

already written extensively elsewhere. A list of relevant titles is included in the Bibliography.

When adopting a 'mix-and-match' approach the trick is, of course, to produce results that look and function as if all the models had a *common* origin. Using modern detailing parts and finishing aids like lining transfers, together with mechanisms embodying sophisticated high-quality drivetrain components, achieving such consistency is entirely possible – although where the best of modern RTR is the benchmark, the job is no casual picnic.

The common specification

A drum I've banged for years in my crusade for realism in railway modelling is the importance of consistency of appearance across all aspects of the model. In the context of the loco stud, such visual consistency comes very much in matters of detail and finish, particularly the latter. In terms of layout *working*, it is obviously important to have a fleet of model locomotives that perform to a similar high level of mechanical refinement and which exhibit proper adherence to the appropriate wheel/track and electrical standards.

In order to decide whether a model is acceptable on any of these counts – and, if not, what needs doing to bring it up to par – a clearly defined 'common specification' is a useful tool. Arriving at such a benchmark need not be an involved or

protracted exercise; at the simplest, you merely pick your best model and proclaim: 'Everything on this layout must be as close to this standard as possible!' More practically useful, however, is to analyse carefully just what it is that makes this 'prize' model so satisfactory – and from this to derive a set of precise criteria which the rest have to meet.

So, for instance, consider for a moment the matter of handrails. On the best hand-built or contemporary RTR models these will all be accurate renditions of the originals, separately applied using appropriately sized and accurately formed wire held in knobs (more correctly, 'stanchions') of scale dimensions. Some kits may come with just such authentic handrail hardware, but many do not. I think it was the late Guy Williams who memorably described many model loco handrails as looking like 'a row of footballs strung along a gas pipe'. On older 'toy market' RTR models chunky handrails were the norm, of course – where they weren't reduced to simple moulded-on protrusions. Either way, they are a fundamental 'case for replacement'. In terms of our common specification, therefore, we might stipulate that 'all handrails are to be of wire of appropriate scale diameter held in scale-sized stanchions of correct length, finished to match the prototype', where shiny, chrome-plated handrails are a decided rarity!

Repeating this sort of appraisal across all the fitments, details and finishing of the model locomotive should give rise to a detailed visual specification sheet along the lines of the one appended alongside – which is the benchmark I use for my own layouts. This sheet is the tool I use to assess the 'look' of all prospective candidates for use on the layout, and to determine what modifications/improvements/alterations will be needed to make the model live happily alongside existing members of the stud. Should the candidate be a complete model, then alongside this visual assessment will sit exacting running trials. If the model is a 'body only to use' RTR rework or a hybrid concoction, then the required replacement or new chassis will also need to be properly specified, as described in Chapter 5.

RTR-based models

'There is nothing made that cannot be made better' goes the old saying – and that applies to RTR model railway locomotives as much as anything else. However, the degree of improvement needed will vary considerably, from a spot of minor titivation for the cream of the contemporary crop, to major reworking in the case of some old stagers. Between these two extremes lie many RTR models that, while basically accurate and possessed of acceptable running qualities, don't *quite* come up to the mark for detail and refinement set by the best of contemporary RTR. To endow them with that 'extra something' is usually a case of making a series of minor cosmetic improvements – none of them of earth-shattering difficulty or huge visual significance in themselves but, when taken in total, just 'lifting' the model through those last few degrees of realism.

If you're modelling to modern fine scale 4mm wheel and track standards like EM or P4, then no RTR 00 loco is going to be of use to you as it comes. Even the most refined of current production is going to need re-wheeling before it can enter

BELOW *A loco stud specification sheet.*

```
Loco Specification: Trerice/East Suffolk/Paradise Fields

Mechanisms:

 1) All wheels P4 profile with steel tyres.
 2) Minimum 1.5mm side-play centre axle 6-coupled.
 3) All 3-point compensated with 1mm vertical travel.
 4) Motors: Mashima 1026, 1220/24, 1424. Sagami 1425
 5) Transmissions: Multi-stage, ratios 50:1 or higher. To
    be arranged to keep cabs as clear as possible.
 6) Wiper pick-ups, minimum 6 wheels (unless 0-4-0!). Gold
    or gold-plated contacts if possible.
 7) Ballasted to pull minimum 15 wagons on level track.
 8) Chassis detail to include brakes/brake-rigging,
    sanding gear with pipes, correctly-configured guard-
    irons, firebox/ash-pan in profile at least, ancillary
    plumbing.
 9) Chassis to be painted/patinated to match super-
    structure.

Cosmetics:

 1) Al plastic/whitemetal superstructures to have thinned
    visible edges.
 2) All mould seams and joint cracks to be eliminated.
 3) All boiler-mountings corrected to prototype. All
    chimneys to be bored out.
 4) Buffers to be correct to prototype but not necessarily
    sprung.
 5) Scale link couplings on all buffer-beams, with
    functional coupler loops as necessary in 0.3mm wire.
 6) All buffer-beam hoses to be fabricated wire type
    correct to prototype.
 7) All handrails to be scale-size wire with Gibson turned
    stanchions or closed-down split-pins.
 8) All lamp-irons to be scale-size 0.8mm strip for use
    with slip-over loose lamps.
 9) Full cab fittings with fall plates on all tender
    locos. Minimum of all readily-visible cab fittings on
    tank engines. Full cab floors. Cab doors to be open on
    shunters if possible. All cab windows to be flat-
    glazed. All cabs to be crewed!
10) All loco/cab steps to be scale depth with scale
    visible edges.
11) All bunkers and tenders to be prototypically coaled.
12) All locos to have patinated finish and weathering
    (varied!). Chassis and superstructure to match!
```

ABOVE *The handrails of the Hornby J52 are not at all bad (top), but they are a touch chunky when compared with the scale handrails on the other locos in my mostly kit-built stud. So, in the cause of consistency, they were replaced with 0.45mm NS wire and Alan Gibson's turned-brass fine-scale stanchions, when the body of my one was being reworked.*

service – which, given the greater complexity of modern mechanisms, is no sinecure, even when using a purpose-made conversion kit. In that context, a complete replacement chassis built from one of the excellent 'aftermarket' etched kits – which can readily be configured for fine scale standards and endowed with all manner of refinements including skew-wound can motors, multi-stage gearboxes and compensated or sprung suspension – can sometimes seem a more-attractive option. Such a kit-built chassis will, of course, utterly transform older and less mechanically refined models; it is the key component in almost any 'RTR rework' or ' hybrid' locomotive.

RTR reworks

What on earth, you may wonder, precisely *is* an 'RTR rework'? Well, by the time you've 'done the necessary' to a vintage specimen such as the Hornby-Dublo R1 for example, the result will be very much an 'Irishman's shovel' – not all that much of the original left! In the case of the R1, involving a completely new chassis, beneath a body moulding

extensively altered to correct errors and eliminate production expediencies, the result being tricked-out with scale handrails, lamp irons, sprung buffers, authentic pipe-work and all those other niceties that used to be called 'super detailing', but which nowadays are 'standard fit'. And – of course – the finished model will be treated to an authentic and refined paint job.

A far-reaching reworking like this almost constitutes more of a 'hybrid' model, in that the RTR starting-point probably only provides 50 per cent or less of the ingredients. Given that you can now buy such a wide range of aftermarket chassis kits and detailing packs intended for use with moulded plastic bodies, this 'reworked RTR' approach has become a very popular and economical way of producing good-quality utility motive power. It is especially suited to layouts using EM or P4 standards as it despatches the proverbial avian duet with one well-aimed pebble.

The classic RTR candidate for such a far-reaching makeover is a model having a basic body moulding that is fundamentally accurate and hopefully free from such olde-worlde production compromises as blanking-in below boilers or unprototypical excrescences. It also needs to be of a configuration that does not preclude the installation of a properly engineered and appropriate drivetrain. The starting-point moulded plastic superstructure can come from one of two sources: poached from a complete RTR model, or ordered from a specialist dealer as a spare part. Given that we are going to be providing a new chassis, a non-functioning 'pre-owned' specimen of the appropriate loco is all we require. So long as this basic body moulding is OK, it does not really much matter what state the rest of the thing is in! The ether (in the form of eBay) or the bric-a-brac, bring-and-buy or swapmeet tables at model railway shows are the usual sources of such low-cost conversion-fodder.

New spare-part loco superstructures, by contrast, are not always easy to source; many recent and current-production

BELOW *Manna! A new spare-part loco body and tender, in this case for a Replica Railways (née Mainline, now Bachmann) LNER B1 class 4-6-0. Add an aftermarket chassis kit from Comet or Bradwell for the basis of a fine-scale layout loco, or order the current Bachmann mech. as a spare for mainstream 00 standards.*

mouldings are simply not available as spares, more's the pity. Older productions, particularly from Hornby, are less problematic and can often be obtained either as completely finished and decorated superstructures, or as bare and basic unpainted body mouldings. Which you go for depends to a large extent on how good and appropriate to your intentions the factory detailing and paint job is, although the extent to which you need to rework the basic moulding also has a bearing on the matter. Not much point in paying extra for a fancy paint job if you're going to end up scraping most of it off!

The other key ingredient for an RTR rework is a suitable aftermarket chassis kit – on the anatomy of which you will find much in Chapter 5. This will typically have mainframes etched in brass or nickel-silver with matching etched side-rods and valve gear (if any). The frame outline will usually match the footplate and body-mounting arrangements of the specific RTR body with which it is intended to be used. These mainframes will mount on to separate spacers, which are

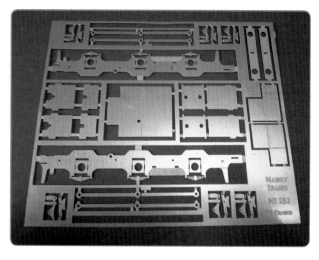

ABOVE *A typical straightforward replacement etched chassis kit for a popular RTR moulded body, in this case the Mainline/Bachmann J72. This is the Mainly Trains version, designed by the author.*

BELOW *A classic hybrid model. This DCC sound-fitted GWR '28xx' uses the Hornby body moulding from the old tender-drive 2-8-0, mounted on a fully compensated Comet 00 chassis. Power is a Mashima 14-series motor driving through a High Level 60:1 transmission. The tender uses a Bachmann body on Mainly Trains underpinnings and is 'loaded' on to the loco (see Chapter 5) to increase adhesion. The resulting loco is very powerful!*

usually available or supplied for 00, EM or P4 standards. The frame design will normally be for a fixed-bearing 'rigid' chassis, but with provision for straightforward modification to suit either three-point equalised (compensated) or sprung suspension, as required. Wheels and drivetrain components are purchased separately to suit the applicable gauge/ standards and performance requirements.

Hybrids

A true hybrid model is one that draws its fundamental components from diverse origins. At its most basic, a hybrid might be a simple mélange of individual models from different makers, a favourite dodge in days gone by. For instance, in a past life I was the proud possessor of a 'super-detailed' Triang SR L1 4-4-0 (old but good), the original cast-block chassis being fitted with an MW005 motor, single-start 40:1 gears and Romford wheels. The resulting loco trailed a Wills white metal-kit Maunsell tender (from the Q class kit) – far more authentic than the LMS-pattern tender Triang gave you. The work involved in creating this model lay somewhere between a straightforward RTR rework and all-out kit-building.

Nowadays, with a far wider choice of RTR models, kits and components to play with, a hybrid model can be a good deal more complex than my old L1, perhaps combining an aftermarket mechanism with a moulded-plastic RTR loco body decked out with a purpose-designed modification or re-detailing kit, all paired with a white metal – or etched kit-built tender. An example of this more free-wheeling approach I can call to mind was a very fetching portrait of one of the 9F 2-10-0s that worked the 'Pines Express' in the final years of the S&D. The model was confected from a Hornby tender-drive *Evening Star* body fitted with a Crownline re-detailing kit for a 'normal' double-chimney 9F, mounted on a coreless-motor-powered Comet chassis built to EM standards, and trailing a DJH cast-and-etched kit-built BR1D tender. Some extremely authentic models have resulted from just such unholy mixtures of components.

The role of the kit

As I think I have established in my ramblings about the prototype, if you're going to assemble a believable loco stud for most layout scenarios, then you are going to need a pre-Grouping 0-6-0 or two about the property, perhaps together with a superannuated suburban tank locomotive to head up a branch passenger train. Given the number of possible prototypes involved, the chances are that the only current source of many such models is going to be a kit of some sort – and, in many cases, likely to remain so. In this context, the kit is seen as resource to be drawn on where an RTR-based model is not an option, rather than as a modelling objective in its own right. The challenge then is to turn the kit into a model that lives happily alongside items of motive power drawn from RTR sources; that 'common specification' applies to a kit-built model as much as any other.

How *much* of a challenge this presents depends on several factors, ranging from personal levels of modelling skill and experience through the facilities and equipment available to – critically – the nature and quality of the kit itself. And yes,

ABOVE *Back before the advent of the Bachmann RTR version, if you wanted a model of a J39 – the LNER's commonplace general-purpose 0-6-0 – it was a case of a substantial rework of the old, inaccurate Wills kit. My model of No 64899 has a scratch-built chassis and a new footplate, among many other modifications. The current South Eastern Finecast version of the kit is correct to scale and has an etched chassis.*

ABOVE *White metal survivor. The ex-LSWR O2 was a personal favourite of Bob Wills and is an old-stager of the Wills range. South Eastern Finecast have tidied the kit up a bit and provided a new etched chassis. This 00 specimen was built for Bob Wills's own layout.*

there are some hoary old rogues out there! Having heard the odd horror story, many modellers today fight shy of loco kit building, which is widely perceived as being a great deal more difficult than it actually is. In fact, most of the skills and equipment needed are little different to those called for a thoroughgoing RTR re-work or hybrid model. When you ask toe-in-the-water kit builders what aspect of the job they find most daunting, constructing the chassis is the most often-cited stumbling block – yet many modern loco-kit chassis are identical in design and constructional demands to the aftermarket RTR-replacement chassis already described. As I hope to demonstrate, screwing-together such a chassis is not exactly rocket science.

Quite apart from the practical matter of providing a necessary and authentic item of motive power, building a model locomotive from a kit can be a rewarding exercise in its own right. Practical necessity apart, possessing a model that you have yourself created and which is unique to you brings its own satisfactions, be it no grander than a humble workaday 0-6-0 goods locomotive. In which context, the good news is that a typical British inside-cylinder 0-6-0 engine – be it tank or tender – is just about the most straightforward of loco-modelling subjects: modest in size, normally straight of footplate, devoid of outside cylinders and valve gear, readily amenable to a simple motor and drivetrain installation, rarely possessed of too much fiddly detail, and almost-invariably finished in plain black. What could be simpler?

All kits are *not* equal

As hinted above, the range of locomotive kits currently available are a pretty mixed bunch (to put it mildly) and they certainly call for a widely varying amount of input from the modeller. It has always been my contention that a kit should solve at least the basic constructional problems inherent in a particular model; it certainly should not add difficulty or introduce errors! Alas, the number of kits that fall at these fundamental fences are legion…

Detailed discussion of all the foibles and failings of the

genus not being possible in the context of a book as wide-ranging as this one, I'm going to confine myself to pointing out what to avoid, and to taking a quick look at factors relevant to the context in which we are considering kits here, as stablemates to RTR-based models. In which context, there are several extensive segments of the kit field I'm going to dismiss out of hand, starting with a few old favourites.

Before I set about them with my hatchet it behoves me to point out that many of the loco kits still available, new and second-hand, have origins that are positively antediluvian. Such offerings thus reflect the standards and expectations current at the time they were originally produced – which were very different to those pertaining today! It is a case of avoiding that traditional Devon *non sequitur* (when asked for directions): "*Woi, Bor, if uz wus goin' thurr, uz wouldn' stairt from yurr…*" So, I regard with a codfish eye, many of the vintage white metal kits of the 1960s and '70s, including most offerings from K's, Bec or Gem, a lot of early DJH/Nu-Cast and those Wills kits which were fundamentally compromised to fit on old Triang or Hornby-Dublo RTR mechanisms.

I also have reservations about of many of the older or more basic etched kits, although given the pioneering role of some of these models – notably the original 'Mallard' range – then a few rough edges are only to be expected. Rough edges are one thing, but embodying highly suspect design criteria is another – which, so far as I'm concerned, rules out most of the extensive Jidenco/Falcon Brass range. Leaving aside the somewhat basic nature of these kits – often unkindly described as 'a starting point for a scratch-build' – in this context I cannot live with a design policy that is based on the use of a scale-diameter driving wheels measured *on the tread* – but with a hefty allowance for over-scale flanges added on, leading to the kits being designed around a grossly excessive overall wheel diameter. The result is a raft of fundamental visual and mechanical anomalies including oversized splashers, wheels sticking into boilers when they have no need to, compromised wheelbases, and lack of room for details like brake and sanding gear – *de rigueur* these days. Put these

ABOVE *Plain commons: a Falcon brass kit. Minimalist is putting it kindly, although at least this specimen – an L&Y Aspinall 'rapid shunting tank' – is spared any splasher or wheelbase anomalies. One-and-a-bit sides of typescript and a sketch provides scant instruction, while a lot of the specification is down to you, but there are some nice turned fittings and enough useful parts to make this a valid starting-point, if you have the skill and experience. A tyro builder would not be in with a prayer.*

things right, and you can make a very nice model out of a Falcon kit – but doing so requires scratch-building skills and loco-modelling experience somewhat beyond the demands of general kit-building.

The other tranche of kits I'm going to excise from this survey are the current generation of ultra-sophisticated, hyper-detailed, complex and costly 'super kits' by the likes of Martin Finney, Brassmasters and Malcolm Mitchell. This is in no way a criticism of these products, which are of superb quality and – in suitably skilled hands – capable of producing models of the very highest calibre, a decided notch up from even the finest of contemporary mass-produced RTR efforts.

And there, of course, lies the rub; the consistency requirement mitigates against a locomotive built to a standard *above* the benchmark just as much as against a model that's below par. One loco with full inter-frame detail and working inside motion serves only to point-up the lack of these refinements elsewhere. The very substantial cost – both in time and hard cash – of such models is also somewhat out of line with the notion of simply supplementing a stud of RTR-based models.

Having carved such a huge swathe through the ranks of the available kits, what are we left with? Well, quite a

reasonable and relevant selection, fortunately. On the white metal or hybrid white metal/etched front, there are three main ranges – South Eastern Finecast, DJH and Alan Gibson – that between them offer a reasonable number of just the sort of utilitarian prototypes we're looking for. Alan Gibson also offers a range of sophisticated etched kits covering a further raft of key loco types, as does London Road Models. More basic – but still highly relevant – are the straightforward etched offerings of Craftsman and PDK.

As well as these main ranges there are some small 'private project' or society-sponsored kits and a few old-but-good survivors to be drawn on – when you can find them! In fact, finding most loco kits nowadays is no sinecure, model-shops with loco kits available 'off-the-shelf' being even rarer than real grocers or doorstep-delivered milk in proper glass bottles; mail order over the Internet or direct-from-the-maker purchase at the better shows are the usual sources nowadays. Many kits have at best, only a spasmodic availability; Alan Gibson's range is now batch-produced on a subscription basis, while many Craftsman products can currently only be found second-hand. Keep an eagle eye on eBay…

Cast white metal kits

The biggest and most readily available of the cast-kit ranges is that of South Eastern Finecast, which has its origins in the old Wills range. Unlike the other 'vintage' ranges, Wills kits came into two distinct categories: the simplified 'popular' kits, more-or-less compromised to fit RTR underpinnings, and the 'scale' kits that used dedicated chassis and were generally far more accurate and refined.

When South Eastern Finecast took over the range in 1989, they set about upgrading the scale kits and providing them with new, dedicated state-of-the-art etched chassis. Although many of the more mainstream subjects have subsequently been eclipsed by new-generation RTR models, the Finecast range still boasts some useful candidates, particularly for Southern modellers.

Specifically, their ex-SECR Wainwright C class 0-6-0 is exactly the sort of prototype loco and well-detailed, builder-friendly style of kit we're looking for – which makes it rather a pity that Bachmann have stolen its thunder! To go with the C, Finecast can also provide you with Wainwright's handsome H class 0-4-4T (classic Southern branch line passenger power), and the supremely elegant and long-lived D and E class 4-4-0s; all cracking good kits with a high level of detail.

Other valuable Finecast kits include the ex-LSWR Adams O2 class 0-4-4T – another branch line stalwart – and the ex-Brighton E5, E6 and E1R 0-6-2Ts – the latter a 1930s rebuild of the veteran Stroudley E1 0-6-0T (also available) that lasted well into the BR era down here in Devon. On a more modern note – prototypically speaking – Finecast have an all-new kit for the Maunsell W class mixed-traffic 2-6-4T of 1931. They can also provide the GE-section modeller with two key items of motive power, the J67/J69 'Buckjumper' 0-6-0T, and the suburban N7 class 0-6-2T – both older Wills models extensively revised and updated (by yours truly, as it happens) in the early 1990s.

For the GW modeller, there's an accurate and well-detailed

version of the GWR '51/61xx' 'Large Prairie' plus, from an earlier prototype era, a very good rendition of the re-boilered 2-4-0 'Metro Tank'. The ubiquitous LMS 4F also features in the range, offered with a choice of beaded or flat-sided Deeley tenders and including a selection of alternative boiler fittings. Being a kit, it is much more readily adaptable to produce the many variations of this type than the plastic-body RTR version; it also has scale-sized splashers! For Scottish modellers, Finecast still list an old-but-good Wills kit for the ex-CR McIntosh 782 class general-purpose 0-6-0T – yet another pre-Grouping type to survive well into the BR era.

The other sizeable range of white metal-based loco kits is that marketed by DJH, and this includes a goodly handful of appropriate prototypes. There are no fewer than six general-purpose 0-6-0s, of which the most useful are the LNER/BR ex-GC J10 and the Southern C2X rebuild of Billinton's LBSCR goods engine; another long-term BR survivor. The remaining four are all Scottish: the ex-NBR Reid J35 plus two old stagers from the extensive ranks of the Drummond 'Jumbos', the Caley 812 series of 1899, and the similar Highland Railway 'Barney' class. The selection is rounded off by a real oddity, the hulking McIntosh Caledonian 30 class, of which there were only ever four examples built.

In the passenger tank engine sector, DJH have the handsome Caley 439 class 0-4-4T, while in the 'heavy general-purpose tank' division they list the 55-ton Gresley LNER/BR J50 0-6-0T. Of these models, the J35 is a 'new-era' DJH offering with a lot of etched brass parts, including the complete tender. The rest are older, traditional cast kits of variable

quality, and all come with DJH's rather basic brand of '00-only' etched-sideframe chassis, designed around older motors and transmissions. Nevertheless, they are still quite buildable – and readily adapted to take modern drivetrain components.

Alan Gibson's white metal offerings mostly owe their origins to the former Models and Leisure range which concentrated on older GWR and LNWR subjects, most of which are more of interest to modellers with a historical bent – although a handful of these older engines did make it through to the dawn of the BR era. Staples include the GW 517 class 0-4-2T, 850 class 0-6-0ST and 1076 'Buffalo' series outside-framed saddle and pannier tanks, with the 'Coal Tank' and 2-4-2T 5ft 6in 'radial' for the LNWR. Another small-but-good range with some useful subjects is Cotswold, now available, intermittently, from Autocom. A couple more GWR panniers feature, the 2021 (big brother to the 850) and the 1949 BR '16xx' 'lightweight pannier', a GWR design built after Nationalisation. There was also a very nice '42xx/72xx' 2-8-0/2-8-2T. These Cotswold kits were notable in their day for chassis blocks milled from a solid slab of brass.

Etched loco kits

There are four main manufacturers to consider here, ranging from the basic and straightforward to the pretty sophisticated. Among them, they cover most of the essential general-purpose 0-6-0s, and many of the older passenger types otherwise absent from the RTR ranks. The oldest and most basic of these ranges is Craftsman, very much the direct descendant of the old Jamieson-style of stamped-metal kit described in Chapter 1.

In a Craftsman kit, the etching process is used simply to cut the bits out, drill the holes and provide the odd fold-up or tab-and-slot assembly aid; no intricate detail overlays or fancy multi-layer fabrications here! Parts that need shaping do come pre-formed however, which is a useful bonus for many. Fittings are cast white metal and the rather dated chassis is a

BELOW *A really useful engine. Pre-Grouping general-purpose 0-6-0s such as this ex-SECR Wainwright C class formed the backbone of everyday railway working well into the BR era. Although the C is now available RTR from Bachmann, kits have long been the main source of this type of motive power. This one is from South Eastern Finecast.*

LEFT *The Craftsman range of straightforward etched-brass kits is not large, but includes some useful prototypes not available elsewhere, such as the ex-MR Johnson 1P 0-4-4Ts. I built LMS No 1339 in EM for Henry Tasker's 'Bath Green Park' layout.*

somewhat-crude '00-only' fold-up design that makes no provision for suspension of any sort. To bring a Craftsman up to the current benchmark takes quite a bit of effort, but they are a good basis to work on and certainly worth the sweat as the series includes some real staples: the ex-MR Johnson 1F 0-6-0T (the charismatic 'Half Cab') as well as the classic Midland 0-4-4T, the ex-L&Y Aspinall A class 0-6-0 in two versions, and the ex-GNR Ivatt C12 class 4-4-2T.

In the same straightforward vein – if somewhat more recent in origin, and considerably more sophisticated in design – are the PDK (formerly Crownline) range of etched loco kits. These also tend to eschew too much use of complex fold-ups or multi-layer construction with overlays, but are rather more complete and better-detailed than a Craftsman offering, with superior (often turned or lost-wax brass) fittings. Some models use moulded-resin boilers and other parts, an increasing trend in modern kit design that can obviate many constructional problems.

PDK's chassis design is variable; most kits offering a basic etched rigid-frame 00 mechanism, plain and simple, but more recent introductions have beam-equalised compensation. This surprisingly extensive range has historically been somewhat erratic as to availability, but things appear to have settled down now with a website-based mail-order service and direct sales at some shows. The range includes some really valuable 'baseline' 0-6-0 prototypes, including the ex-LSWR Drummond 700 class 'Black Motor' and the Maunsell Q for the Southern, and the ex-GER J17, J19 and J20 classes plus the ex-NBR J36 for the LNER.

The PDK range is also strong on pre-Grouping (but BR-surviving) express-passenger 4-4-0s, including the ex-LSWR D15 'Big Drummond', ex-NBR 'Scott' and 'Glen', ex-GCR D10/D11 'Director' series and the ex-GER 'Claud Hamilton' in several incarnations. The LNER man also gets the useful and compact ex-GER B12 and the versatile ex-NER mixed-traffic B16 class 4-6-0s as well as the 'missing link' LNER Gresley O2 class 2-8-0.

The next up in the pecking-order of etched-kittery, comes the extensive London Road Models range. This embraces models originating from a variety of sources, some of them dating back a few years, but also boasting some real 21st century state-of-the-art super-detailed composite kits using resin mouldings as well as metal components. Generally speaking, LRM kits are pretty user-friendly, with good instructions and a basic chassis design that offers the choice of simple non-suspended 'rigid' construction as well as allowing for springing or compensation.

LRM kits are adaptable to 00, EM and P4 standards, but a few of them do require special scale wheels due to specific diameter or crank-throw requirements. These wheels – from the

BELOW *No layout based on the old Lancashire & Yorkshire Railway, set any time between 1890 and about 1960, can do without at least one of these: a 23 class 0-6-0ST, as rebuilt by Aspinall from the old Barton Wright 0-6-0 goods engines. My P4 model is from the London Road Models etched kit, which uses a resin moulding for the tricky saddle tank.*

former and much-missed Sharman range – are available through LRM. Body-wise, these kits are fairly sophisticated, with fold-up and multi-layer construction embodying overlays. They are generally, very well detailed and the supplied fittings – in turned and cast brass as well as white metal – are of high quality. Not quite 'beginners fare' – but not too daunting either.

The LRM range is very much biased towards older pre-Grouping subjects and includes some real veterans dating back to the 1860s and '70s. In the context of this book, there are some choice survivors in the general-purpose 0-6-0 and passenger tank categories. The list includes the LNWR 18-inch 'Cauliflower' goods and both sizes of LNWR 2-4-2T 'Webb radials', with 4ft 6in or 5ft 6in wheels. From the LYR come the Barton Wright 'Ironclad' 0-6-0 goods and its saddle-tank rebuild, the 23 class, together with the characteristic 2-4-2T 'Radial tanks' in several variants. For the LNER modeller, there are the ex-GNR J6 0-6-0 and C12 4-4-2T, the ex-NER J21 and J25 0-6-0s, and a selection of ex-GER 'Buckjumper' 0-6-0Ts of classes J65, J68 and J69/2 (originally my own 'Riceworks' kits). For the slightly more ambitious, LRM also does a very nice kit for the original Gresley GNR/LNER K2 Mogul.

Finally, a little more complex to build and rather more finescale-biased, are the Alan Gibson range of etched kits, which make use of some multi-layer and composite constructional techniques. Etched Gibson locos generally come with a sprung chassis that uses profile-milled brass rather than etched mainframes, incorporating slots into which the supplied sprung hornblocks are intended to fit directly. These kits also come complete with Gibson's own push-fit, plastic-centred wheels, on which more in Chapter 5. It must be said that such a chassis is not really a good proposition for the tyro kit-builder. A basic rigid-frame version is not on the cards and a fair bit of experience is needed to get a sweet-running result from the components supplied, or to adapt the chassis to an alternative set-up.

Gibson's superstructures, by contrast, are far more conventional – in etched-kit terms – and do not usually present any particular constructional problems. They are generally very well detailed, come with plenty of high-quality lost-wax cast brass and white metal fittings, and have nice scale handrails. A few also use resin or cast-metal boilers.

There are some truly useful subjects, starting with just about every variant of the Midland Johnson/Deeley 2F/3F/4F 0-6-0 goods engine family, plus the MR and LMS 'Standard' 2P 4-4-0s. Some modellers combine these Gibson superstructures with the Comet etched-frame aftermarket 4F and 2P chassis kits for ease of construction. For the GE modeller, the Gibson range also has some key types: the essential J15 0-6-0 and E4 'Intermediate' 2-4-0, as well as three 2-4-2T Radials: the large F5/F6 and the smaller F7. There are also an ex-GCR

ABOVE *A full-house etched loco kit – Alan Gibson's J15 0-6-0, a key model for East Anglian enthusiasts. Not shown are the comprehensive instructions, which include a full set of accurate scale drawings. The kit is very complete, although in this case I have substituted Sharman driving wheels for the Gibson originals, which have a spoke too many.*

J11 'Pom-Pom' 0-6-0 and two important ex-LSWR types, the O2 0-4-4T and G6 0-6-0T.

Conclusion

As the above skit around current offerings has hopefully revealed, most of what you could possibly need is available, from somewhere or other; all you have to do is find it! As far as possible, availability details of all these models are included in the Sources index at the back of this book.

BELOW *The last word in liveries, if not in kits! My old friend Vincent de Bode built his lovely GER T26 class 2-4-0 from an Alan Gibson etched brass kit. He also painted and lined it, probably while wearing sun glasses!* Vincent de Bode

5 MATTERS MECHANICAL

Getting a small-scale model railway to run really well has always been a challenge, as several factors come into play. Leaving aside the quality of the trackwork and layout wiring/control system – somewhat outside the scope of this book – it is the design and functioning of the locomotive mechanisms that probably have the biggest impact on overall performance, so high quality here is a *sine qua non*. Fortunately, that's getting ever easier to achieve, with dramatic improvements in both RTR and 'aftermarket' drivetrain components. And, of course, the huge increase in the range of models of diesel locomotives has given rise to a whole family of sophisticated bogie-based drivetrains.

However, apart from a little interbreeding between some designs of diesel power bogie and steam-locomotive tender drive systems, steam and diesel locomotive mechanisms have very little in common. As has probably become apparent by now, I'm no great fan of tender-drive set-ups generally, and the commonly available RTR types in particular. So, in the context of this book, I'm going to limit myself to looking at loco-mounted steam locomotive drives – of which there are some truly excellent examples about nowadays.

Modern 4mm/1ft scale RTR locos are, of course, made to '00 standards'; or they would be if there *was* a properly defined and universally applied 00 standard – which, alas, there isn't. So even today's super-refined models don't yet exhibit unanimity as to wheel profiles, running clearances, back-to-back gauging and so on. Things are a very great deal better than they were, of course; the days when wheel profiles and gauging varied wildly between makers are thankfully past, and most current production generally falls within the somewhat broad church of the old BRMSB 'Scale 00' parameters, although the rather more delicate American NMRA 'RP25' wheel profile is gradually displacing the BRMSB flange outline.

So, if you're working to mainstream 'fine 00' norms then most current-production RTR will come on wheels that will function adequately both on H0-standard Peco 'fine scale' Code 75 track with flat-bottom rail – the current 'default option' – as well as on scale 16.5mm British-prototype, fully chaired track from C&L or SMP, using scale-section Code 75

ABOVE *The chassis of Ken Northwood's prize-winning* Eaton Mascot Hall *shows the sort of lengths that top modellers of the 1950s went to in their search for a concealed drive, mechanical refinement, and good traction. There is a 'big Pitman' in the tender with a shaft-drive to a two-stage transmission in the loco, modified Romford drivers and wiper pick-ups all round. For all this effort and sophistication, a modern RTR Bachmann 'Hall' is quieter, more refined, and just as powerful. It also possesses the correct 15in crank throw, something that Ken could not achieve with his modified* Romfords. *Ken Northwood/Author's collection*

bullhead rail. However, older RTR wheels of the Airfix/Mainline era and earlier, together with original BRMSB Romford/ Hamblings 'scale' types won't run on the C&L bullhead track, as the deeper flanges hit the scale-height chairs. SMP's chairs are more petite and don't cause a problem.

I have already remarked on the extraordinarily high levels of scale accuracy and detail embodied in recently introduced RTR model steam locomotives. Praise be, this excellence usually also extends to the chassis of these models, which are very much 'all of a piece'. 'Twas not ever thus, however; old saws of the model railway hobby like your author can well remember those days – broadly, from the 1950s until the mid-1970s – when the chasm that separated 'proprietary' from 'scale' model railway locomotives very much started with the chassis.

Even where the upperworks of an off-the-peg offering from this 'first generation' were somewhere near the mark for authenticity, the chassis invariably let the side down both in terms of mechanical refinement and, particularly, scale appearance. Often, this was due to the use of a single 'standard' mechanism for a variety of different prototypes, with the result that the frame outline, coupled wheelbase, driving wheel diameter and overall length were often wrong. Although the running gear of the more-authentic and refined 'second-generation' RTR models that started to appear from 1975-onwards – from Airfix, Palitoy/Mainline and revitalised Hornby – was a great improvement on this traditional fare in terms of scale conformity and fidelity to prototype, the new mechanisms did not generally *run* any better; in fact, they often ran worse!

Traditional RTR mechanisms

Traditional 'toy-orientated' mass-produced mechanisms all came with unrealistic coarse-scale wheels. Triang's original solid 'steam-roller' efforts were among the crudest – miles too wide,

ABOVE *The later Ringfield two-rail Hornby-Dublo 8F was mechanically (and aesthetically) about as good as it got in the era of traditional, first-generation RTR models. Allied to that torquey, smooth-running, but cab-fillingly massive motor, came an accurate wheelbase, scale diameter wheels with correct balance-weights and spoke/crank configuration, a complete set of Walschaerts valve gear, and scale-sized cylinders. Wheel profiles were well over-scale, while 50 per cent of the driving wheel flanges were missing, with pick-up consequently only from a miserly two contact points a side. While the valve gear may have been all there, in the cause of 'toy' levels of robustness it was chunky and rather crude; where's the fluting and motion bracket? Of other chassis detail was there ne'er a vestige.*

and with monstrous flanges; Trix were even worse. Hornby-Dublo (at a mere twice scale width!) were very much better; they had see-through spokes and wheel-hubs and cranks that at least vaguely resembled the real thing, with some of them even boasting accurately shaped balance weights…

Centre-axle wheelsets on six-coupled locos of any provenance, however, were invariably bereft of flanges and very often of reduced diameter, so that they rode some way clear of the railheads; not a lot of help for traction or pick-up! Coupling rods were generally clunky and of crude outline, while valve gear was often somewhat approximate. The best was Hornby-Dublo's Walschaerts, which was commendably delicate and at least gave you a full complement of waggly bits – Triang left half of 'em off! Of other chassis fittings – like brake gear, sand-boxes or guard irons – was there rarely a trace.

Not only was the appearance of these older chassis wanting, but they all-too-often ran like a peg-legged jack-rabbit – not helped by the crude 'all-or-nothing' resistance devices usually used to control them. RTR locos of this era were essentially intended as toys and hence configured to run at the unrealistically high speeds beloved of small boys, your author not excepted! That said, both the Rovex/Triang and Hornby-Dublo mechanisms were basically well-engineered and manufactured to high standards of quality, especially in the matter of bearings and gears. Let it not be forgotten that most of Guy Williams's early Pendon locos used Triang drivetrain components to excellent effect.

Although powered by simple three-pole motors and single-stage transmissions using relatively small reduction ratios – typically 18:1 or 20:1 – some of these mechanisms were actually capable of running with surprising refinement, especially when used with a more-sophisticated controller like a variable-transformer Hammant & Morgan Powermaster. The smoothest off-the-peg drivetrain you could buy pre-1960 was undoubtedly Hornby-Dublo's Ring Field, with its excellent adjustable bearings, substantial armature, and close-fitting 'ring' magnet'. By contrast, the worst offender – Farish's two-pole 'trembler' – was, frankly, dire beyond description.

The modern RTR chassis

The vast majority of recently introduced Dongguan-built RTR locos from both Bachmann and Hornby, come with mechanisms that not only look the business but generally run very nicely, thank you. They have wheels with tyres as fine in profile as any BRMSB 'scale' contender, but are usually far more authentic about their spokes and hubs. Indeed, the best modern RTR wheels rival the fabled Beeson product in matters of exact diameter, prototypical rim profile, correct spoke configuration, appropriate crank throw and crankpin location. Balance weights nowadays are authentic not just for profile and position, but also come complete with detail such as attachment bolts and edge chamfers. Coupling rods and valve gears are likewise complete, accurate to prototype and to scale, with delicate bracketry and even refinements like lubricator drives. They are assembled using fine, turned rivets and exhibit a commendable lack of lateral slop.

All the supplementary chassis detail is likewise present and correct: brakes (in line with the wheel-tyres and replete

BELOW *The state of the modern RTR mechanical art: the mechanism of Bachmann's SR N class Mogul has, thanks to a discreetly concealed high-tech can motor and multi-stage transmission, the power, torque and smoothness to better the best efforts of a well set-up Dublo Ringfield mech. It also possesses fully flanged 00 scale wheels of accurate diameter, configuration and spacing, with pick-up from all drivers. Valve gear and cylinders are complete, of scale proportions, fluted as appropriate, with fully modelled bracketry and crossheads, while brake and sanding gear are all present and correct.*

with linkages), sandboxes and sandpipes, guard irons, ashpans, injectors, frame access points and washout plugs, blow-down and cylinder drain cocks, ATC gear; you name it – it's usually there.

These hi-fi chassis mostly perform as well as they look: smooth, quiet and controllable, with a realistic speed range and excellent slow-speed performance. Drivetrains marrying skew-wound can motors with multi-stage transmissions – allied to very accurate component production and precisely jigged assembly see to that. Haulage power is likewise uncompromised; a combination of sprung axles, adequate ballast combined with intrinsic weight from cast components in the chassis and body and the odd discrete neoprene traction tyre generally produces all the tractive effort you could ask for. Put simply, for all normal use there is little or nothing you can do to improve such a chassis, bar a spot of discreet weathering. Only where there is a requirement to accommodate fine scale standards (EM or P4), need the thoroughly modern 4mm scale modeller contemplate any spanner-work below the footplate.

'Throwback' mechanisms

Now that Hornby have all-but eliminated their last tender-drive survivors there are very few models in their current catalogue (outside the budget-price Railroad range, which is home to a few old-stagers) that still employ unsatisfactory 1970s-era 'throwback' mechanisms. Even the former Airfix LMS 4F at last has the benefit of a modern skew-wound mechanism with the drivetrain where it should be, in the locomotive. Over at Bachmann, all the dreadful pancake-motored Mainline chassis have thankfully been long ago laid to rest, replaced initially by chunky can motor/worm drive mechanisms that retained the split-frame pick-up system in ameliorated form. In many cases, these in turn have been superseded by chassis employing modern drivetrains with miniature can motors, multi-stage gearing and wiper pick-ups.

All of this means that almost any current-catalogue 'premium range' RTR locomotive purchased new should be possessed of a decent drivetrain and respectable performance. Any poor running among such models is most likely to be down to a dud individual specimen, a matter which can at least be readily addressed care of the supplier or manufacturer. (Although, in my experience, a quick check of the pick-ups will very often identify the problem!)

The snag is, of course, that we are not all in a position to populate our locomotive studs entirely with brand-new, state-of-the-art models straight off the boat, especially since most of them now command three-figure prices. With popular and presentable RTR models originating in the 1970s and 1980s being available in large numbers on the second-hand market for a few pounds apiece, a lot of us perforce look to such pre-owned specimens as a basis for our motive power needs. This means the problem of second-rate mechanisms hasn't entirely gone away! Given that the reason so many of these older models are on the pre-owned market in the first place is that they don't run acceptably – if at all! – then a certain amount of mechanical rectification and improvement is going to be necessary. The question then comes down to the two basic

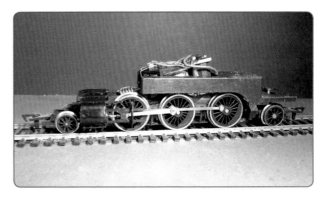

ABOVE *An oldy but not-so-goody: the mechanism of the ex-Airfix (latterly Hornby) GWR '61xx' is pretty crude by modern standards, lacking both realism and refinement. The current iteration of the 'Large Prairie' has a mildly upgraded body and an improved chassis insofar as the carrying wheels and rods go. Hopefully, the motor and gearing have also been breathed on, but the whole thing is some way from the state of the RTR-art. The current list price of just under £100 makes a second-hand Airfix body and a Comet chassis kit an appealing proposition in my book!*

options that apply to any piece of machinery past its best: repair or replace?

Well, some of these older mechanisms *can* be rescued and even improved. The 'traditional' Triang-Hornby locos – like the LMS 'Jinty' and its similarly powered brethren – or those Airfix locomotives employing conventional chassis – the GW '61xx' 'Large Prairie', LNER N2 0-6-2T, and the GWR '48xx/14xx' 0-4-2T – are amenable to the sort of tune-up techniques that were popular in the 1960s. Truing-up out-of-square motor frames, polishing commutators, careful tweaking brush-spring pressures, hi-tech lubrication, fitting better and additional pick-ups, and so on can produce notable improvements, just as fitting a twin-choke carburettor and a free-flow exhaust could pep up a Ford Cortina of similar vintage.

The fact is, though, that whatever you do to such an old Airfix or Triang-Hornby mechanism, it's never going to hold a candle to a current RTR drivetrain, just as the souped-up Cortina would be hard-pressed to keep up with a modern shopping hatchback. The world has moved on, and to my mind fiddling about with superannuated mechanicals is a waste of time and effort (unless you're restoring a historic collector's model – but that's a different branch of the hobby entirely!).

The transplant option

No; faced with a tolerable body powered by a dodgy drivetrain (especially if it's in the tender) then my invariable preference is to go down the replacement mechanism route. In which case, you have two possible options: where something suitable is available for the model in question, buy a modern RTR chassis as a spare part; or build your own replacement mechanism by drawing on the wide range of kits and components now available for just that purpose.

The first option is really limited to those specimens – such as the former Mainline engines that are now part of the

Bachmann range and the Airfix and Dapol models absorbed by Hornby – where a current product uses an original older body moulding (or a close derivative of it) in conjunction with a new mechanism. In these circumstances, it is usually possible to fit the original body on to the new chassis, albeit with the need for a few modifications or adaptations. In economic terms, such a strategy usually results in a reasonable saving over the cost of the current-production model, although there may also be some cosmetic leeway to make up. This 'new-for-old' approach is, of course, only applicable where you're sticking to mainstream 00 standards. If you're working to EM or P4, then the case for a DIY replacement chassis is unanswerable. Personally, even in 00, I still prefer to 'brew my own' – not just for the satisfaction of producing something myself, but for the freedom it gives me to evolve my own specification and to tailor the locomotive to its precise role on the layout.

Many old-but-useful RTR models can be utterly transformed both in appearance and performance by fitting them with replacement chassis built using the excellent etched kits produced for the purpose by a variety of makers. Assembled with a modicum of care and equipped with decent wheels and a state-of-the-art drivetrain, such a kit-built chassis can hack it with the best of current RTR drives for both performance and appearance. And, of course, such replacements can just as readily be built to EM or P4 standards as 00.

Indeed, the combination of a suitably titivated RTR body with a purpose-built finescale chassis is probably the most popular and economical way of putting together the bones of a loco stud for an EM or P4 layout. Tackling one of the simpler examples of these chassis kits is also a first-class introduction to the whole business of model railway locomotive engineering. The combination of the Airfix '14xx' body with an etched chassis, scale wheels, a decent drivetrain and a re-detailing kit is probably the most popular of loco-building toe-in-the-water projects, especially among new converts to EM or P4.

BELOW The starting point for this splendid GWR Churchward '31xx' 'Large Prairie' in original straight-bunker form, was none other than the Airfix old-stager mentioned above. The body underwent startling surgery (see next chapter), while the chassis was replaced with an etched version from South Eastern Finecast. This was built for fine-scale 00, with a Maxxon coreless can motor driving through a High Level gearbox. Wheels are Gibson and the model also features three-point suspension and full on-board DCC sound. The model was built by Andrew Duncan. It runs like a Rolex and pulls like an ox.

Chassis kit alternatives

As noted above, there is a very good selection of kits and components available in the 'scale replacement mechanism' market, with several alternative choices for the more popular prototypes. Somewhat naturally, not all these kits take the same approach, ranging from pared-down simplicity to ultra-fine-scale sophistication. Some of them, in fact, are designed exclusively for adherents of EM/P4 and cannot be built for straightforward 00. So in choosing something apt for your needs, it is necessary to start out with a clear idea of what you are trying to achieve, mechanically and aesthetically. In other words, it will be necessary to make your choices in conformity with the benchmark 'Common Specification' advocated in Chapter 4.

At the most basic these etched chassis kits give you the essentials: a pair of frames with matching coupling rods, some frame spacers – sometimes for 00 only, but often offering alternatives for EM/P4 as well – together with simplified brake gear and (hopefully) a set of balance weight overlays. Plus, of course, bogie or pony-truck frames, outside cylinders and valve-gear where appropriate. The design of these basic kits is biased very much for simplicity of construction, and towards mainstream 00 standards. Motor, transmission, pickups and any additional chassis detail are down to you, as is any sort of suspension system – although most of the current ranges incorporate half-etched guidelines or partial etching-out of the horn guide cut-outs to aid this provision.

Now that the trend-setting Perseverance range is defunct, the largest and most comprehensive of these 'basic' chassis kit ranges is Comet, which covers the vast majority of the RTR subjects for which anyone is ever likely to require a replacement mechanism. Indeed, they also produce chassis kits for several of the current generation of RTR 'super models', which I find somewhat puzzling.

I can perhaps see the logic of such kits as a basis for a no-holds-barred, all-singing EM or P4 chassis for a modern RTR model – but given Comet's strong 00 bias, that doesn't seem to be the intention. Frankly, I think you would have to be a bit barking to junk a costly current-production RTR mechanism in favour of a DIY 00 alternative which is unlikely to confer any discernible mechanical or aesthetic advantage, while demanding a considerable expenditure in time and hard cash. If one could readily purchase the current generation of RTR bodies separately as spares then things would be rather different – but, alas, the current policy of both Bachmann and Hornby seems dead set against this possibility.

Also providing no-frills etched chassis kits, albeit on nothing like as comprehensive a scale as Comet, are Branchlines and Mainly Trains. Southern-biased Branchlines covers, amongst things, the ex-SECR R1 0-6-0T (Hornby-Dublo/Wrenn) while Mainly Trains offers chassis for the LNER/NER/BR J72 0-6-0T (Mainline/Bachmann), and the ex-GNR J52 0-6-0ST (Hornby), together with useful underframe kits for several popular RTR tenders.

Also available – if not that easy to track down – are a few specialists offering kits related to their specific field of interest. So, Scottish-prototype modellers can look to Eastfield/NB Models for a chassis for the LNER ex-NBR J83 0-6-0T that can

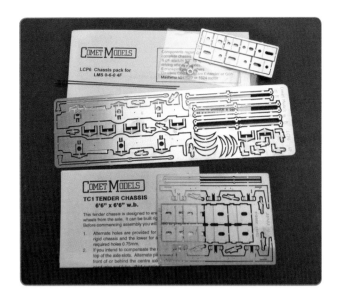

ABOVE *The staple diet of the RTR loco-converter: a no-frills Comet etched chassis – in this case for the LMS 4F and its accompanying Fowler 3,500-gallon tender. (The two kits are sold separately.) Just add some wheels and a suitable drivetrain and you can turn a lame-duck tender-drive Airfix sow's ear into a smooth-running, powerful and realistic silk purse.*

be adapted to the Hornby model, while industrial railway enthusiasts will be seeking RT Models' competent and economical kit for the Dapol/Hornby Hunslet 16-inch 'Austerity' (BR J94) 0-6-0ST.

The other source of good-quality and mostly straightforward chassis kits is white metal loco-kit maker South Eastern Finecast, which will happily supply the etched chassis provided in its loco kits, several of which are for prototypes also covered by the RTR makers: the LMS 4F, LNER J39, A3 and A4 Pacifics, SR N class Mogul and 'Schools' 4-4-0, and the GWR 'Castle' 4-6-0, among others. Not being purpose-designed for RTR conversions per se, these kits may need a little adaptation in the matter of body-mounting, but they are generally well-designed and, in some instances, very well-detailed.

Sophisticated chassis designs

At the opposite extreme to the no-frills offerings of Comet are the no-compromise finescale-only chassis produced by Dave Bradwell. Like everybody else's kits, these give you frames, rods and spacers – but there the similarity ends! Bradwell's frames are absolutely true to prototype in outline and fully detailed with overlays, push-out rivets and all the twiddly bits, mounted on (P4, adaptable to EM) frame spacers correct for position and configuration. Rods are multi-layer for scale thickness and correctly knuckle-jointed. As for 'suspension to choice' – with Bradwell it is full wire-leaf springing without the option. The drivetrain is designed-in to the kit and uses high-end components throughout, while valve gears are in full relief with proper forked joints. The brake gear too, is all there – compensators, adjusters, pivot mountings, cross-beams and pull-rods.

These kits provide complete underframing – loco and tender – together with adaptation and detailing parts for the RTR bodies, while castings are generally lost-wax brass or nickel-silver of superlative quality. Instructions – thankfully – are very comprehensive and beautifully produced. In other words – these kits are the full works, with a price to match. Although, given the quality and the niche fine-scale market, the amount asked is by no means unreasonable.

A little less puritanical in intent and a good deal more pragmatic in execution are the excellent High Level kits. Although also incorporating a high level of prototype detail – including dummy inside valve gears and accurate frames on prototypical spacers – these kits can be constructed for 00 gauge, and without suspension, although the designs are generally slanted towards fine scale and three-point compensation. The most notable feature of these chassis is the incorporation of custom-designed transmissions using High Level's super-smooth gear-trains, as featured in their outstanding range of stand-alone gearboxes – of which, much more anon.

Like Bradwell, Chris Gibbon at High Level gives you a cracking set of instructions, and all the castings and other components are of the highest quality. Again, this quality doesn't come cheap, but that said, for what you get, the sticker price is actually pretty competitive. The only nagging worry I have is that these high-end chassis are just a bit *too* good when viewed as simple replacements for dog-eared RTR mechanisms on tired old engines. With many of the bodies for which they are intended, *serious* cosmetic refinement is going to be needed to bring the upperworks up to the standard of the underpinnings!

These sophisticated chassis kits, while being of exemplary fit and quality, are obviously more complex as constructional projects than the simpler affairs peddled by Comet *et al*. And of course, in the case of the Bradwell offerings, they are limited to EM or P4. Although the detail and refinement of the High Level kits are appealing, to me their outstanding virtue is the super-smooth performance endowed by the combination of a silky transmission with the current generation of powerful, quiet-running and powerful can motors. With that Rolls-Royce drivetrain you can – courtesy of the stand-alone

BELOW *The epitome of the truly useful layout loco: Andrew Duncan's 00 GWR Dean Goods combines a mildly reworked Airfix loco body and tender with Comet underpinnings. A Mashima motor, High Level gearbox, three-point suspension and Ultrascale wheels complete the specification.*

ABOVE *Here is High Level's complete kit-built chassis for the LMS 'Jinty' 0-6-0T, which, as well as being compensated and very fully detailed, incorporates a custom-designed transmission that keeps the motor clear of the cab. High Level designed the kit with the Bachmann model in mind, hence the Bachmann sandboxes on this example. It makes an interesting contrast with the Comet-based 'Jinty' chassis that features in my main example later in this treatise.*
High Level

High Level gearbox kits – install happily and simply in 'lesser' chassis based on more prosaic offerings, giving you the best of all possible worlds. The advent of comprehensive ranges of versatile and well-designed gearboxes has been, in the opinion of your 'umble scribe, the best thing to happen in the whole field of model locomotive mechanism construction in recent years.

A bespoke chassis specification

Some people complain when they have to go hunting for the bits – motors, gears, wheels, pick-ups, suspension components – to complete their Comet or Branchlines chassis

BELOW *Mix and match: here's my choice of components for a specialised application – in this case a J72 destined as a shunter for a compact P4 colliery layout, a role in which it will rarely get much above walking pace while negotiating rough track. Hence the drivetrain choice of a three-stage 108:1 High Level Hump Shunter gearbox in combination with a compact Mashima 1026 motor, and the provision of Flexi-Chas three-point compensation using hornblock assemblies from London Road Models.*

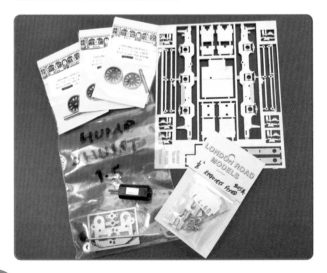

kits. But not I! Far from it; the freedom to select and specify the components making up the drivetrain, for example, is something I value for the opportunity it gives me to come up with an arrangement that not only physically suits the particular model in question – keeping the cab clear and preserving the 'daylight under the boiler' – but which also enables me to fine-tune the model for its role on the layout by optimising its performance characteristics. No more 100mph shunters or gutless heavy haulers.

When it comes to wheels, I can opt for those that best suit both my practical requirements in matters such as tyre material, flange profile or quartering system – as well as best pleasing my discerning eye. Pick-ups are very much something I'm happiest devising for myself – for reasons that will become apparent – so these don't figure on the shopping-list anyway. Suspension components – hornblock bearings and guides – on the other hand, very much do. While a compensated chassis is by no means *essential*, in my book it is definitely *desirable*…

With this mix-and-match approach, I can come up with locomotives that will always start on command, run smoothly and sweetly at all likely speeds and exhibit a high degree of controllability, even without the benefit of sophisticated DCC electronics. It is certainly readily possible to produce performance that will match the best of modern RTR mechanisms; pull out all the possible stops, and you can go a notch or two higher… And don't forget that all this performance comes wrapped in a package that also looks the business, being accurate in outline, well-detailed and sitting on wheels of the correct diameter and spoke configuration. Well worth the effort, I'd say.

Desirable chassis characteristics

So what are the key ingredients of a sweet-running DIY model locomotive mechanism? Well, the first attribute it must possess is to be truly free-running, in the strictly mechanical sense; friction in bearings, rods and gear-trains must be kept to an absolute minimum. This comes down to a clear understanding of the causes of such friction, together with the steps that can be taken to avoid it – matters addressed in the detailed notes that follow. The second key ingredient in our optimum chassis is, of course, the drivetrain – the motor and transmission together with any 'enhancements' such as flywheels.

As we've already noted, with a wide choice of components of excellent quality for both parts of this equation freely available, coming up with a refined and powerful drive for just about any locomotive type is a relatively straightforward proposition. Closely allied to these mechanical aspects of the drivetrain are the electrical characteristics – which, at the basic level, are concerned with the essential business of supplying the motor with appropriate *and consistent* electrical power. While the 'appropriate' part of this requirement is down to the control system in use – be it an external 'layout' set-up or an on-board DCC decoder – the even-more-fundamental consistency requirement is the province of those vital-but-neglected components, the pick-ups. The quality and reliability of the pick-up system is one of the most influential factors in determining the overall performance of a model locomotive mechanism. It's a pity then, that it is so overlooked…

ABOVE Yes, I know it's a chestnut and no, I don't expect to trample smooth-shod over stray sleepers left across the rails, but if a suspension system can cope with this situation it will certainly live with any likely dips, humps, bumps, dropped joints or track twist/cant, while keeping the wheel-treads firmly and consistently on the rail-head. This is a key factor when it comes to those two fundamentals of chassis performance: traction and pick-up.

This brings us finally to the matter of suspension and its impact on the reliability of the electrical pick-up of a locomotive chassis and the 'grip' it can exert on the rails. It's a sobering thought that a wheel that loses contact with the railhead, even by 1/1,000th of an inch, will effectively contribute a big fat zero to either of these vital functions! There are those who will assure you that their rigid chassis are precisely in square for alignment and level, their wheels are absolutely true for circularity and consistency of diameter and their track is flatter than anybody's billiard table, so perfect contact is assured at all times. While attention to all these factors will undoubtedly help to improve pick-up and traction, I fear that anyone who really believes that they can build to, let alone maintain, tolerances of ± 0.025mm is kidding themselves!

Nowadays, it is rather the opposite approach that has gained credence, where track and chassis imperfections are accepted as inevitable and steps are taken to address the consequences by use of some form of suspension, on the driven axles at least. Such a refinement is often associated with fine-scale standards, particularly P4, where the fine flanges certainly demand secure rail contact at all times if derailment is to be avoided. But, so far as maintaining electrical continuity and grip is concerned, a functional suspension system is a substantial asset no matter what the gauge or wheel standards in use. Contrary to popular conception, simple suspension is not *that* difficult to contrive on most of the modern aftermarket chassis kits.

Wheels

A pretty vital component of any chassis, I think you'll agree, although these days the choice of ranges and fundamental designs is broadly limited to two very different alternatives: the all-metal Romford/Markits design, and the plastic-centred Alan Gibson range. Although differing in detail design, manufacturing process and tyre profiles used, both types of wheel can be used for mainstream 'scale 00' and for EM standards. When it comes to P4, however, only the Gibson range offers wheels of appropriate profile and matching axles for 18.83mm gauge.

Both ranges offer a wide choice of prototype-conformant 'dedicated' driving wheels, correct as to diameter, spoke count, rim profile, crank throw and crankpin alignment (in line with spoke or between-spoke), together with matching and appropriate bogie and tender 'carrying' wheelsets. They both use 'standard' driving axles of eighth-inch diameter, available for 00 or EM, with 3mm diameter axles available as an alternative for re-wheeling recent RTR models, which mostly use this size.

Bogie and tender wheelsets universally use a 2mm axle diameter. Flangeless driving wheels are not available from Gibson, which can cause the occasional problem. While the non-prototypical fitment of flangeless wheelsets on the intermediate axles of 00 six or eight-coupled locos 'to get around model railway curves' has long been shown to be quite unnecessary (vide all current RTR locos), there are a handful of prototype engines that *did* have such 'blind' wheelsets at full size: the ex-LNWR G2 0-8-0 and the BR 9F 2-10-0 are the ones you are most likely to come across.

Romford/Markits

The Romford driving wheel has a long history – over 60 years of continuous production – although the current version and its Markits derivative are far more refined and of far better quality than the Romford wheel of yore. There are effectively, two ranges in production: a small selection of the original Romford 'generic' wheels and the much larger Markits range of 'dedicated' wheelsets. The generic driving wheels are not very authentic – useful for restoring historic models, but not up to the mark for a modern realistic chassis. All Romford/Markits wheels have turned nickel-silver tyres mounted on blackened metal centres cleanly die-cast in zinc alloy made self-quartering by means of a square axle-hole mounting on a square-ended

BELOW The all-metal Markits wheels are derived from the long-running Romford design, with its self-quartering, square-ended axle system and screw-in crankpins. Current production wheels all use the finer, RP25 profile and are prototype-dedicated. The old generic wheels with BRMSB tyres and cast-in balance weights – the bare alloy-centred specimen at upper left – have now been phased out. Markits wheels suit fine-scale 00 and EM; a P4 wheel is not available.

axle, with a 10BA threaded spigot and a countersunk 10BA 'cheesehead' nut to hold the wheel in place.

The turned-brass Romford crankpins also use a 10BA spigot, which screws into a pre-tapped hole in the wheel centre from the front. The rods are held in place on the pin by either a push-fit retaining collar on the basic crankpin or, on the latest 'super de luxe' variant, by a circular 14BA screw-down nut. The crankpins are supplied in sets but – de luxe model aside – do not include 'top hat' crankpin bearing bushes (see the section on coupling rods following), although these are available separately.

Romford/Markits driving wheels come in rim-insulated or all-live formats and use the American RP25 tyre profile. This last falls within the BRMSB 'scale' parameters while having a more delicate, shallower and better-engineered flange which usefully reduces overall wheel diameter (often vital for scale splasher clearance), and runs on scale chaired bullhead track without fouling the chairs. The bogie and tender wheels are of similar construction to the drivers. All these wheels are 100thou/2.5mm wide, which strictly speaking falls outside the standard for EM gauge use. However, as the RP25 flange profile and the back-to-back dimension on Romford EM axles are conformant, the extra 10thou of wheel-width on the front face makes no practical difference. Blackened etched brass wheel boss overlays (to hide the axle securing nuts) and appropriate etched balance weights are supplied for each prototype wheel type. Details of both ranges are in the Markits price list, available as a pdf download at www.btinternet.com/~markits/. Alas, it takes a bit of deciphering and lacks much information and a proper website would, as always, be a boon.

Gibson wheels

The Alan Gibson wheel range has its origins in the original P4 Studiolith wheels of 1970, which married a turned steel tyre with a centre moulded in ABS plastic. From the outset, these wheels followed specific prototypes and over the years the range has grown to more than 80 types. There are very few prototypes for which a suitable driving wheel is not available! Bogie and tender wheels – of which a wide choice is also available – are made in exactly the same way as the drivers.

Nowadays, Gibson wheel-centres are injection-moulded in black nylon and press-fitted to bright-steel turned tyres, which come in two distinct formats: a 90thou wide 'Fine 00/EM' profile based on the EM Gauge Society standard, and an 80thou tyre turned to P4 standards – incorrectly described as 'S4' on the Gibson lists. The wheel-centre mouldings are common to both types – which means that on the 00/EM wheel, the rear of the tyre stands slightly proud of the centre, calling for an appropriate spacing washer on the axle to ensure that the wheel-rims don't contact the frames. This is a factor that needs to be taken into account when considering side-play requirements, as discussed below. Gibson will sell you a pack of very nice turned spacing washers of graduated thicknesses to take care of these issues.

Gibson's axles are plain steel rod accurately turned to length, on which the wheels are a firm push-fit; quartering is thus down to the user. P4 wheelsets are supplied with an appropriately finished axle, while the 00/EM wheels come with an axle for each gauge in the pack. Crankpins – sold separately in sets or bulk packs – are based on an M1 1mm-diameter metric-thread steel screw, which self-taps from the rear into a pilot hole moulded-in to the wheel centre. Turned-steel top-hat bearing bushes in two lengths – for single or doubled rods (coupling rod + connecting rod on outside-cylinder engines) are supplied as standard, and rod retention is by circular screw-down crankpin nuts that have the added virtue of looking very much like the real thing. Range details can be found on website www.alangibsonworkshop.com, which also includes a downloadable pdf list.

Unless you're a P4 modeller, which type of wheel you go for is very much a matter of personal priorities. If ease of use is the predominant factor, then Romford/Markits – with their self-quartering design and screwdriver assembly – win hands down. If closer-to-scale wheel profile, delicacy or spokes and rims and ultimate conformity to prototype form the goal, then Gibson has it by the neck over Markits, which to my eye, are still a shade on the chunky side and with those hub overlays are not quite convincing in the appearance stakes.

The other key difference lies in the tyre material. Here, Gibson's steel tyres both look more convincing in fidelity-to-prototype terms (nothing looking more like steel than steel…) while offering superior tractive grip, especially on steel rail. In my experience, steel wheels also stay cleaner for longer, which helps pick-up and reduces the need for wheel-cleaning. Many folk worry about rusting however – in which case, Markits

LEFT AND RIGHT *The steel-tyred, nylon-centred Gibson design is essentially a fine-scale wheel. The fine 00/EM versions conform to the EM Gauge Society profile and the 18.83 variant uses the P4 standard. Axles are plain steel finished to the correct lengths, but quartering is down to the modeller. The inset gives a close-up of the crankpin and coupling rod bearings.*

combination of nickel tyres and stainless steel axles should allay their worst fears.

Practical chassis engineering

Unfortunately, within the context of a wide-ranging book such as this, it is just not practicable to explore the stage-by-stage nuts and bolts of chassis kit construction in terms of the specifics of the various different designs touched on in my whistle-stop survey above. An example does figure in Chapter 9, which should give an idea of what is typically involved. There are, anyway, a number of books available covering the 'how to' side of the chassis-building business in exhaustive detail – not least, my own *Locomotive Kit Chassis Construction in 4mm*, 158 pages covering the theory and practice of mechanism-building in considerable detail; see Bibliography. Although that book is now a little dated in terms of the components currently available, taken in conjunction with the notes here, it should answer most questions. The rest of this chapter is, therefore, devoted to the mechanical and electrical requirements germane to model locomotive chassis as a species, and the practical means by which the y can be addressed.

Axle bearings

I've made much of the importance of arriving at a truly free-running basic chassis. Attaining this state of mechanical nirvana calls, first, for decent axle bearings *of the right size* – not 'tight' obviously, but not sloppy either. What we are after is a good 'running fit' which calls for truly round axles (which, thankfully, all the main commercial sources provide) revolving in truly circular bearings with an overall running clearance of around 2–3thou. Meeting this requirement is, you may think, down to the manufacturer and by and large, that is so – but any production engineer worth his salt is going to work on the basis that a bore a bit on the tight side can be 'eased out' to a running fit, whereas if the hole is too big in the first place there's not a lot anyone can do about it. So most 1/8in bearings are turned to be 'spot on' for diameter, typically producing a stiff push-fit on the axle, which we need to ease by a thou or two. This is a job I always do *after* the bearings are aligned and fixed in the frames – see below – as a tight fit is a help when setting up a chassis.

The tool for opening-out a tight bearing is *not* a 1/8in twist drill, as often suggested, but rather a 1/8in parallel reamer. Actually, the perfect implement is a 0.127in 'clearing' reamer, but these are difficult to find and expensive, so we normally make use of the fact that an eighth parallel reamer twiddled in the fingers (rather than being used in a lathe) normally cuts 'oversize' by a couple of thou. Before reaming a bearing in this way, I use a finger-twiddled twist drill of about ¼in diameter to bevel the ends of the bearing bore slightly. This removes any turning burrs from the bore-ends and

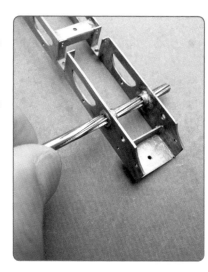

RIGHT *Reaming bearings: the bearings are aligned and fixed in the frames before reaming, which is accomplished with an 1/8in parallel reamer used in the fingers and twiddled gently to and fro. No force is necessary and power tools are a no-no!*

eases the axle entry; the bevel also provides a useful oil-ring reservoir to retain lubricant when the bearing is in service. Then just keep twiddling the reamer in the bearing until the axle slides smoothly into place and revolves freely.

The axle bearings also need to be aligned accurately in the chassis. A bearing that is skewed in relation to the axle is effectively 'tight' and, worse still, not symmetrically so, which can cause high levels of wear. What this comes down to essentially, is keeping the frames – and hence the axles and bearings – truly 'in square' while the basic chassis is being assembled. This is a prime function of the various sophisticated chassis assembly jigs that have recently come on the market. Such devices are of necessity expensive and hard to justify if you only knock up the odd chassis now and then, but they are a good purchase though, for a club or other modelling group.

However, Neanderthals like Rice somehow managed to build sweet-running mechanisms long before such things burst upon us, and a method of achieving accurate frame alignment without resorting to 'hi-tech' gadgetry is illustrated overleaf. The main requisites are a couple of 4–6in lengths of

BELOW A worthwhile refinement is to use a larger drill to cut a tiny bevel on the outer faces of the bearing, which makes it easier to insert the axle and provides a retaining groove for axle lubricant.

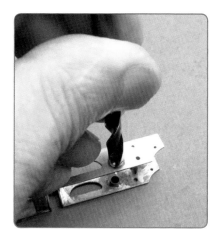

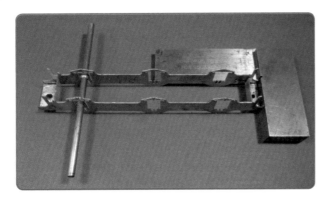

ABOVE The basics of frame-checking; a decent length of ¹/₈in rod as an alignment aid, one or more small engineer's squares, and plenty of Mk 1 eyeball. Laying the parts out on squared paper can also help.

eighth-inch diameter steel bar (which Markits sell for this very purpose), a couple of engineer's steel rules and a small engineer's square with a 3–4in 'long leg'. These are arranged as shown to provide plenty of reference points by which to judge the axle alignment; the rest is down to the (surprisingly accurate) Mk 1 human eyeball. There's much more on frame assembly and bearing fitment in the chassis construction book mentioned earlier.

Side-play allowances

The other factor which needs a moment's consideration before erecting a chassis is the prevailing track curvature on the layout over which it is to run, and the related need for side-play (unhindered lateral movement), on one or more of the coupled wheelsets on six- or eight-coupled engines. There is a golden rule in the matter of side-play, which runs along the lines of 'You can't really have too much, but you can sure as heck have too *little*!'

The available side-play allowance is determined by the difference between the *total* width of the chassis frames (over the faces of the axle bearings) and the back-to-back distance of the wheelsets. On a typical RTR chassis, this difference will often be 2mm or more, while most of the aftermarket chassis kits give you the potential for 1–1.5mm in 00 using the spacers supplied. The latter allowance, allied to the generous running clearance (difference between the distance over the face of the flanges and that separating the inside faces of the railheads) inherent in 00 standards, should be enough to get most 00 locomotives around curves of 24in radius, or a bit less.

The problem usually comes where EM or P4 standards are being applied. Here, running clearances are far smaller and the need for adequate side-play correspondingly greater. Unfortunately, some fine-scale chassis are designed more along 'idealistic' lines that eschew the pragmatism of generous side-play in favour of a 'scale width' chassis. Great for showcase models… So look out for frame spacers in kits that set the chassis width at close-to-scale values, resulting in a paucity of side-play – allowances of less than 1mm. Yes, you don't expect an EM or P4 loco to run around curves as tight as those associated with 00, but few of us have space for true-

scale curves (5ft minimum radius), so fine-scale modellers still need reasonable side-play to get around the 3ft 6in or 4ft minimum radii commonly forced upon them.

Bearing the golden edict in mind, I like to try to stick to the 1–1.5mm frame/wheelset difference used in 00:1mm for curves of 4ft radius and above, 1.5mm if values stray below this figure, calling for frames 15mm or 15.5mm wide over bearings in EM and no more than 1mm wider in P4. In fact, I often err on the generous side and use EM spacers giving 15.5mm frame width for P4. Do bear in mind that all these numbers are the extreme widths over the bearing faces, which are often 0.5mm or so proud of the actual mainframes on each side.

Kit frames are usually etched in metal 18 or 20thou thick, giving a total frame thickness of around 40thou/1mm. Making allowance for these values means that a 15.5mm extreme frame width will call for spacers 13.5mm wide – a common figure for kit-supplied EM spacers. By the same token, 00 spacers are usually 11.5mm wide. Any unneeded side-play is, of course, simply taken up by the use of spacing washers, already noted as being available in a variety of thicknesses for this very purpose.

Coupling rods

Unwanted friction – most notably, *uneven* friction – in the coupling rods is without doubt the most prevalent failing of many self-built model locomotive mechanisms, not to mention the odd RTR product. This friction has six usual

ABOVE Loads of side-play (1.5mm+) on all three driven axles is the recipe that enables RTR mechanisms like this Mainline Collett Goods to get round ultra-tight train-set curves with a full set of flanges. The downside of this arrangement (still current on many RTR locos, although not so pronounced as this), is the side-to-side shimmy that occurs when the loco is running on straight or gently curved track.

BELOW On more reasonable curves – 24in+ in 00 – you can get away with restricting the side-play to one or two axles, as on this J52 chassis. Keeping side-play to a minimum – 0.5mm or so – on the leading and trailing axles makes for steadier running, when 1.5mm clearance on the centre axle will still squeak the loco round a 21in radius curve, as here.

sources: a tight fit and/or poor bearing surfaces in the coupling-rods where they ride on the crankpins; over-tight crankpin retaining nuts/screws/washers; lack of clearance between the inside faces of the rods and the faces of the wheels causing the rods to rub on the wheel-hubs; a miss-match in the actual centres of the coupling-rod bearing holes in relation to those of the axles; inconsistent 'throw' of the driving wheel cranks, and quartering errors. Any of the three latter conditions will cause 'dot and carry one' running, with 'tight spots' one or more times per revolution.

Tight crankpin bearings, rubbing rods and over-fierce retaining arrangements just make the whole chassis 'stiff'. My test for a truly free-running chassis is that the wheels should revolve freely when the bare chassis (i.e., sans motor and with no extra weight or down-force applied) is pushed along on a flat, smooth surface (such as a piece of MDF) by means of a fingertip applied delicately to one end or the other. This is a good test because if there are any tight spots, the point at which the wheels lock and the chassis starts to skid will usually give a pointer to the problem.

Straightforward crankpin bearing friction is avoided by a properly designed set-up with an adequate (but not excessive) running clearance, which good engineering practice says should be 2–3thou. That is, the bearing hole in the coupling rods needs to be around 3thou greater than the diameter of the crankpin. Easy to write, not so easy to achieve! How do you determine what the dratted clearance actually is? In fact, it is not something you can practically measure without specialised equipment, so we need to fall back on subjectives – in this case, 'a little bit of waggle', the best description I can come up with for the 'feel' of a well-set-up coupling rod when you try to move it fore-and-aft on the crankpins. If you can *just* feel a bit of movement in each direction, then you're about right. What the actual resulting clearance is I haven't a clue; it is probably considerably more than 3thou! But what I *do* know is that an engine whose rods are set up thus will (all else being well) normally run sweetly.

The rule-of-thumb way to achieve this sort of fit is to start with the rods as a tight fit on the crankpins, then using the appropriate-size of taper brooch progressively ease out the bearing holes. Rather than guessing each hole individually, I use an ancient 'dodge', which is to put a stripe of permanent marker along the brooch then, selecting one 'master' hole in the rod, I twiddle this out to get the desired 'waggle fit' of that hole on a crankpin. As the taper brooch goes into the hole, the marker ink gets cleaned off the cutting edges, giving you a handy reference mark which you can then use to brooch out all the other holes to the same size; 'seemple', as the Russian rodent says.

Opening holes out with a brooch in this way has two further benefits; you get a nice, smooth finish to the bore of the hole which makes a decent bearing surface – a surface which will also be truly circular, the other key requisite of a good bearing. In the matter of free-running coupling rods, it is also worth noting that multi-section 'divided' rods overlapping on the crankpins – as now fitted to virtually all RTR locos and provided for by the majority of the aftermarket chassis kits to facilitate the installation of suspension – are much easier to set up to run

smoothly and freely than long rigid rods. They also allow unimpeded sideways displacement of those wheelsets with side-play allowances. For these reasons, I always opt for a multi-section rod approach even on 'rigid' non-suspended chassis.

A further refinement in the matter of coupling rod bearings is the use of proper turned insert bushings or 'miniature top hats' made in an appropriate bearing material, These bushes give an increased bearing area, which is less prone to wear. The actual bearing surface is the *outside* of the bush, which is of larger diameter than the crankpin, hence providing the increased bearing face on which the rod rides. This, contrary to what a lot of folk think, means that these turned bearings do not need to be a free-running fit on the actual crankpins; a nice push-fit is what we want, leaving the 'waggle fit' clearance to be between the hole in the coupling rod and the *outside* of the bush.

The use of these 'top hat' turnings imparts two further virtues; first, the flange of the bearing, sited inside the rod next to the wheel, acts as a spacer and ensures the rods run well clear of the wheel-faces, avoiding any rubbing. Secondly, by trimming/filing the front of the bearing so that it sticks through the front of the rods by a small amount – roughly the thickness of a sheet of copier paper – we can ensure that the crankpin retaining nut (Gibson) or retaining collar (Romford/Markits) can't be fitted 'too tight'. If it is screwed/pushed down hard onto the top of the bush, running clearance will be maintained with the bearing held securely in place.

Rod centres, crank throws and quartering

The *exact* matching of coupling-rod and axle centres is an absolute prerequisite for proper functioning of any rod-coupled chassis, and no amount of tweaks, dodges and clever bodges will overcome a deficiency in this vital correlation. There are three ways of ensuring this match is accurate: by sophisticated close-tolerance manufacture of the components (the way the RTR makers do it); by designing the artwork for an etched chassis such that the rod centres and frame bearing

BELOW *Traditional chassis kit design best practice puts the rods and frames on common artwork and centres to ensure an accurate match between rod and axle centres. Nowadays, computer-aided design and tool-making can undoubtedly achieve accuracy even on separate artwork and etches, but it is not so easy to check the correlation.*

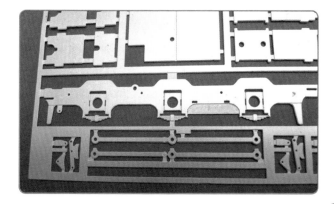

holes are on common alignments and produced on the same sheet of metal (to keep any production error constant 'twixt rod and chassis and hence maintain an accurate match), and by the adoption of 'jigged' chassis assembly techniques using the coupling rods as the reference for setting up the axle bearings in the mainframes.

The first two methods are the prerogative of the manufacturer rather than the user and, these days, problems with such fundamentals are rare. The 'jigged' approach is usually associated with the construction of compensated/sprung chassis using separate hornblocks/horn-guides set into cut-outs in the mainframes. It is a process described in detail in the chassis kit construction book already referred to and illustrated alongside, and 'en passant' in Chapter 9.

The other cause of 'lumpy' running is some derangement of the actual cranks themselves, either in matters of consistent crank throw or – most usually – quartering. The former glitch is most common on models using plastic-centred wheels by Alan Gibson, which leave the final fitting of the crankpins to the modeller. Although the current production wheels have the crankpin hole in the wheel moulded right through (in days gone by, you only got a centre-mark and had to drill your own holes!) it is important to drive the 1mm-diameter steel screws forming the actual pins home very carefully to ensure that they go in true and parallel to the axle in all planes. Go gently without any use of force and let the screw 'find its own way'; I find that they almost invariably go through nice and 'plumb' if you don't try and chivvy them.

Quartering This is the setting of the cranks of the driving wheels on a given axle so that they are at right angles to one another. It is either very easy, in that the design of the wheel uses a 'square-ended' axle that takes care of the problem for you (Romford/Markits), or a bit of a headache, in that you have to establish the relationship yourself (Gibson). Quartering a Romford wheelset is merely a matter of getting the correct 'lead' on the cranks. The normal convention with British steam

BELOW *For truly smooth running of a coupled chassis, the axle and coupling-rod centres must match exactly. Using tapered jig axles enables you to establish this match with precision; the process is described in the suspension section following.*

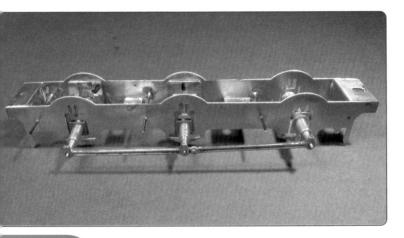

ABOVE *Quartering the wheels on the 'Jinty' chassis, one axle at a time by 'controlled sequential adjustment' (trial-and-error!), using a small mirror as an aid to compare the relative positions of the cranks on either side of the engine. This process is not as hard as it looks, especially when tackled in stages with divided rods and axle locations that are accurately matched.*

locomotives is that the right-hand crank – looking forwards from the footplate – is 90° in advance of the left-hand. That is, with the left crank at 'top dead centre', the right-hand crank will be pointing forwards. The rest of the job just comes down to screwing the wheels on in compliance with this rule.

Quartering 'DIY' wheels like Gibson's is a bit more of a job, again described in detail in my chassis kit book. Suffice to say, there are some excellent wheel-mounting tools and quartering jigs available to help take care of this particular difficulty. Failing this, you can resort to the old-fashioned trial-and-error approach, which relies upon the principle of setting the cranks on one axle as a 'datum' and adjusting all the others to match this by eye, and plenty of suck-it-and-see trial running. In this context, it matters not one jot if you don't quite get the cranks at an exact 90° side-for-side; so long as the error is the same for every axle, all will be well!

One thing you will find no mention of, either in these pages or those of the chassis book aforementioned, is the oft-advocated but extremely ill-advised notion of attempting to address quartering, crank-throw or rod/axle alignment errors – and the consequent 'lumpy' running – by 'ovalling' the bearing holes in the coupling rods. This is a total 'no-no' in engineering and practical terms as it destroys the fundamental relationship between the axle-spacing of the chassis and the corresponding centres of the crankpins in the coupling rods, as well as causing the holes to cease functioning in any way as proper bearings.

The only way to cure such lumpy running is to track down the exact cause and address the underlying error. Again, considerable space is devoted to this sort of fault-finding and the necessary remedial work in the chassis book. The only exception I would ever make to this 'don't monkey about with the coupling rod holes' rule is the case of a very slight (almost imperceptible) 'tight spot' once per revolution in an otherwise free-running chassis. Sometimes, this can be eased by brooching out the coupling rod bearing holes to give just a smidgeon more running clearance. Note well that this maintains the circularity of the bearing. While a slightly loose but concentric running fit is quite acceptable in sound engineering circles, an egg-shaped bearing is never anything but abhorrent.

The drivetrain

You might expect the section of this chapter devoted to the very guts of a model locomotive mechanism (the motor and transmission) to be lengthy and involved. In fact, the converse is the case as there is comparatively little to say in the context of a general practical treatise such as this, for the simple reason that nowadays providing a high-quality drivetrain is pretty straightforward. There are no bad motors or dodgy gears produced these day, while what is available offers such a wide choice and such excellent quality that it is hard to go far wrong.

Smooth, powerful five-pole can motors and hi-efficiency multi-stage transmissions with decent reduction ratios are now the norm for both RTR and self-built mechanisms. Comparatively speaking, these modern drivetrains aren't even expensive. In real terms, a modern Mashima can motor and a High Level gearbox at around £35 the pair is far better value for money than the £3 16s 6d (£3.83) or so that a Pitman DC66 and a set of Romford gears would have set you back circa 1960. (Just to put things in perspective, in those days you could buy a brand-new family car for well under £1,000!) Not only is the modern drivetrain more economical to buy, it also turns in a performance that would knock the Pitman/Romford combo clear into a cocked hat in terms of both tractive effort and running refinement.

Modern miniature electric motors are generally classified by minimum width x length, all quoted in millimetres. Mashima's range of flat-sided can motors – nowadays pretty much the model railway 'standard fit' – come in three widths for use at 4mm scale and below: 10mm, 12mm (both with 1.5mm-diameter armature shafts), and 14mm (2mm shaft).

BELOW A selection of Mashima can motors, the most popular and widely available range. Those seen here are a 1026 at bottom left, with a 1424 and 1428 (fitted with a High Level Loadhauler Plus gearbox and flywheel) above it. Mounted in the Beattie well tank chassis at top left is a 1224 on a Roadrunner Compact Plus transmission, while at bottom right is an older round-can 1624. For many years this was my 'standard fit'; the 1424 is essentially a more compact version of the same thing.

The smallest is the 1015, followed by the 1020, 1024, 1220, 1224, 1420, 1424, 1426, 1428 and 1430. Many of these motors have skew-wound armatures, where the armature poles are set at a slight angle to the armature shaft rather than being parallel to it. This eases the entry of the pole into the magnetic field, reducing the 'cogging' effect often prevalent where high-strength fields are involved.

Mashima's combination of manly magnets with small 'air gaps' (spaces between the magnets and armature) produces some pretty fierce fields! These features largely account for the high power and torque (twisting force) outputs of these motors. Coupled with tightly wound armatures, good balance and accurately aligned bearings due to the can design, this puissance comes allied to refinement and sweetness, with quiet running and a general lack of vibration. With the wide range of sizes and high specific outputs, there is an apposite Mashima motor for just about any application.

What is still apt to leave old-stagers like Rice with jaw a-gape is the sheer grunt of these devices. When you have been brought up on a doctrine of 'bigger is better', it is hard to come to terms with the fact that a skinny runt of a 10-series Mashima can blow a traditional open-framer several times its physical size clear into the weeds for torque and power output. The joy of this is that you can create truly compact yet powerful drivetrains that offer far more options for concealment as well as leaving a lot more space for ballast or DCC electronics.

If Mashima can sell you the power source, High Level will provide you with a gearbox to get the best out of it in the context of just about any locomotive. High Level's ingenious transmission design centres around a modest menu of high-quality gears machined in brass or moulded in high-quality acetal engineering plastic, cleverly combined to give a wide choice of configurations and overall reduction gear ratios, ranging from 30:1 right up to 108:1. The basic design uses a primary-stage worm and pinion set of 15, 20 or 27:1 reduction, followed by one or two further 2:1 spur reduction stages to give ratios of 30, 40 and 54:1 (two stage), and 60, 80 and 108:1 (three stage).

The primary worm gears are available at 1.5mm or 2mm bores to suit the different Mashima motors and the final drive can be specified to suit a 1/8in or 2mm-diameter axle. Final drive gears similarly, are located on the axle with either a Loctite-fit or grub screw fixing, to choice. Not only do you get a wide selection of ratios, but these reductions are available in a number of different configurations, distinguished by descriptive names such as Loadhauler and Hump Shunter. There is also a swivelling 1:1 'reach extender' (on gearboxes with a 'Plus' suffix to the name) that provides an even wider range of mounting options.

The gearbox frames are straightforward fold-up etched nickel-silver assemblies and incorporate a motor-mounting plate matched to the various Mashima motors, which are simply screwed into place. Assembling the whole thing is pleasingly logical and surprisingly unfiddly, aided by first-class instructions. High Level have scale gearbox outlines on their excellent website (http://www.highlevelkits.co.uk) that will help you choose the right set-up for the particular locomotive in question.

RIGHT *This little sequence shows the High Level Roadrunner Plus 54:1 gearbox of the guinea-pig 'Jinty' going together. The first picture shows the unformed main gearbox etch screwed to the front of the Mashima 1424 motor. In the second view, the gearbox sides have been bent up and the first stage of the gearing – the 27:1 worm gear-set with integral spur gear on the pinion – installed on a layshaft cut from the 2mm rod provided, using a mini-drill and cut-off disc. Note the neat turned-brass spacer keeping the gear-wheel centred under the worm. Also shown is the simple fold-up reach extender that makes this a 'Plus' gearbox, fitted with the turned axle bearings provided.*

The third picture shows the second stage gearing assembled on a further layshaft, which also forms the pivot for the extender. The second-stage gear is held in mesh by virtue of being trapped by the pinion of the worm gear-set. The final view has the completed drivetrain installed in the basic 'Jinty' chassis for test-running, with a dummy axle of $^1/_8$in rod. It ran as sweet as a nut, as usual.

There are some other good gearboxes on the market – most notably from Comet and Branchlines, but in my experience nothing to match High Level's flexibility, wide configuration choice, and versatility. Not to mention the silky smoothness and near-silent running imparted by those ultra-low-friction Celcon plastic gears, with their generous tooth profiles and high-quality finish. The design, manufacturing quality and accurate meshing of the gears is the key to the refinement of any transmission – something especially true of

BELOW *A 50:1 Comet two-stage gearbox, installed in the chassis of my J52. With a nylon worm and high-precision Ultrascale gears, it runs very sweetly and quietly, but with its generous side-frames and lack of a reach extender as offered by High Level, the gearbox intrudes into the loco cab more than somewhat. A portly driver provides the necessary disguise.*

fine-tooth worm-pinion gears with relatively high single-stage reductions (38 and 50:1) as used by Comet, *et al.*

Carefully assembled and set up and appropriately-lubricated, such metal-on-metal multi-stage gear trains can turn in a very good performance – my P4 J52, illustrated at several points in this narrative, has a notably sweet-running Comet 50:1 gearbox – but I have always found them more demanding to build. The High Level gearbox design, by contrast, more or less falls together. It has, for some considerable time now, been my own 'standard fit' – and I have yet to encounter any problems with it. On that basis, I commend it.

In a situation where almost any modern motor will produce more than sufficient 'oomph', the most significant factor in our drivetrain specification is the choice of gear ratio. Here, the object is to choose an overall reduction that will keep the motor running as far as possible at those mid-range speeds at which it is sweetest when the loco is working normally. The exact gear ratio needed will depend on the typical running speed and the locomotive's driving wheel diameter. Given that, on most model railways, speeds are generally slow-to-moderate, and the rule-of-thumb is very simple: the slower the average speed and the bigger the driving wheel diameter, the higher the reduction ratio required in the gearbox.

With the wide range of reduction ratios and configurations available, it is possible with equal facility to produce a fleet-footed free-running passenger engine, a real 'slogger' of a goods loco powerful enough to walk off with whatever you care to hang on behind it, or a shunter that will happily crawl along all day at less than a scale walking pace. In the first instance, a double-stage gearbox with an overall reduction ratio in the range 30–54:1 would probably suit, unless it is a Victorian high-stepper with really big drivers (7ft or more), which might call for 60:1.

The goods engine, on the other hand, with driving wheels of 4ft 6in–5ft 3in and no need for speed, will be happiest with a ratio in the range 50–80:1. Slower still, the shunter will benefit from the 'big step' ratios from 60–108:1. A small-wheeled shunter with a 108:1 ratio will be flat out at less than a 'scale' 20mph and should be able to run smoothly and steadily at less than a 'scale' 1mph.

Suspension

As I think will have become apparent by now, I am a firm advocate of the value of fitting model locomotives with some form of suspension, with the aim of optimising and maintaining the vital wheel/railhead contact on which so much depends. That said, while suspension is undoubtedly a good idea, it is by no means *essential*; there are plenty of rigid-chassis models that turn in a perfectly adequate performance on the layout which, after all, is the ultimate benchmark. So, chassis flexibility can perhaps best be viewed as a refinement rather than a fundamental, certainly for 00 and EM locomotives.

Model locomotive suspension systems can take many forms and be applied to all the axles in a chassis, to the coupled axles only, or to one or two axles from within the coupled group. Two basic principles are used: equalisation (often called compensation), which uses beams and pivots to load the axles, and sprung suspension, in which the load is applied to the axle through springs of some sort – wire leaf, coils and even soft rubber. In the most sophisticated systems, both principles are used in combination, which is what the prototype usually does.

The subject of model locomotive suspension is one that has long delighted the mathematical theorist and those of an experimental bent, with the result that the topic has, over the years, generated a considerable and often complex literature full of forbidding formulae, grim graphs, convoluted charts and joyless jargon. Unsurprisingly, this sort of stuff puts a lot of folk off and they pass the whole business by without ever giving it a try. This is a pity, because the benefits are well worth the effort.

However, the present volume is not the place for yet another diatribe on suspension, theoretical or otherwise. I have written in some detail on the subject in my chassis construction book, and in the context of the sort of kitchen-table engineering around which my suggested approach to the provision of effective motive power for a layout is based, I'm going to plump for simplicity rather than sophistication, by suggesting the adoption of straightforward three-point equalisation along the lines developed by Mike Sharman under the Flexi-chas banner. I make no claims as to this being the 'ultimate' system, but it is effective, consistent and relatively easy to install. There are no tricky springs to set up and once the system is installed it remains consistent even when worn.

I have built over 200 Flexi-chas engines, some of which have been running for 30 years and more, without problem. Flexi-chas also addresses a number of other chassis-construction issues, most notably the vital matter of obtaining that truly accurate match between axle centres and coupling rod centres already touched upon.

So what additional work is involved in the installation of suspension? The principal difference between a traditional rigid chassis with axles fixed firmly in the frames and a sprung or compensated one lies in the axle bearings, some or all of which will need to be able to slide up and down as well as being free to tilt slightly in the frames (to accommodate the situation where one wheel on an axle is riding higher than the other due to a track inequality). While it is possible to use normal 'top hat' axle bearings riding in a slot provided directly in the frames, this arrangement is difficult to set up accurately

BELOW *The essentials of a suspended chassis: frames with provision for hornblock cut-outs and a beam pivot hole, hornblock assemblies for the floating axles, and divided rods that allow the axles to rise, fall and tilt. This is the chassis from South Eastern Finecast's J69 'Buckjumper' with the hornblock cut-outs duly cut out. The hornblock assemblies are from MJT.*

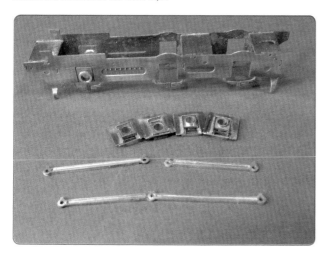

BELOW *The hornblock assembly is the key component of a model locomotive suspension, be it sprung or beam-compensated. This assembly has two basic components, the horn guides and the axle bearings, which are normally square-sided. The key requirement is that the bearings should slide freely and smoothly in the guides without being a sloppy fit. This often calls for careful fitting work – the normal convention being that the bearing is a push-fit in the guides as supplied, being eased to a sliding fit with a fine file. These are London Road Models assemblies, which use a cast brass horn-guide; other makers use etchings. The green pen stripes are for identification purposes.*

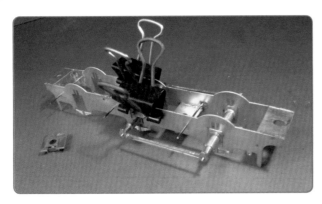

ABOVE *Jigging the Comet 'Jinty' chassis using taper-ended jig-axles and the finished coupling rods to set the horn-guides and bearings of this compensated chassis at exactly the right centres. The horn-guides are held in place with spring-clips while the alignment is adjusted, then tack-soldered in place when all is well. To ensure accurate location of the rods on the jig-axles, the axles are set up as pairs in sequence starting from the fixed-axle location.*

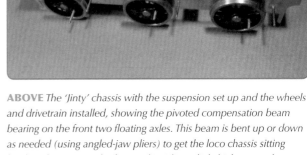

ABOVE *The 'Jinty' chassis with the suspension set up and the wheels and drivetrain installed, showing the pivoted compensation beam bearing on the front two floating axles. This beam is bent up or down as needed (using angled-jaw pliers) to get the loco chassis sitting level. In this picture, the fore-end is riding a little high, as can be seen by comparing the relationship of the tops of the wheels with the upper edge of the mainframes.*

as it is effectively non-adjustable. The bearings can also rotate in the frames, leading to high rates of wear.

So the usual practice is to use a hornblock system, which consists of a machined square-block bearing sliding in an etched or cast-brass horn guide. The guide normally incorporates 'guide cheeks' as well as the slot for the bearing. These cheeks help locate the bearing accurately and stop it from turning, as well as providing plenty of contact area for the sliding surfaces to reduce wear. The whole hornblock assembly is installed on the inside face of the chassis mainframes, which have rectangular openings 6mm wide cut in them to clear the axles and sliding bearings. The hornblocks are aligned in the frames using the coupling-rods as a jig, which ensures a spot-on match between rod and axle centres. To facilitate this setting-up, special 'jig axles' are used, turned to 1/8in diameter to fit the bearings, but with fine tapered ends on which the coupling-rods make a nice tight fit. A suspended chassis, of course, uses multi-section rods, but those are provided in virtually all the kits and are, as already noted, a good idea even on rigid chassis.

The difference between a compensated and a sprung chassis comes in the way the weight of the loco is transferred to the axles. A straightforward six-wheeled compensated chassis (0-6-0, 2-4-0 or 0-4-2) – probably the most common case – will have one rigid driven axle located at one end of the chassis, usually the rear axle of a 2-4-0 or 0-6-0, and the leading axle of an 0-4-2. The other two axles will be 'floating', and these are loaded by a beam (normally a length of fine rod) pivoted at its centre and bearing on top of the mid-point of each axle. The round rod beam resting on top of the round axle at right-angles gives a very low-friction bearing arrangement. The pivot for the beam usually consists of a short length of fine brass tube set crosswise in the chassis and swivelling on a rod or pin located through holes in the frames.

Sprung locos, by contrast, don't normally have any fixed axles. All the axles float and have either a captive coil spring fitted into the horn guide assembly and bearing on the top of

the square axle bearing block (a set-up known as a sprung hornblock), or use a separate wire-leaf spring – one for each axle – resting on top of the bearing block and attached to the frames at either side. The latest thinking favours a single continuous wire spring linking all the axle boxes on each side of a chassis, supported by bearing points at the ends of the frames and between each pair of adjacent axles. The idea is that the reactive flexure of this 'continuous springy beam' provides a measure of compensation as well as the spring action. Very neat!

Pick-ups

Ensuring uninterrupted and unimpaired electrical supply from the railheads to the motor brushes is an absolute fundamental of a successful model locomotive chassis. We have already looked at one critical link in this vital chain, the contact between wheel-tread and railhead and the ways in which this can best be maintained. This leaves the second part of the equation, conducting the power from the wheel-rim to the motor. There are basically two routes we can use to transmit this supply: through some form of sliding contact – a wiper or plunger – between an insulated wheel-rim and then via a feed-wire to the insulated motor brush, or from an uninsulated wheel-rim through the wheel, axle, bearings and frames to a 'live-to-frame' motor brush.

The traditional approach was a mix of these two methods with insulated wheels and rim-contacts on the feed side of the model energising the isolated motor brush, the return side of the circuit being through the live brush, motor frame, chassis block, bearings and axle to a non-insulated wheel. Hornby-Dublo two-rail and Triang both adopted this system and it was for many years normal practice for 'scale' modellers using the old Romford BRMSB wheels, which came insulated or plain to suit the arrangement.

The big drawbacks to such an arrangement are two-fold. First, in the days of flangeless centre axles on six- and eight-coupled mechanisms, for all practical purposes, the majority of locos were

ABOVE *The traditional 1950s-era pick-up system, here seen on the chassis of my vintage B12 (see Chapter 1!). Motor brushes are insulated on one side only, taking a feed from wipers on the insulated wheel (RH) side and returning via the live brush through the motor frame and the plain (uninsulated) wheels on the near side. It amazes me how many modellers still use this archaic set-up, in spite of its manifold disadvantages!*

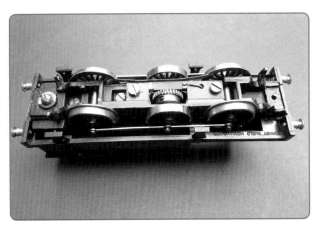

ABOVE *A traditional one-side-only wiper pick-up in flat strip bearing on the wheel-backs, here seen on a vintage Hornby-Dublo R1 chassis. A strip pick-up like this is fairly stiff and has a large contact area – good for power-handling, but bad for drag. It is also visually intrusive.*

effectively 0-4-0s, with only two contact points a side at the best of times. Add in a little dirt, uneven track and a rigid chassis, and that would often come down to a single point a side or, all-too-easily, 'nul points', and an unscheduled halt. In terms of consistent running it is certainly a truism that you can never have too many pick-ups, but you can very easily have too few!

The other big drawback to this traditional system was that the whole of the chassis – and the loco body too, if it was a metal one – was 'live' to the return side of the pick-up circuit, greatly increasing the chances of a short-circuit, and more unwanted halts. When you start adding chassis detail like brake gear and sand-pipes – not to mention coupling locos for double heading – the scope for such unwanted electrical fireworks goes up exponentially! For these reasons, many of the better scale models of yore used rim-insulated Romford wheels all round, with contact pick-ups for both sides of the circuit and both the motor brushes isolated to give a chassis and body assembly which was electrically 'dead'.

With the advent of the modern ranges of plastic-centred scale driving wheels, this double-sided rim-contact pick-up arrangement has now become the norm for RTR conversions and kit-built chassis and, indeed, the vast majority of modern RTR models. I would certainly commend it, even where Romford/Markits wheels are used; after all, these days a 'plain' uninsulated wheel is no cheaper than an insulated one, removing the cost-saving that often lay behind the choice of 'live chassis' return.

Contact pick-up systems

There are basically two forms of contact pick-up in use for small-scale model locomotive mechanisms: flexible wipers, or spring-loaded plungers. The former are by far the most prevalent system as they are infinitely more adaptable and versatile in the possibilities they offer for mounting and positioning. A plunger, by contrast, can only be mounted directly in line with and behind the wheel-rim on which it acts, where it is relatively inaccessible and difficult to clean or adjust.

If, as is usually the case, the spring supplying the contact pressure to the plunger is a coil, then this will exhibit a variable rate as it compresses – which gives inconsistent loading and often creates a lot of frictional drag as the coils close up. Under full compression, they can even 'bind', when the spring becomes all-but solid and the plunger acts more like a disc brake pad! It is also very difficult to adjust or tune the characteristics of a coil spring, especially when it can't be accessed. Plunger pick-ups also don't sit well with suspension systems, can interfere with axle side-play, take up valuable space between the frames, and are difficult to connect to the motor leads. From all of this negativity you may have inferred that the author is no fan of the plunger pick-up. You'd be right!

The flexible wiper pick-up, by contrast, is a very adaptable beast that can be configured and positioned to collect power from the wheel-tread, the edge of the flange or the back of the rim. By varying the effective length, material and cross-section (round wire or flat strip) it can be made as supple as might be desired, with the resulting contact pressure being readily adjusted by simply tweaking the wiper with a pair of snipe-nosed pliers. A criticism often levelled at wipers by advocates of split-frame or other contactless pick-up systems is that they create drag and generally interfere with the overall free-running nature of a chassis This is certainly possible, but only when the pick-ups are badly conceived using unsuitable materials, which, alas, they all-too-often are!

The ideal wiper

Virtually all the unsuccessful wiper pick-ups I have encountered in forty-plus years of railway modelling have been too stiff; almost invariably, they have been made from too hefty a size of often-unsuitably rigid wire or strip, have lacked sufficient length for adequate flexure, and have had much too large an area in contact with the wheel-rims, creating unnecessary drag.

There was a time when manly motors with a current draw of an amp or more supplied through only a couple of contact

ABOVE *By contrast with the Dublo R1, here are a set of home-made fine-wire (0.33 hard brass) wipers on my EM gauge NER E1 0-6-0T. They are mounted on two electrically linked PCB pads, a large one for the combined pickups of the rear and centre axles, and a smaller one – mounted vertically on the L-shaped frame spacer – for the front axle. The wipers are sleeved in fine PVC sheathing to avoid any short circuits where they pass close to the dummy loco springs.*

points a side demanded hefty pick-ups with a generous contact area to avoid arcing and overheating, which is why flat phosphor-bronze strip used to be the norm. And a very good brake it made too! But for modern low-current motors, the very much smaller contact patch resulting from a nice fine wire wiper bearing on a flange-edge or tyre-back is quite adequate, especially when applied to as many wheels as possible; the more contact points you have, the smaller the electrical load each has to carry.

Over the years, I have tried all manner of wires for pick-ups, gradually reducing the size as more efficient motors became available. These days, I find straight-drawn wires of 0.31–0.35mm diameter to be quite hefty enough. Such small diameters give a suitably minimal contact patch combined with a nice supple spring action that produces plenty of

BELOW *Here are the sophisticated and very discreet wiper pick-ups of a modern RTR loco – the Bachmann '45xx'. Tailor-made to shape in thin phosphor-bronze, they have embossed dimples at the business end to reduce the area in contact to a minimum, maximising contact pressure while reducing drag. There are, of course, similar pick-ups on the other side of the chassis.*

contact pressure with insignificant drag. Decent contact pressure is what we need for reliable current collection; the tiny contact patch both helps create this desirable pressure while minimising friction. (If you want the theory behind all this, it's in my chassis kit construction book mentioned earlier.)

The wire I usually use these days is 0.33mm brass or nickel-silver sold in straight lengths by suppliers like Alan Gibson or Eileen's Emporium. Avoid wire that's been coiled as it has a 'set' that makes it harder to adjust pick-up pressure accurately. You will note I have given phosphor-bronze – often cited as the traditional pick-up material – the cold shoulder. That's because it doesn't work too well when in contact with my favoured steel-tyred wheels, where it is prone to something apparently called 'sympathetic oxidation' – a build-up of black gunk on the contact patch. This does not occur with nickel-silver wheels.

Installing wiper pick-ups

As with the amount of ballast, the degree of spring force keeping the pick-up in contact wants to be the least that will do the job. Having more than you need serves no useful purpose and can interfere with free running, side-play and – where applicable – suspension movement. The joy of the very small contact patch produced by fine wire is that even a very soft spring action will give adequate contact pressure for reliable current collection, combined with self-cleaning of the contact patch.

The natural suppleness of these relatively wimpy wires also means that you don't need much of an active length of spring to give this desirable softness, which is very handy where there's not a lot of space available to fit the pick-ups unobtrusively. Wire wiper pick-ups can take many forms, but on typical mechanisms they are generally mounted to isolated PCB pads secured beneath the chassis, either directly, or via busbars, with the wipers below the frames bearing on the flange-edges or tyre-backs. Of course, there are always awkward customers that won't permit this simple and convenient mounting. Possible alternative locations and configurations are, once again, dissected in the dedicated chassis kit book. In the context of the present opus, I've sailed on the 'picture being worth a thousand words' tack and illustrated some successful (and a few dud!) wiper arrangements hereabouts.

Wheel cleaning

No matter how sophisticated the pick-up and suspension system you contrive for your model locomotives, all will come to naught if you end up with a nice insulating layer of dirt and oxides building up on wheel-treads and railheads. This plays merry hell with your hard-won continuity. Alas, that's something which comes into the same unavoidable category as the Grim Reaper and HMRC. Even steel wheels on steel rails – in my experience, by far the 'cleanest-running' combination – don't obviate the need for cleaning; they just reduce the required frequency somewhat.

However, it is an uncomfortable fact that to get the best quality running – especially where frequent starting and really smooth slow speed with ultimate finesse of control are the

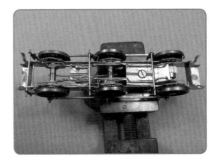

ABOVE AND RIGHT *This sequence shows the wiper pick-ups being fitted to the guinea-pig 'Jinty' chassis. In the first picture, a pair of busbars have been bent to shape from 0.7mm brass wire and soldered to PCB mounting pads installed on the chassis. The motor connecting wires are also fitted at this juncture. The actual wipers (the second illustration) are soldered in place as simple lengths of straight wire (0.35mm brass, in this instance), being bent to shape and trimmed to length in situ. The third view shows the finished result. The loco's brake gear was fitted before the pick-ups, to ensure there were no conflicts between the two.*

BELOW *And here's what you do if there's no room beneath the chassis for normal side-acting wire wipers: fit top-acting ones in fine phosphor-bronze strip (to allow for sideways movement of the wheelsets). These have tiny contact pads in brass or, better still, gold or gold-plated copper (old computer edge-connectors are a source of such material). Tucked tight up under the footplate, such pick-ups go unseen.*

name of the game – then cleanliness is definitely next to holiness. Well before the point at which gross malfunctions of the jerk/stammer/unwanted stop/refusal to start nature begin to intrude, I find that the 'edge' has gone off the ultimate performance – an edge that can be instantly restored by a quick wheel de-tox. (Oddly enough, this even seems to apply to DCC set-ups as well as conventional DC control, for all that the higher on-track ac voltage and on-board nature of the control should theoretically mitigate the effects of impaired continuity.)

Much will depend, of course, on the environment in which your models are operating; dirty surroundings beget dirty track and wheels, so where a little preventative housekeeping is possible it will lessen the need for the often-tedious and tricky cure. Keeping the rail-heads bright and polished will obviously help lessen the build-up of crud on wheel-treads, but that isn't always easy to achieve, especially on large and complex layouts, or those possessed of delicate scenery, structures and detailing. Whether your chosen approach to rail-cleaning is chemical or abrasive, it is a tricky and time-consuming process that you don't want to be doing too often.

Unfortunately, the nickel-silver rail usually encountered does need fairly frequent cleaning to keep it oxide-free. It's amazing just how much black oxide crud you can wipe off a clean-looking nickel rail if you run a tissue along the railhead. Steel does not seem to pull this trick, remaining clean and oxide-free unless the environment is hostile enough to cause rusting. Whatever the rail material, however, there is no doubt that keeping the track truly clean is a thankless and usually near-impossible task, although using one of the rolling rail-cleaner systems (usually a heavy brass roller set at a very slight angle to the track centreline and sheathed with an abrasive or fabric cleaning surface) will usually help.

Cleaning techniques

Wheel-cleaning being thus unavoidable, the trick is to make it as easy and as non-aggressive as possible. I've seen more

damage done to model locomotives in the cleaning of wheels than I ever have, due to accidental mishap or fair wear-and-tear. As with the rail-heads, there are two basic approaches to wheel-tread cleaning: chemical, using some kind of solvent or de-greasing agent, or mechanical, where dirt is physically scraped or burnished off the wheel-rim. Both methods have drawbacks and, if not carried out carefully, can easily cause problems. I use both techniques, opting to chemically clean the tyres of powered wheels – drivers and coupled axles on rod-driven steamers, power bogie wheelsets on diesels, while buffing-up carrying/tender wheels by mechanical means.

My usual chemical cleaner is common-or-garden lighter fluid, which forms an effective de-greaser and 'gunk solvent' that is not too volatile and relatively benign to paintwork, fingers, and the long-suffering lungs. Another suitable choice is non-lubricating switch/contact cleaner, which you can buy from electronics suppliers like Maplins in aerosol cans. I do not use powerful organic solvents like Butanone; they work well enough, but at some hazard both to the operator and to the paintwork of the model. For mechanical cleaning, my weapon of choice is likewise relatively mild-mannered: a suitably supple brass or nylon-bristle flat-disc brush used in a motor tool or mini-drill.

I always clean driven wheels with the loco 'right way up' and sitting on a suitable length of track – usually my test-track, or in the fiddleyard somewhere – over which is draped a pad of solvent-soaked tissue paper; cheap toilet paper is ideal. The loco is run slowly on to the tissue under power and stopped with the fingers when at least one axle is still picking up power. It is then allowed to slip *gently* under its own

ABOVE AND BELOW *This is the way I clean loco driving wheels – under power and on the track, one axle at a time, with a piece of loo-roll folded as necessary and wetted with a volatile de-greasing solvent as a cleaning pad. The loco is held gently in position with the wheels resting on the pad under its own weight. There is no need to press down. Several solvents are effective: meths, non-lubricating switch cleaner, purpose-brewed 'mechanism cleaner' and, as here, good old-fashioned lighter fluid. The amount of gunk that comes off even from wheels that look clean is surprising, as seen in the second picture.*

ABOVE *Cleaning unpowered wheelsets I find, calls for a rather different approach – the use of a high-speed mini-drill and a burnishing brush-wheel. The brush is run at high revs (5,000rpm+) and touched lightly on the tyre of the wheel at an angle of about 20°, so that the brush both rotates the wheelset and polishes the tread bright. Again, no pressure is needed and the process only takes a few seconds. This technique will also get rid of unrealistic chemical blackening from wheel tyres.*

weight for a few moments, with one or more driven wheelsets revolving slowly on the solvent-laden tissue, which can be topped up as required with a syringe. Once the first group of wheels is nice and clean, the model is swapped end-for-end (or reversed and the tissue suitably relocated) and the process repeated for the remaining powered axles – the accompanying illustrations should make the process clear.

The thick black stripes that build up rapidly on the tissue are testament to the effectiveness of the method, as well as being a stark reminder of just how much dirt manages to get into the issue in the first place! Used with due care, such on-track cleaning avoids the need for too much handling and is kind to the paint and detail. It also avoids loading the motor/gears excessively and, most importantly, does not put a lot of strain on the quartering of push-fitted wheels like Gibson or Ultrascale. And take it from me, it's all-too-easy to accidentally shift a driving wheel on an axle when employing more robust cleaning methods like running the loco upside-down at high speed and using abrasive papers or fibreglass brushes on the wheel-rim.

Unfortunately, you can't use the on-track-tissue method of wheel-cleaning for unpowered wheelsets as there's no real practical way of rotating them. The best answer I've found so far is to polish these wheel-tyres using a mildly abrasive flat disc brush running at high speed in a hand-held motor-tool. The other essential implement for the task is a cradle which

can support the inverted model in a firm but safely cushioned manner – a generally useful piece of kit for a variety of constructional and maintenance tasks. These cradles can be bought (avoiding any foam-plastic versions which spell death to delicate lamp-irons and the like), but they are easy enough to make. The illustration should show what's involved.

The brush I use for the actual polishing has either fine brass or nylon bristles, not too stiff. Such brushes are a stock line with the tool-and-supply merchants like Eileen's Emporium. To clean a wheel, the brush is simply run up to speed (fast as you can!) and touched *lightly* on to the tread at a slight angle. It will spin the wheelset rapidly and burnish the tread and flange face mirror-bright in only a few seconds. No pressure or force is needed; the rapid scrubbing action does the work, making the whole process surprisingly delicate. This technique also works for rolling stock, and keeping wagon and coach wheels clean is a big help in controlling the amount of crud being spread around the track generally and hence accumulating on driving wheel tyres. In my experience, time spent on such preventative maintenance is rarely time wasted. I believe the same applies on real railways…

Lubrication

It is a well-established tenet of model railway maintenance that more damage is done by an excess of lubricant in the wrong places than ever arises from lack of it in the right ones. Nevertheless, it is equally true that a spot of an appropriate lubricant 'in the right spot' can work wonders in terms of low friction and smooth, quiet running. Note that word 'appropriate'; all lubricants are *not* the same and the wrong one can be more harmful than a dry bearing.

Many popular general-market products – like 3-in-1 and WD40 sprays – are designed for purposes (silencing squeaky hinges or preventing rusting) far removed from the precise spot-lubrication of small and delicate mechanisms. To do our models any favours, we need a light, low-to-medium viscosity, non-degrading oil for bearings of all sorts, with perhaps a lightweight high-slip grease to anoint the teeth of all-metal or combination metal/plastic gears.

There are two readily available oils suited to our purposes: high-grade mineral clock oil, or lightweight silicone-based synthetic 'instrument' lubricants. Example brands are J.D. Windle's Clock Oil or LaBelle 101 synthetic oil. Details of availability are in the Sources index. Although either type will suit normal metal-on-metal bearings, the synthetic oils can attack and degrade plastics – something to look out for where a metal bearing is housed in – or close to – a plastic moulding, as on Mashima motors, Gibson wheels, and many RTR mechanisms. For this reason, I stick to the clock oil for motor and gearbox bearings and any composite Mazak/Plastic RTR chassis, as well as in the crankpin bearings on Gibson wheels.

LaBelle 101 – used very sparingly as you only need a trace – is very good for axle bearings and valve gears. It penetrates even a long bearing bush and stays put on valve gear pivots and the sliding faces of horn guides. This oil comes in a container with a capillary-tube needle applicator, which enables one to 'spot' it just where needed. Clock oil, by contrast, comes in a plain bottle, so here I use a length of fine (0.33mm) wire to dip just the merest drop to apply to the bearing. That's usually all that is needed. When you're convinced that 'just a drop more would be a good thing', it is probably the time to stop!

Suitable greases for gears are also no problem. Plastic gears moulded in 'slippery' low-friction engineering materials like Celcon or Delrin do not call for lubrication in the first place, so it is only the all-metal and hybrid metal/plastic gear-trains we need to worry about. With a lot of modern mechanisms ranging from digital cameras to office copiers incorporating just such hybrid gear trains, suitable non-degrading, chemically inert greases are now readily available. The one I use is the American Super Lube synthetic silicone grease, sold in the UK under the Loctite brand, which you can buy from electronics suppliers like Radiospares. It comes in an 85-gram tube, one of which will last you and all your friends a modelling lifetime!

As with all these lubricants, apply very sparingly and as precisely as possible to the gear-teeth. A syringe is a good

tool, but be aware that the grease will do funny things to the rubber of the plunger if you leave it in protracted contact. I only put a small quantity of lubricant in my syringe and withdraw the plunger after use. The tip of a cocktail stick makes an alternative applicator.

Maximising tractive effort

For many modellers – eternally short of space and hence not in a position to run any but the most modest of trains – the ultimate tractive effort of their locomotives is usually of academic interest only. But where trains are longer and/or heavier or – more particularly – where over-steep gradients or ultra-tight curves have been introduced into the design of the layout, then grip and tractive effort at the head of the train suddenly take on a new significance. Wheel-rail frictional loadings and lateral drag can dramatically increase train resistance on sharp curves, while gradients have an even more profound impact.

In the real world, a locomotive that could haul a thousand tons on the level would typically only manage to drag a bit over two hundred tons up a gradient of 1 in 50, a factor of more than 4:1! The same order of gravitational impedance typically applies on model railways, where gradients markedly steeper than 1 in 50 are far from unknown. So there are times when we need to look to the tractive performance of our model locomotives, be they off-the-peg RTR or hybrids of our own devising.

The amount of 'grunt' (technically, drawbar pull) that a model locomotive can exert is determined by two basic factors: the power and particularly, torque available from the drivetrain, and the grip of the driving wheels on the rails. Nowadays, the former is rarely a problem; a modern can motor driving through an appropriately geared transmission will produce more than enough torque to happily spin the wheels of just about any model locomotive when we hang a decent load behind it. It is getting enough frictional grip on the railheads to use this torque productively that is the problem.

It is a problem for the prototype too, as discussed in the 'adhesion' section in Chapter 2, and many of the remedies we can apply to counter a lack of railhead grip are strategies used at full size. These are choosing materials for our wheel-tyres and rails (steel-on-steel if possible) that have a good coefficient of friction; using a suspension system that keeps the wheel-treads in firm contact with the railheads at all times, and, of course, applying enough weight (ballast) to the driven axles to ensure adequate frictional grip between the driving wheels and the rails – on which topic, more directly. The thing we *can't* do as modellers is to introduce abrasive sand into the wheel-rail interface, but then, the prototype can't sneak a neoprene traction tyre on to the odd driven wheelset!

In this regard, you may well ask why such traction tyres are not therefore more widely used by modellers building their own chassis? The answer to that comes in two parts: first and most problematic, is the total lack of suitable grooved-tread wheels and matching neoprene tyres in the currently available 'component' wheel ranges, but secondly, there is the not-so-small matter of the adverse effect traction tyres have on the

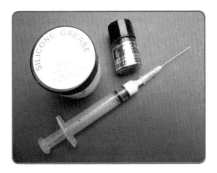

BELOW A little drop of the right stuff does you good; too much of the wrong stuff spells trouble. Here is my basic lubrication kit: high-quality non-degrading watch or clock oil for bearings, and plastic-friendly silicone grease for gears, with a syringe to get just enough of it in exactly the right place. The watch oil is Anchor (from a specialist jeweller's suppliers), while the grease came from Eileen's Emporium.

ABOVE *The RTR-makers secret weapon in the train-haulage stakes – the neoprene traction tyre, applied to one or more driving wheel treads to give greatly enhanced grip. The downsides are the loss of a wheel for pick-up purposes, and a thoroughly unprototypical appearance.*

pick-up arrangements, especially on smaller locomotives with less wheels to play with.

All of this is not to say that DIY traction-enhancing wheel tyres aren't possible; in the USA, you can buy – under the apt but un-alluring trade name of Bullfrog Snot (I kid you not!) – a self-curing latex 'traction aid' designed to be brushed on to the wheel tread to form a 'grippy' rubberised coating. I'll confess I have never tried it, although I can see no reason why it shouldn't work. The problem is, once again, that it will effectively eliminate any wheel to which it is applied from the pick-up equation.

Ballasting

It has long been an established principle of model locomotive engineering that if you wanted an engine to pull more and pick up reliably, you added extra weight to increase the contact pressure between the driving wheels and the rails. This was an approach that some veteran modellers took to extremes; my old mentor Ken Northwood (of North Devonshire Railway fame) would tender-mount a large motor with a shaft drive through to a gearbox on his locomotives, which were otherwise entirely full of lead and Cerrobend ballast to maximise their weight. The North Devonshire's 'King' – built from a Wills white metal kit – tipped the scales at all but 3lb, with a Pitman DC71 motor (intended for 0 gauge) in the tender to provide plenty of 'oomph'. It was required to be capable of starting a 16-coach train of all-metal Exley coaches weighing nearly 1lb apiece up a 1-in-100 gradient, which it would do, albeit with a modicum of genteel slipping.

That ability to slip was important; one of the big drawbacks to this 'heavy metal' approach is that it is all-too-easy to overload the motor. If the motor stalls under full power before the wheels slip, or the controller cut-out trips, the inevitable result is a nasty smell shortly followed by a bill for a new motor! So the golden rule is always ballast to allow 'slippage before stalling'. Even when things are not thus *in extremis*, a heavy loco puts greater demands on its drivetrain and bearings; motors consistently draw heavier current levels – often uncomfortably close to their operating limits – and pick-

ups and brushgear suffer accordingly. The motor will also tend to run very hot, which can adversely affect the magnet.

That old North Devonshire 'King' drew a good amp or more in steady-state running and probably twice that on starting – the lights would go dim when you really cranked it up! By contrast, a modern RTR drivetrain will typically rarely demand more current than a modest quarter-amp or so even on starting, and few modern electronic controllers or DCC decoders, will deliver more than an amp or so at maximum output. Also, it is not only the electrics that can suffer overload; in spite of careful lubrication and adjustment, the gears and shaft-drive components of North Devonshire locomotives also suffered heavy wear. The 'King' (still going strong!) is now on its third set of gears…

The modern approach to ballasting might be summarised as the complete antithesis of this traditional 'as much as you can get in' approach; the watchword nowadays is more along the lines of 'the minimum amount that will do the job'. So long as the loco has enough weight to produce the tractive effort required for the work it has to do, any excess serves no useful purpose. There are a number of reasons for adopting this minimalist approach, starting with that requirement to slip well before stalling, and ranging through the reduced requirement for drawbar pull resulting from modern free-running pinpoint-bearing lightweight plastic-bodied rolling stock, to the superior wheel-rail grip provided by traction tyres, steel-on-steel and suspension systems.

We also need to take into account the much lower current-handling capabilities of the newer electronic control systems, be they conventional DC or on-board DCC. On which tack, the advent of DCC – and especially, on-board sound systems – has also led to a greatly increased requirement for internal space in model locomotives, needed to house all the extra electronic 'gubbins'. The compact nature of modern drivetrain components has helped a bit, but lead has not got any denser in the interim and packing substantial amounts of ballast into a locomotive superstructure takes as much space as it ever did. So anything that can reduce the amount required is a decided bonus.

In the right place…

With the development of model locomotive suspensions and consequent greater understanding of axle loading and weight distribution, has come the realisation that adding extra ballast per se is only of limited effectiveness, and can even be counter-productive. Rather than simple overall mass, what counts is sufficient weight *acting in the right place* – that is, positioned so that it bears on those driven axles of the locomotive that can put it to good use. By contrast, weight in the *wrong* place – as in the front end of a 4-4-0 or the bunker of an 0-4-4T, for example, can actually serve to *reduce* the loading on the driven axles. To be effective, we need to position our ballast so that it acts within the coupled wheelbase of the locomotive. Notice that word *acts*; so long as the weight is effectively borne by the driven axles, it doesn't necessarily have to be located physically above them – space often given over to the model's drivetrain or DCC electronics.

So long as the weight is well balanced, it can be outside

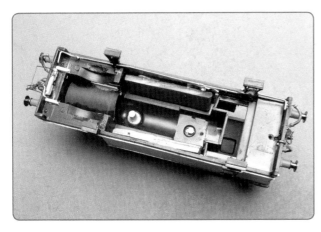

ABOVE *Here is the ballast I added to the body of my modified Hornby 'Jinty' – a small slab of doubled-over Code 3 (3mm thick) roofing lead inside each side-tank, held in place with pads of Blu-Tack – which helps damp out any resonance in the plastic body. This brought the total weight of the body up to a little over 70 grams.*

RIGH *This is the complete 'Jinty', tipping the (rather battered!) scales at a modest 135 grams – not enough to tax the drivetrain, but plenty enough for reliable track-holding and pick-up while ensuring the model slips well before it stalls. As for tractive effort, the longest train I can assemble on any of my layouts – 24 pin-pointed P4 wagons – caused it no problems whatsoever. I would happily back it for ten more!*

the coupled wheelbase altogether. A hundred grams of ballast in a small tank engine divided 50:50 between the smokebox and the bunker will be just as effective as the whole hundred placed amidships over the driving wheels. Indeed, it is not always necessary to put all the weight actually in the loco. If it's trailing a tender, then this can readily be modified (by allowing the front two axles to 'float' vertically) so that ballast in its fore end acts through an inverted draw-hook riding on a loop on the loco's drag-beam to 'load' the rear of the coupled wheelbase – a loading balanced by a similar amount of ballast in the front of the engine. This is a highly effective arrangement for 4-4-0s, which anyway, often tend to intrinsic nose-heaviness. It can also be used to produce a six or eight-coupled engine with *serious* tractive effort. Such an arrangement is usually referred to as a 'loaded tender'.

Leaden tales

One last (cautionary!) word about ballasting concerns the actual nature of the ballast and the way it is fixed in place. With depleted uranium not being too freely available in the model trade, lead remains the usual option – most often obtained in block or sheet form. Popular sources are stick-on car wheel-rim balance weights – try your local tyre-fitting outfit – or lead roof flashing. This last comes as code 3 or code 4 (3mm or 4mm thick respectively) and can usually be bought 'off the roll' at the more helpful builder's merchants in widths from 150mm upwards. Half a metre of 150mm code 3 will keep most loco-builders in ballast for a modelling lifetime. To fix such sheet lead in place I advocate either small foam adhesive pads (Sticky Fixers and the like) or Blu-Tack adhesive putty, which is clean and easy to use, non-reactive, and no problem to remove if (or when) you get a weight in slightly the wrong place. Lead weights resiliently mounted in this way also act as very effective resonance-dampers, making for quieter-running locos.

However, a popular ballasting option in recent years has been to use fine lead shot, sold as 'liquid lead' or similar. The

advantage of this stuff is that you can get weight into irregular spaces, cavities and closed voids by simply pouring it into place and then retaining it by adding a liquid adhesive. This is where we encounter a problem; solvent-based cements or contact adhesives can attack plastic body mouldings, while cyano is both difficult to control and somewhat final. If you need to get the ballast out at any point, you'll need Semtex! Therefore, a lot of people have opted to secure their shot with thinned PVA white glue, which on the face of it, is an ideal solution. Unfortunately, over the course of time, the acetic acid in the PVA sets up a chemical reaction with the lead shot which causes the volume of the lead/PVA mixture to increase substantially. The result has been that a number of models have literally been split asunder by the forces exerted by the expanding ballast within! Definitely 'one to avoid'…

BELOW *The anatomy of a loaded tender – in this case, a GWR 3,500-gallon Collett example for a worked-over Mainline Collett Goods. Note the inverted draw-hook intended to rest on a loop at the rear of the loco. A good slab of ballast is positioned in the fore end of the tender body, while the Comet etched tender chassis has the rear axle fixed and the leading two running in vertical slots and lightly sprung – just enough for reliable track-holding.*

6 REFINING AND REWORKING

The contemporary state-of-the-art 4mm scale RTR model locomotive is a pretty wondrous thing just as it is when it comes out of the box. Wondrous – but not perfect, for it still incorporates compromises. For a start, there are obvious practical constraints. If it is to be a practical manufacturing proposition and affordable in the end market, there must be limits to the complexity and delicacy of the finished model, which has to be mechanically reliable and robust enough to stand shipping and normal handling – whatever *that* is! More fundamentally, it will be built to '00 standards' – thus incorporating a whopping (if pragmatic) error: a track gauge 12½% below true scale value – a pretty large liberty to take in anybody's book!

Furthermore, the model will be engineered to negotiate the 'train-set' 00 curve radii still prevalent in the thinking of the big RTR manufacturers, with a 'first' or innermost radius of only 371mm – call it 14½in – and a 'widest' or third radius of a whole 505mm – a shade under 20in. Any of these are absurdly tight curves in the context of anything approaching a scale model! The normal *minimum* running-line radius for a full-sized main line engine is around six chains (396ft), which is a shade over 62 inches at 4mm scale – more than *three times* the *easiest* of the train-set curves! Such drastic departures from true scale values inevitably have consequences for the 'look' of RTR models. The surprise these days is that the deviations aren't more obvious! I discussed the practical implications of 00 standards and the related side-play allowances in Chapter 5. For the present, I'm more concerned

OPPOSITE When it comes to the cream of the current crop of 4mm scale RTR locos, there is not a lot of call for refinement of the basics. All you can really do to improve a model like this Bachmann 'Crab' 2-6-0 is to do something about the couplings, add some decent bufferbeam detail, and close up the loco-tender gap, plus a little work on the finish to make it look more realistic. There may also be the odd bit of re-detailing to individualise it to a particular prototype locomotive, but that's about it!

ABOVE *Older RTR models on the other hand, can call for a lot of work to bring them up to the required spec for our stud. This GW '93xx' Mogul – a Bachmann product of the mid-1990s that is still around second-hand – needed a considerable amount of basic refinement and detailing/re-detailing to produce this convincing character study. The work involved shortening the over-long front end, closing up the loco-tender gap, eradicating mould seam lines, thinning the visible edges of the cab sides/roof and tender copings, and re-profiling the lip of the safety valve bonnet.*

New Comet cast cylinders replaced the undersized originals, and an etched Comet front bar-frame pony truck replaced the solid Bachmann item. The chimney is also a replacement casting, and bufferbeam details, lamp irons and fall-plate were made as described in the next chapter. The mechanism is the original Bachmann can motor type, but the wheels have been modified with new balance weights. The paint job is the original, worked on as described in Chapter 5. Altogether, not exactly a five-minute job!

with the impact of these compromises on the realistic *appearance* of our model locomotives, and ways we can minimise this.

A useful start is to forget any notion of getting the things around anything approaching those toy-town curves. In the context of the 'realistic railway modelling' standpoint from which this book is predicated, such things have no place – except, possibly, in enabling one to take a few liberties with unseen 'off-stage' trackage. The whole complex matter of appropriate track curvatures is considered in detail in the Layout Design volume in this series, but in practical terms, setting some reasonable limits as to minimum radius enables us to make a number of useful visual improvements to our models.

Models converted for EM or P4 use will perforce be limited to the minimum curvatures practically permitted by those standards (also touched upon in Chapter 5), but by 'voluntarily' adopting a reasonable limitation for 00 as well, we can address some of the more obtrusive compromises embodied in RTR motive power. In my experience, adopting a minimum 00 radius of 30in strikes a good balance between minimising the use of space for the layout, while maximising the authentic look of the locomotives.

Visual effects of RTR compromises

Fortunately, modern RTR design practice eschews most of the grosser eyesores so painfully prevalent on mass-produced model locomotives of yore: no more super-wide wheel-treads or monstrous flanges, flangeless centre drivers, incorrect wheel diameters (most notably, grossly undersized bogie and trailing wheels), wrongly dimensioned and positioned splashers, exaggerated ride heights, shrunken cylinders and incomplete valve gears, yawning chasms 'twixt loco and tender, missing steps, or general lack of below-the-footplate detail. No, praise be, the modern RTR locomotive chassis is usually every bit as much a model as the upperworks, rather than a mere rude mechanical afterthought. These days, the Walschaerts valve gear will not only be complete and to scale, but be the right *sort* of Walschaerts; likewise, wheels won't just be the right size, but have the right number of spokes and rim profile, authentic crank arrangements, and appropriate balance weights. Only in the head-on view will things appear other than they should be.

Getting the wheels right is fundamental in realistic loco-modelling – in which respect, I'm glad to say, modern RTR designers (unlike some of their kit-making brethren) appear to have taken to heart Guy Williams's dictum that, so far as model locomotive driving wheels are concerned, what matters is that these are of scale diameter *over the flange*. This permits accurate wheel spacing and allows any splashers to be of the correct radius, with the running plate set at the appropriate

BELOW One of the more obvious compromises afflicting older RTR outside-cylindered locos is shrunken-cylinder syndrome, usually found in conjunction with displaced steps and an excess of daylight. The bogie is also a bit of a travesty. The afflicted engine here is a Mainline 'Jubilee' – in terms of authentic appearance and refinement of detail, a very good model for its day, and very much a candidate for a makeover.

height – all factors fundamental to preserving the essential proportions of the locomotive being modelled and hence its realistic appearance.

Modern RTR also avoids the old chestnut of laterally displacing the splashers in relation to the footplate edge, either in 'squeezing' them inwards to suit the incorrect 'over 00' total wheel-width, or shoving them outwards to accommodate grossly over-wide 'steamroller' wheels or lashings of sideplay. With the finer wheel profiles now in use, side-play adequate even for acute curve negotiation by wheelsets with a full complement of flanges can be obtained within the space liberated by the 00 under-gauge error, while still keeping the splashers in the right place.

The ride heights (and hence vertical buffer centres) of modern RTR engines are also commendably correct. Gone are the days when Triang and Lima locos teetered along on tiptoes with the footplate a scale six inches too high above the rail – a deviation made, believe it or not, to permit leading bogies enough unencumbered vertical movement to accommodate an abrupt transition from flat track on to the 1-in-12 gradient needed to allow a figure-of-eight 00 layout *with flyover* to fit on the once-traditional six-by-four baseboard! Fortunately, these days nobody expects a 'Duchess' to negotiate the Big Dipper at Butlin's, even if the poor thing *is* still expected to hurl itself around hairpin bends! So at least we have correct ride heights and scale-sized bogie wheels.

The worst errors around the front end of most modern RTR bogie engines usually result from excessive bogie swing, calling for frame narrowing or oversize frame cut-outs, and usually adversely impinging on the loco's front steps. Nowadays, the most sophisticated solution is to make these last as an add-on part to be fitted by the modeller 'where curves permit'. This is decidedly preferable to the alternative dodges of putting them in the wrong place, making them woefully undersize, or setting them far too far apart, resulting in a lamentable lack of relief with regard to the actual steps, which presents a decidedly odd appearance. But even this is marginally better than the 'step solution' so prevalent in an earlier RTR era – just ignoring their existence!

Couplings and coupling distances

The other main area of curvature-induced compromise is the coupling of an RTR locomotive to its tender (assuming it has one, of course). One of the usual consequences of the acute curve-rounding requirement is that the gap between locomotive and tender ends up miles too wide, sometimes comically so. Some older RTR engines apparently had Olympic long-jumpers for firemen! More recent models go some way to addressing this anomaly and tender drawbars incorporating an alternative short coupling distance have been around for a while.

A number of the latest offerings

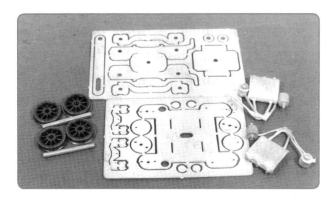

ABOVE AND BELOW *Fortunately, you can usually do something about the typical RTR front-end compromise. Here are the ingredients I used to improve the look of my 'Jubilee': Comet cast/etched cylinders and etched bogie frame, plus some fine-scale 00 bogie wheels. The second picture compares the scale-sized Comet cylinders with the under-sized Mainline offerings. I modified the latter by cutting and filing them down until the Comet cast wrapper fitted on as an overlay; this enabled me to retain the Mainline slidebars and cylinder mounting system.*

BELOW *This is the reworked 'Jubilee' with modified front end, loco-tender gap closed up, and all the usual detailing/re-detailing refinements, which included new Plastikard front steps in the correct location. The original Mainline mechanism (a good one, for a change) was retained, but the modifications help the model sit right on the track.*

make use of the clever NEM coupler-box technology that allows close coupling on the straight, but opens the gap proportionally on curves – which does at least mean that the loco looks convincing for at least part of the time. Sticking to the suggested 30in radius ruling curve permits the closing-up of loco–tender gaps to realistic proportions.

Production values

I think that most modellers would cite the refinement of detail and finish to be the most obvious area of improvement on the current generation of RTR locos, but to my eye there's been an equally notable improvement in the fit, finish and overall quality of the underlying basic superstructures. With the accuracy, economy and versatility of modern CAD/CNC tool-making techniques, together with the greater labour input permitted by Far East production, and higher retail prices, we have seen a shift away from the traditional one-piece body moulding in favour of multi-section assemblies. This often involves a mix of plastic mouldings and sophisticated die-cast metal components.

These new techniques have eliminated most of the compromises and expediencies that characterised older RTR models, while the extreme precision in the fit of modern multi-piece injection-moulding tools has not only permitted the production of far more complex shapes, but has also virtually eliminated the visible mould part-line – let alone any suggestion of good old-fashioned 'flash'! Modern die-making using inserts – removable interchangeable segments of the mould – which also permits prototypical variations to be produced from one basic set of tooling.

All this means that the current crop of RTR models do not call for the sort of basic remedial work that used to be needed to remove production compromises and surface blemishes, from the basic body mouldings. Such baseline cosmetic operations nowadays are likely to be confined to RTR upgrades or reworkings involving older body mouldings. However, it has to be said that a few truly vintage plastic mouldings, notably those from the old Hornby-Dublo stable, are of astounding quality for their day and can bear

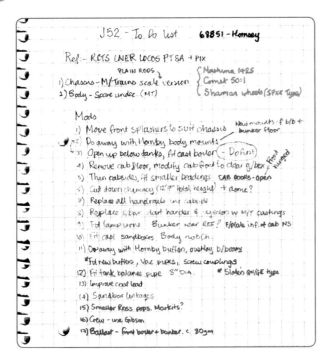

ABOVE *The job list – just as much a tool as a file or a saw. It is no work of literature or thing of beauty, but it can help avoid mistakes and oversights, and save a lot of valuable modelling time. In my experience, time spent thinking through and planning a modelling project is never time wasted.*

comparison with current production. On the other hand, a lot of what was produced by Hornby, Palitoy/Mainline/Replica/ Bachmann, Dapol and Airfix from the later 1970s through to the early 1990s, often calls for a touch of tidying-up and 'de-seaming', as well as the refinement of over-thick visible edges and attention to handrails and other details.

Preliminaries

Before setting-about a model of whatever pedigree, a necessary preliminary is to give the thing a thorough and detailed examination to decide exactly what needs doing. This examination comes in two parts: the quest for manufacturing imperfections, and the quest for authenticity. The first part requires the unfettered use of the Mk I eyeball to seek out and note such defects as unwanted seams, cracks, gaps and holes, any over-thick visible edges, ill-fitting moulded parts, and so on. Also at this stage, the model is assessed for its conformity to the common specification noted in chapter 4. Handrails fine enough? What about the lamp-irons? Are etched plates needed? Are bufferbeam fittings up to par? Bunker or tender properly coaled-up? Convincing-looking smokebox door dart handles? Is all glazing present and convincingly flush? Is there a crew? And so on.

The part two exam is all about fidelity to prototype – hopefully, with an eye to a particular engine. With almost any class of locomotive there will be myriad minor variations in detail between individual engines within the class. Larger and – especially – older classes will often exhibit a veritable plethora of alternative combinations of detail fittings, boiler

mountings and finish. Some of these variations, such as the fitment of alternative chimneys, are very fundamental. The chimney shape is such an important determiner of the character of a locomotive that getting it absolutely right is the key to creating a convincing model. All of this is why sticking to a single prototype is the best bet; picking on a particular engine at a specific date (hopefully, that for which you have most photographic reference!), is often the only way of arriving at anything approaching an authentic model.

The end result of all these deliberations is a detailed list that can form the basis of a 'job sheet' on which can also appear the location of useful prototype references, a shopping list of the necessary bits and pieces, and notes of just how you intend to address the model's various shortcomings – together with details of any useful and relevant 'how to' articles in the modelling press. The intention is that when you actually get around to tackling the job, all the information, ideas and components needed will be to hand. A dog-eared hardcopy example of just such a testament of good intentions is illustrated.

Smoothing the wrinkles

The mould part-line manifesting itself as a narrow-but-obtrusive ridge along the top centre-line of the smokebox/ boiler/firebox is a persistent characteristic of many older plastic RTR models. While it is true that a few prototype locomotives did have centre-top joints in their boiler cladding sheets, these were in the form of a narrow groove rather than a raised line. So such protrusions have to go. This is easy enough to accomplish with the aid of a sharp, three-sided scraper, with an abrasive burnisher or rubbing-stick, and some fine abrasive papers for finishing.

The trick to avoid any 'flats' or tool-marks on the highly visible boiler top is to minimise any cutting or scraping *along* the line of the offending seam, as far as possible. Work with the tools used *around* the boiler top in a direction of at least 45° to the blemish. Resist also the temptation to try to take any hefty cuts; *gentle* but repeated passes with the edge of a sharp scraper (far less prone to dig-in than a knife-blade), is the key to getting rid of the protrusion without damaging the underlying surface.

To restore the surface to a smooth finish, I find fine wet-and-dry abrasive paper used wet and with a spot of washing-up liquid added to the water, is the way to go. The rubbing-sticks are the best tool for this job, starting with 240-grit paper and finishing with 400 grade. Again, as far as I can, I work at 45° or more to the direction of the seam and once again avoid applying too much 'oomph', just rubbing gently and letting the abrasive do the work. Dip the rubbing-stick in the soapy water frequently to clean away the plastic residue and keep the cutting action nicely lubricated. A few minute's-worth of such careful work can completely eliminate a part-line – and it is amazing what a difference *that* can make to the look of a model.

Of course, not all such part-lines conveniently occur on nicely unobstructed, smooth surfaces like boiler-tops. Boiler bands can often intrude, while smokeboxes in particular are prone to outbreaks of hard-to-avoid rivets. The boiler-bands I never worry about too much as with care, it's possible to work

RIGHT AND BELOW *This sequence details the removal of mould part lines, in this case along the boiler top of a Bachmann B1. Gentle use of a sharp scraper and a fine abrasive-paper rubbing stick used wet serves to smooth the intrusion away.*

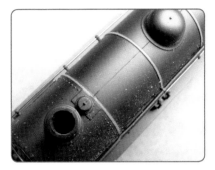
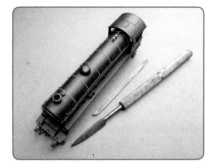

around them. Very often though, I find that on many older body mouldings they are too thick and chunky anyway for realism. (See the section in the next chapter for more information on what they *should* look like.)

In such cases they fall into the same category of unwanted protrusions as the part-lines – and hence merit the same summary treatment with scrapers and abrasives, being suitably reinstated at the detailing or painting stage. Rivets, on the other hand, are *desirable* protrusions, so I take considerable trouble to either avoid them or to reinstate them where this is not possible. Single rows of rivets don't usually cause too much of a problem – just work up to either side of the row with the scraper and then nick out that last little bit with the tip of a knife-blade. But double and triple-row rivets are a real pain, so unless a mould part-line is very obtrusive or pronounced where it passes through them, I find it best to leave it alone and just work up to the outside of the riveting on either side. Where that's not acceptable, I lop off the minimum number of rivet-heads needed to clean-up the part-line, then reinstate them, as described in the next chapter, which covers rivets in general.

Refining edges

Plastic moulding technology – especially older plastic moulding technology – requires the moulded material to be kept to a certain minimum thickness to ensure it flows into all the mould cavities when liquid, and is stable and robust

when set. Where such a plastic moulding on a model is being used to replicate a part on the prototype – like a cab or tender side – which in reality is less than an inch thick, then inevitably the result will tend to be a tad on the chunky side. This is an area where modern injection-moulding technology, with higher injection pressures and sophisticated high-strength, high-stability styrene plastics, has made great strides. The older models often present visible edges such as tender or

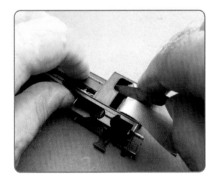

ABOVE AND BELOW *Thinning a visible edge on a plastic body moulding – in this case, Hornby's J52, where the cab sides adjacent to the doorway are something over 1mm thick. A three-sided scraper and a craft knife are used to bevel the edges of the opening to leave an edge of about 0.75mm – a lot closer to the prototype's beading width of 2¼in (0.73mm). Note the strip of Gaffer Tape being used to protect the cabside while the scraper is deployed.*

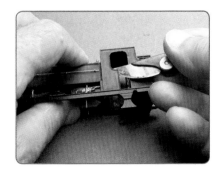

bunker copings, cab doorways/cut-outs/windows, roofs, footsteps and so on, which look far too thick to convince.

Fortunately, when we look at such a feature, what our eye takes note of ('reads') is the thickness of the actual 'edge surface'. So; as long as this is in the 'ballpark', the thickness of the rest of the moulding is far less apparent. Simply tapering-off the edge of the moulding by an appropriate amount usually tricks the eye into believing that what is too thick is actually prototypically thin. Some recent RTR models and many of the better cast-white metal loco kits (which also suffer from over-thick components) incorporate just such 'feathering' of visible edges in their manufacture. Where this has been omitted it is a simple enough task to undertake as a 'refinement'. I use the three-sided scraper or small flat file to remove the excess material, working by eye on my usual 'if it looks right…' principle. The cut edge is smoothed and finished with rubbing-sticks and abrasive papers. The whole process is illustrated in the accompanying pictures.

The quest for daylight

The current generation of RTR locos all have custom-designed mechanisms using compact 'can' motors and multi-stage geartrains that permit a wide range of motor locations within the locomotive superstructure. This has led to fully concealed drivetrains becoming the norm nowadays. 'Twas not ever

ABOVE AND BELOW *Removing the below-boiler infilling from the Hornby 'Jinty' body involved drilling a series of holes at the corners of the desired opening and along the lower edge above the front splasher. These holes were then joined-up using a craft knife and, at the upper edge, a straightedge. The resulting (rather ragged!) opening was then tidied up using first-cut (coarse) Swiss files, to give the result seen in the second picture.*

thus; many older RTR locos were saddled with a 'one-size-fits-all' choice of drivetrain componentry which often meant bits of mechanism were obtrusively visible beneath boilers or within cabs.

The relatively unsophisticated tooling often associated with older one-piece RTR body mouldings also placed fairly severe restrictions on the degree of 'undercut' that could be achieved. Such limitation also called for compromise – particularly in the awkward gap between boiler and footplate. Many models of this period are missing the bottom segment of the boiler barrel – sometimes comically so! Others suffer the partial or complete infilling of the below-boiler gap by unprototypical solid 'skirting'.

In reworking these older models to live alongside current productions, getting rid of such skirting and reinstating the full curvature of the underside of the boiler is obviously a priority. Similar reinstatement is also called for when basing models on some ex-Mainline body mouldings where the nether regions of the boiler formed part of the chassis casting of the mechanism: the J72, 2251 Collett goods, and '57xx' all suffer from this, as does the Bachmann J39 0-6-0.

Removing unwanted infilling from beneath boilers is often a tricky job, particularly where splashers, sandboxes, lubricators and other detail have to be worked around. The accepted technique for this sort of piercing-out operation is to drill a series of small holes just inside the outline of the area to be removed, then to join these up with a saw or craft-knife. Where possible, for this work I use a jeweller's piercing saw fitted with a fairly coarse blade – size 5 or 4. If I can't get the saw into play, I either use the Swan-Morton knife (which has a nice strong blade) or the tips of the jaws of the flush-cutting nippers to chew out the plastic between the holes. The resulting ragged-edged orifice is tidied up with the craft-knife and files, finished off with abrasive rubbing-sticks and papers.

Missing boiler bottoms

Providing a missing bottom segment to the boiler is an operation very often called for when reworking older RTR body mouldings. Fortunately, it is a fairly straightforward task in most cases. The basic technique is to pre-form an oversized piece of plastic sheet to the appropriate radius to match the rest of the boiler, then carefully trim this to size and cement it in place on to a pair of 'ledges' set in place to align the boiler surfaces. To make the boiler segment I generally use 30thou thick black Plastikard, which is shaped by taping it firmly to a former (a piece of dowelling) slightly *below* the desired finished radius. The plastic is then softened by heating, either by dunking it in boiling water or by giving it a modicum of grief with a hair-dryer on the 'hot' setting. It is then allowed to set to the curved form before being un-taped for trimming to size.

Making the insert fit the hole in the moulded boiler is a classic case of trial and trim, starting with a craft knife and straight-edge followed by a medium-cut flat file and finishing with a rubbing-block. As with all fitting jobs, I proceed on the principle that filing a bit more off is a lot easier than putting a bit back, but if the last becomes necessary then any slight gaps between boiler and insert can be filled with styrene putty

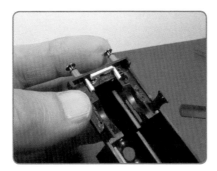

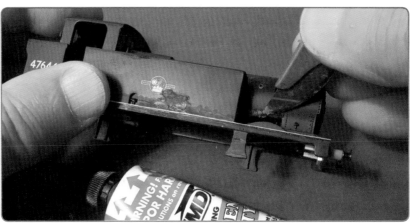

ABOVE AND RIGHT Making a boiler bottom for the 'Jinty' from .030in black Plastikard. A hair-dryer and a suitable round tool-handle used as a former produced a suitably curved blank, which is carefully trimmed to fit and mount on a pair of .060in-square Microstrip ledges cemented inside the boiler. Any imperfections in the resulting join are made good with fine body putty, and sanded smooth with an abrasive rubbing stick.

(Squadron 'Green' or similar). The joint is finished with rubbing-sticks or fine wet-and-dry paper used wet with soapy water, for a really smooth finish.

Almost invariably, fitting an insert like this leaves the matter of missing boiler banding to address. As noted a while back, I very often find that moulded-on boiler bands are worth replacing anyway – and this is almost always the case where a boiler-bottom insert has been fitted. So I lop them off and reach for the Microstrip.

Boiler mountings

It does not matter how spot-on the rest of a model steam loco is, if the boiler mountings – especially the chimney – miss the mark, then it will never capture the essential 'look' and character of the prototype. A dimensional error or missing detail might pass unnoticed, but botch the chimney and it positively shouts at you! Unfortunately, this is an aspect that even the best RTR and kit makers sometimes fall down on. Unsurprisingly, many RTR old stagers dating back to Triang/Hornby-Dublo days were suspect in this regard, including the original Triang 'Jinty' and 3F 0-6-0, the Dublo BR 2-6-4T and almost anything by Trix.

Older kits were often even worse, with some pretty wild approximations being foisted on the hapless modeller. Things have improved since then, but even among the ranks of much more recent RTR (including some models still in the catalogues) there lurk some notably naff boiler fittings, at least to my eye. The Airfix/Hornby '14xx', Hornby's tender-drive LMS Compound, the Mainline/Bachmann GW Mogul, 'Manor' and 2251 come at once to mind.

For these fundamentally flawed apparitions, replacement is the only satisfactory option, an operation described in detail in the next chapter. The latter requirement isn't always down to a dud specimen on the model, mind; on real steam locomotives, chimneys were a wearing part and called for replacement at intervals – and such replacements were often of a different pattern to the original. Modifications to draughting arrangements also resulted in a change of

BELOW Some detailing/reworking kits for specific RTR models provide you with a cast-white metal boiler bottom, as here on the Mainly Trains scale chassis conversion for the Hornby J52 body. The rather untidy filler here is stopping gaps resulting from moving the front splashers and doing away with the Hornby body mounting holes.

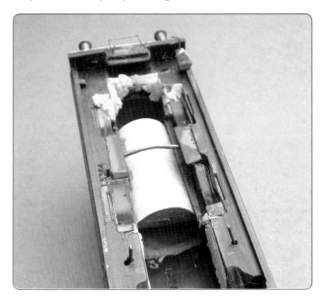

ABOVE AND BELOW *Two-part chimneys often suffer from an overly obtrusive joint, as on the Bachmann GW '45xx'. The remedy is to separate the two halves and file the seating(s) truly flat to get a better fit. A little gap-filling adhesive on reassembly, and a coat of paint can help disguise the join.*

chimney type – often to multiple-blastpipe designs. Domes, too, got cut down, or replaced with later patterns, while many a loco that started life with 'cased' safety valves ended up with exposed Ross 'pops'. Top-feed apparatus was another boiler detail that came and went with boiler changes. Recent RTR models take account of such variations and offer different versions to suit, but on older RTR models it may be that you're stuck with the wrong type of fitting for the particular engine you are portraying, calling for substitution.

Chimney refining

Good though most of the current production is, there are still a couple of aspects calling for a touch of refining. In particular, quite a lot of modern RTR chimneys come as a two-part moulding, an approach that dates back to Hornby-Dublo's R1 of 1958 – which had a separate (and very fine) chimney cap and rim. The advantage of this approach is that it enables the chimney base and skirt to be moulded integrally with the smokebox – ensuring accurate seating of the skirt and secure fixing – while still allowing for a correct rim profile, even where this incorporates undercuts or other production impediments.

Airfix came up with a variation of this two-part chimney idea with their Dean Goods, where the main chimney barrel, complete with cap, was moulded separately from the chimney base, with the join at the bottom of the barrel. Bachmann have subsequently used this approach for a number of their engines, including the Collett Mogul and the '45xx'. Where a really good close fit is achieved between the two sections, such a divided chimney can look fine, but in my experience this fit is often less than perfect, which then looks decidedly odd. Bear in mind that the prototype is either a seamless one-piece casting or an assembly in which the barrel fits *inside* the base. In neither case is there a visible gap, groove or seam.

The Bachmann '45xx' illustrated here is very much a case in point. In reality, there *was* a joint between the chimney base and barrel, with the latter locating into the former; but the fit was virtually flush and hence barely visible. Bachmann's chimney barrel is spot-on for diameter where it meets the seating, but the top of the seat moulding is slightly rounded – not by much, but enough to result in a slightly too-visible groove where the two parts come together.

I hummed and hawed for quite a while before deciding to try to do something about this. In the end, I carefully pulled the cast-metal chimney barrel from the plastic seat and filed the latter to a dead flat finish with a fine flat file and a rubbing block. Once I had a really good fit between the two parts I carefully pushed the barrel into its base and ran a drop of Zap a Gap into the join. The result, once painted, is far less obtrusive and hence more realistic – very much the point of this sort of refining work.

The rim-slim

The other aspect of moulded-plastic RTR steam engine chimneys that sometimes falls a little short of acceptable, is

LEFT AND BELOW *The same moulded chimney – that of the Mainline/Bachmann J72 – before and after a session with the rim-slimming files. A good photo is an invaluable guide to getting the right look to a chimney crown – which is an important step in producing a model that looks the part. The prototype chimney, as seen on J25 class 0-6-0 No. 5648, below, is what we are aiming at.*

the profile of the chimney cap and the size of the internal opening in the chimney top. Caps often suffer from over-thick and chunky chimney rims and errors in the height of the chimney lip above the rim. Usually, the moulded offering is pretty well in the ballpark dimensionally and for general shape, but calls for just a touch of 'fining down' to reduce the vertical thickness of the rim and the finesse of the visible edges to restore the proper degree of delicacy to the cap outline.

Insufficient internal chimney diameter leads to a (highly visible) 'thick' top lip that also lacks prototypical delicacy. In reality, chimney wall thickness here was typically under an inch. The other chimney-cap detail that sometimes needs attention is the position, size and thickness of the capuchon, where one is fitted.

Fining-down portly chimney-rims is a matter of undertaking a little careful work with rat-tailed (round-tapered) and warding (tapered flat-faced) Swiss files. It is a difficult process to describe in print, but I hope the accompanying sketches and photos will help convey what's involved. Basically, the rat-tailed file is used to adjust the *lower* profile of the rim by taking material from beneath, applying gentle upward pressure on the rim, but avoiding inward loading as far as possible. It is a case of working right around the chimney as evenly as possible, with the taper of the file fitted to the radius required for the 'flare' twixt rim and barrel.

You will not achieve a *completely* even result (the other boiler mountings invariably get in the way at some point!) but with care it is possible to remove the small amount of material

required to 'crisp up' the visible edge all the way around the rim. Then, using the warding file, material is similarly removed from the top face of the rim, taking care to maintain the appropriate slope and curvature. I always attack chimney rims with a prototype photo or two propped on the bench where I can see them while I'm working.

The trick is to file a little and look a lot… The one-eye squint with the chimney held up against the light to get a silhouette is an effective way of evaluating the profile you've achieved. It is not only chimney-caps that can call for a touch of this sort of slimming-down – the top edge of the characteristic GW safety valve bonnet is another fitting that is almost invariably moulded too thick. Not surprising, when you look at the real thing and realise just what a knife-edge it is.

With the rim slimmed down, the next job is to assess the amount by which the chimney-lip projects above the upper face. On many models, this projection is far too great; on the prototype, the top of the chimney often surmounted the rim by little more than an inch or so – a mere 0.33mm at 4mm scale! Both the Bachmann/Mainline J72 and Hornby's 'Jinty' suffer from this fault – easy enough to rectify with a small flat file, taking a little off at a time and doing plenty of squinting.

Capuchons – those fore-mounted upward projections from the top of the chimney barrel proper – usually suffer from one of two faults. They are either too big and chunky, or they are in the wrong place relative to the chimney rim – an error particularly evident on ex-Mainline GW engines like the 2251 and 'Manor'. Over-size and over-thick capuchons can be cut

The stages in slimming and refining a chimney top: a rat-tailed Swiss file is used to take off material from beneath the lip, and a warding-file from above. The height of the rim is adjusted with a flat engineer's file, and twist-drills held in the fingers are used in successive sizes to open out the diameter to give a realistic wall thickness. Quarter of an hour's careful work can transform the look of an engine.

down to size with a little work with the files and as part of the boring-out of the chimney, as described below. Those in the wrong place (not aligned with the outer diameter of the chimney barrel) need cutting off and replacing with a new capuchon fashioned from brass strip and attached with cyano – although replacing the whole chimney with an accurate cast item may be a better bet.

Last job on many RTR chimneys is to open up the internal diameter to give a chimney-top rim thickness a lot closer to the prototype dimension. There is no need to try to hollow out the whole chimney – so long as the topmost few millimetres are in

the ball-park, the eye 'reads' the appropriate rim thickness. Strictly, we need a tapered hole that broadens towards the top. Such an orifice is obviously *de rigueur* on a tapered chimney, but even where the chimney barrel is parallel-sided the inside bore is usually shaped thus. So the best approach is to bore the chimney undersize with a suitable drill then open it out to the final size with a tapered reamer – in which role the ever-useful three-sided scraper functions very well. See the accompanying illustration. Drilling-out a plastic chimney is a ticklish operation calling for a delicate touch, best accomplished using finger-power with a pin vice or bare drill-shank in place of any hint of the Dremel.

BELOW *The same approach works wonders with clunky GWR safety valve bonnets. Here are before-and-after shots of the bonnet on the Bachmann '93xx' Mogul.*

BELOW *Correcting the capuchon on the Mainline/Bachmann GW '22xx'. As it comes, this is moulded as part of the chimney barrel, which puts it inside the chimney rim, not on top of it as it should be. The offending item is cut off and replaced with a small piece of 0.5mm square brass strip bent to shape and attached to the (very nice) turned cap with cyano. The internal bore of the chimney can then be opened up to a realistic size.*

RIGHT *Opening out a taper-bored chimney with the ever-useful three-sided scraper used as a taper reamer; horrid, but effective. Twiddle it, don't force it, and it does the job very effectively!*

Splasher correction

One other major feature that often needs attention, particularly on, older RTR locos is the wrong-sized or misplaced splasher. The latter is quite a common case where a chassis of incorrect wheelbase was used beneath the original RTR body, as on the Hornby J52 that figures from time to time in these pages. Adapting this body to a correct-to-scale chassis involved shifting the centre splashers forward a tad to align with the driving wheels and filling in the resulting hole in the footplate. The errant splashers were simply sawn off the footplate with a fine-bladed razor saw and the wheel-openings suitably trimmed out at the fore end to clear the driving wheels. The splashers were then cemented into the correct location with Plastic Weld and small pieces of .020in black Plastikard cut to fit the resulting holes aft of the relocated splashers and similarly welded in place. When all the joins were hard, the job was smoothed and tidied with rubbing sticks. This was a typical straightforward splasher relocation exercise.

Far trickier was basically the same job undertaken on the old Hornby-Dublo/Wrenn R1 0-6-0T, which also has a wheelbase error that causes a jarring visual misalignment when a scale (Branchlines) chassis is fitted, even though the wheels still clear. The complication is that the front sandbox is

ABOVE *It is always a good idea to know what things are supposed to look like; here is a real R1 front splasher.*

integral with the splasher; the resulting shenanigans needed to relocate the splasher, while aligning the sandbox with the smokebox rear and wing-plate, are illustrated here.

Loco-tender gaps

One of the most eye-socking consequences of the RTR manufacturer's obsession with fairground track curvatures is that all-too-often there is a vast chasm between the cab rear

RIGHT *Here is an unaltered Wrenn R1 body sitting on a Branchlines scale chassis; the error in the front splasher location, both in relation to the wheels and to the smokebox is obvious and unacceptable, calling for remedial action.*

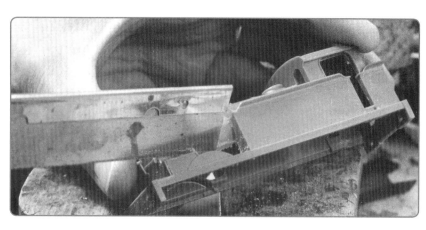

ABOVE, LEFT AND BELOW *Modifying the Dublo R1 front splasher first involves cutting away the infilling below the boiler as already described. A razor saw is then used to cut the sandbox top free of the smokebox. A small hole is drilled in the footplate at the front corner of the sandbox and a piercing saw threaded through to cut the splasher free from the footplate and the smokebox wing plate. The front of the sandbox is then trimmed so that its rear coincides with the back of the smokebox. The splasher can then be cemented back in place. The result is not perfect – the splasher radius is too great – but it is a lot better than it was at the outset!*

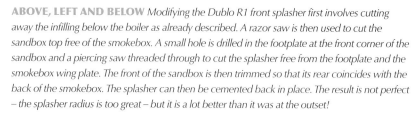

BELOW *The paragon of the contemporary RTR art it may be – but Bachmann's superlative 'Crab' still has a downright silly gap between the loco and tender; this is the 'close' coupling! Pity the poor fireman…*

and tender front of tender locos. In reality, this gap is typically a foot or so, easily spanned by the hinged sheet-metal fall-plate which the prototype generally used to bridge the gap 'twixt loco and tender. Adding a fall-plate and the associated dragbox details in reality to occupy the loco-tender gap is covered in the next chapter; what concerns us here is the modification of the loco-tender drawgear to give a much more believable coupling distance.

How close to scale you can make this gap depends, of course, on the radius of curvature which the engine is expected to negotiate. As an absolute minimum, few prototype tender locomotives were capable of negotiating anything sharper than about 4½ chains radius, taken dead slow. That is a shade under 4ft in 4mm scale, a figure generally regarded as pretty generous and often unattainable on typical layout sites. However, if you adopt my suggested 'pragmatic compromise' of a 2½ft minimum radius for 00, you will find you can usually close the loco-tender gap up to around 5mm or so – only slightly over scale distance.

What this actually involves in terms of hardware modifications depends on the arrangement employed by the particular model. Where a drawbar and pin is used, it may be possible to simply drill an additional hole in the drawbar at the

ABOVE AND RIGHT *Typical modified tender draw-gear on my 'Jubilee'. I generally prefer a hook-and-loop set-up to a solid drawbar as it is easier to couple up and adjust (especially where a fall-plate is fitted), and allows unhindered lateral movement. It is also compatible with the loaded tender arrangement described in the previous chapter. On this 'unloaded' engine, a downward facing hook on the drag beam was used. The second picture shows the resulting gap – all but true to scale; the modified loco (with a slightly narrowed fall-plate) readily copes with 33in radius curves.*

appropriate location; or it may be preferable or necessary to make a new, shorter drawbar. The same is usually true of permanently coupled drawbar systems, where the loco and tender are linked by a drawbar held with screws at both ends.

I find fibreglass-backed PCB sleeper strip a good material for making drawbars. If loco-tender isolation is needed, it is easy enough to gap the copper film. Older and cruder hook-and-loop or hook-behind-dragbox set-ups are usually more difficult to modify and hence are best replaced by something a little more discreet, compact and adjustable – a wide wire loop (to allow sideways movement) and a matching wire hook that can be tweaked fore-and-aft to fine-tune the coupling distance works well, and is amenable to the loaded-tender arrangement mentioned in Chapter 5.

Tension-lock couplings

There is no getting away from it – the standard-fit British tension lock coupling is a right eyesore. No matter how good the rest of a model locomotive is, all comes to naught if you decorate its nether extremities (especially the front end) with a monstrous claw and a chunk of motorway crash barrier. Such desecration is not unavoidable; there are a number of alternative 4mm scale coupling systems that are far more discreet, as well as offering sophisticated magnetic uncoupling, often with delayed-action capability. But even on layouts retaining

the tension lock system, disfigurement of locomotives can be simply avoided without impairing the functionality.

This calls for the replacement of the full hook-and-bar set up with a far-less-obtrusive fine-wire loop, set at the appropriate height to match the tension lock, as on the GW Collett Goods illustrated below. Not only does such a loop look a great deal better, it also permits the fitment of a scale link coupling and a full set of bufferbeam hoses. It also makes it a great deal easier to uncouple the loco from a train when required – only one hook to disengage. If you do nothing else, fit such a loop on the front end of your tender engines! Double-heading? Couple the engines in tandem using the scale link couplings, or retain a full hook-and-bar coupler on the tender rear of locomotives regularly used for piloting.

BELOW *This 00 gauge Mainline GWR '22xx' Collett Goods, which I built for my old friend Andrew Boyd in Massachusetts, has had the full range of refining treatments detailed in this chapter, including reworked boiler fittings, a new boiler bottom, thinned cab and tender sides, and mould seam removal. The tension-lock couplings have given way to unobtrusive wire loops. The replacement chassis is, once again, by Comet.*

7 DETAILING

There was a time when adding or improving detail on RTR (and, indeed, many kit-built) model locomotives was a staple of the railway modelling diet. Not any more, though; the need for such work seems to get less and less with every new introduction, to the point that the best of today's RTR is so well-detailed that there's nothing much left to add or improve! But more vintage offerings do generally leave scope for additions and refinements – tasks which I, for one, find rather rewarding. In particular, such models will often lack many quite basic fitments we now expect or take for granted: decent scale buffers, buffer-beam hoses and standards, smaller grab-rails and pipework, lubricators, lamp-irons, sanding gear, various operating linkages, cab fittings, cab doors, tender fall-plates, and internal tender detail.

The 'in need of upgrading' category also gets smaller as the models get newer. Boiler and cab handrails, for instance, have gone from moulded-on approximations or wire of gas-main proportions held by split pins, to delicate filigree confections of scale-diameter wire and turned stanchions, on the cream of the contemporary crop. Carving off vintage crudities for replacement by handrail knobs and wire is a basic necessity in the cause of realistic modelling, whereas replacing the factory-fitted handrails on something like a current-production Hornby M7 takes you well into the territory of diminishing returns. That said, even on the loftiest of modern RTR paragons there is still some scope for improving things like lamp-irons, where the need for production-friendly robustness mitigates against the delicacy of the true-scale item.

Basic detailing options

Adding the sort of basic superstructure detail listed above is essentially an exercise in fixing bits on to plastic body mouldings, together with a spot of mild fabrication. The parts to be fixed will include commercially produced plastic moulded, cast or etched-metal detail components, small turnings like handrail stanchions or smokebox door handles, and home-fabricated details in a variety of materials. These are wire and metal strip in a variety of sizes, milled sections and the odd bit of sheet metal, styrene sheet, Microstrip and plastic rod, a few scraps of paper, glazing materials and an epoxy putty or filler – Milliput or similar. These detail parts will be attached to the plastic mouldings in one of four ways: force-fitted or pegged into holes, retained with screws or nuts and bolts, glued on, or melted into place.

Rather than spending a lot of ink in attempting to discuss the various detailing options and fabrication techniques in

ABOVE *Some of the moulded detailing that comes 'out of the box' on the latest RTR models is simply stunning, like this steam manifold on Bachmann's BR Standard Class 4 Mogul, subtly weathered by Philip Hall. Fabricating this little lot from wire and odds and ends would be a pretty tall order; bettering Bachmann's efforts verges on the impossible!*

BELOW *There are plenty of commercial detailing parts from a wide range of sources available to the 4mm loco-improver. Admittedly, some of my random selection shown here are a bit long in the tooth – but eBay is a ready source of bits like these, and some of these older items are of excellent quality.*

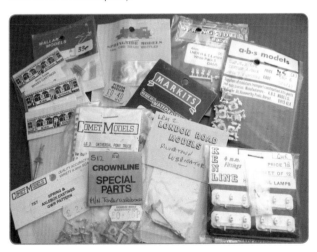

abstract, it seemed more useful to describe my own methods in the context of the type of detail being represented. So I have divided the body of this chapter into sections centred on the various aspects of a locomotive's anatomy and the ways the relevant details might be modelled. As there are a number of ways of tackling some of the common jobs, this enables me to offer alternatives where appropriate.

Detailing decisions

The first step in the detailing or re-detailing/upgrading process is the thorough assessment of the base model, as already touched upon in previous chapters. The key aid here is a good selection of prototype photographs against which to judge the model, both for the quality/authenticity of what has been provided by the manufacturer, and conformity with the actual

OPPOSITE *Yes, it is my long-serving '57xx' pannier tank, based on an early Mainline body moulding and a Perseverance chassis. This model was extensively modified and fully detailed, including all-new scale handrails, fully fretted-out injectors, a full set of lamp-irons (although I notice a few have gone AWOL in 25+ years!), fire-iron brackets, extra plumbing, a full cab interior, all the complex sandbox linkages, AWS gear, refined boiler mountings, and a replacement safety valve bonnet with dented rim, and various dings, dents and kinked handrails. The finish is far from pristine, to complete the workaday look of the model. Definitely not a showcase specimen!*

loco you are intent on modelling. It never ceases to amaze me just how much diversity of detail there can be between engines of nominally the same class, or even sub-class. Sometimes it seems as if no two steam locomotives were *ever* identical, certainly after a year or two in service and the odd visit to 'shops'.

Good though the modern RTR loco undoubtedly is there is a limit to how far the authenticity requirement to match every prototype variation can be taken in the context of mass production. Indeed, you may be surprised at just what you sometimes need to do even to state-of-the-art modern RTR to accurately replicate individual prototype locomotives. A good example of the sort of pit that lies in wait for the unwary is my own experience with Bachmann's GWR '45xx' 2-6-2T, widely (and rightly) regarded as a very good model of this useful prototype. When I came to examine my own specimen – a 'straight-tank' BR lined-green version numbered 4569, entirely appropriate for the line I was modelling and for which I had a good selection of photos and a nice set of etched-brass plates – I found that Bachmann had fitted a 'low' safety valve bonnet; correct for almost every straight-tank '45' except – of course – 4569, which had a 'tall' one.

What to do? Well, there are undoubtedly various after-market GW cast safety-valve bonnets about, but they are invariably made integral with the associated top feed. Bachmann's bonnet, by contrast, is a separate component that fits over a top-feed moulded integrally with the boiler. Carving this off will almost invariably wreck the superb paint job – something I was anxious to preserve! Bachmann do make a tall valve cover, fitted when appropriate to other versions of the '45xx' model – but it is not available as a separate item, and buying another complete locomotive just to get my hands on a tuppenny-ha'penny bonnet moulding seemed rather an extravagant solution!

BELOW *Exchange is no robbery! The joy of the separately applied details found on most modern RTRs is that you can easily remove a fitting that is not quite right and replace it with one that is. Hence, I was able to swap the short valve bonnet on my Bachmann '45xx' for a long type from another model, by drilling out the locating pins and popping the bonnet mouldings off the top feed.*

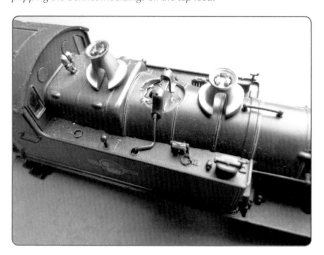

The pragmatic answer would have been to pick another member of the class as subject, one that *did* have a squat bonnet. I got lucky, however, and found a fellow modeller possessed of a tall-bonnet 4575, but intent on modelling an example with low headgear. This marriage-made-in-Dongguan was duly cemented by a little exchange transplant surgery.

Substitute boiler fittings

However, such a convenient swap is not always possible. Should you find yourself foisted with an unconvincing or incorrect-to-prototype chimney or other boiler mounting on an RTR model, then changing it for something more appropriate from an alternative source is not that onerous a task. As always, the first thing to do is to take a really good look at the prospective replacement to ensure that it really *is* an improvement. I've come across a good few 'chimney upgrades' that, while being sexily cast in lost-wax brass, were neither as refined in profile nor as accurate to prototype as the plastic original. So cast a cod-fish eye on what you are offered; brass is nice but a crisp, delicate white metal casting is preferable where it does a better job of catching that all-important outline. A photograph, Watson: truth lies ever in a photograph…

Practically, the worst part of the job lies in getting rid of the original moulded-on chimney while preserving all the surrounding rivets, lamp-irons and other details. This calls for careful work with the piercing saw, a first-cut (coarse) flat jeweller's file and three-sided scraper, and finished off with fine files and rubbing sticks. A good first move is to apply strips of masking tape to any rivets in the vicinity, in the hope that this might save them from decapitation. A piercing saw with a fairly fierce blade – a 4 or 3 – is then used to make the unkindest cut of all, right through the chimney base as close to the smokebox top as possible. The bulk of the resulting stump is then removed with the flat coarse file, followed by some careful work with the three-sided scraper to get rid of the remains of the chimney skirt. A final dressing with a fine file and rubbing-stick should serve to prepare the smokebox top to accommodate the base of the new chimney. If any rivets have been damaged during this process, all is not lost; they can usually be reinstated, as described in the 'riveting' section below.

Chimney fitting

Getting a cast chimney accurately seated on a plastic smokebox often calls for some careful work to get a good match between the chimney skirt and the smokebox top. This is where a readily malleable white metal casting often has the edge over something manly in cast or turned brass, as it is easier to 'roll down' the skirt to match the smokebox diameter. The key aid to this fitting work is a former – a bit of hardwood dowel or, better still, steel or brass bar – of a diameter equal to, or very slightly less than, that of the smokebox, over which the chimney skirt can be formed and sanded to get a really good fit.

If the chimney casting has a spigot – whether central, or offset as a mould feed as on the popular Alan Gibson

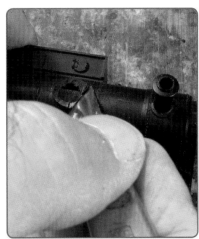

ABOVE *Removing unwanted boiler fittings is a progressive job calling for a variety of implements. I start by sawing off the fitting as close to the boiler as I can using a piercing saw. I then carve away the residue using a craft knife followed by the three-sided scraper. Lastly, I resort to abrasives – a small first-cut file to get rid of the last remnants, finishing off with a rubbing stick to smooth the final surface.*

castings – then this will get in the way of the fitting process, so it has to be sawn off carefully with the piercing saw and the cut smoothed flush with files. The seating face of the chimney casting is then prepared by removing any mould part-lines or other surface protrusions. This is done away with by rubbing the casting to and fro on some nice fresh abrasive paper (180 grit wet-and-dry used dry) wrapped around the former. This technique is also useful for reducing the thickness of over-chunky chimney skirts; on the prototype, they are very thin sheet metal, usually no more than a quarter of an inch or so thick.

With luck, the result of this rubbing-down will be a chimney that sits snugly atop the smokebox with the outer rim of the skirt nicely feathered to a fine edge, leaving no unseemly gaps. All-too-often, however, the skirt will be found to be of slightly too great a radius to match the smokebox top, leaving the skirt 'flying' slightly with an unrealistic gap around the lower edges. Remedying this fault calls for the skirt

to be rolled down to the right radius to get a proper fit, an operation accomplished using the former and an ordinary engineer's scriber.

First, though, if the chimney is brass – especially turned brass – then it will probably need a bit of annealing to make it soft enough to work. Heat the chimney skirt in a flame or with a resistance soldering probe until it is at least dull-red hot, then quench it in cold water. To form the skirt down, the chimney is clamped firmly on the former in a vice or clamp, then the side of the tapered portion of the scriber is used as a 'roller' to apply pressure to the top of the skirt, forcing it down to match the former radius, working around the whole circumference of the chimney. It is a lot easier to do than to describe!

Once the chimney has been accurately fitted to the smokebox top and has had any mould part-lines or similar blemishes cleaned up with fine files and abrasive paper, it can be stuck in place on the moulded body. Some people like to provide a locating spigot from brass tube or plastic rod to ensure accurate alignment – but I don't usually bother, preferring to trust the Mk 1 eyeball, sighting against an engineer's square for reference, as in the illustrations. It is especially important to check that the chimney is truly upright when viewed from the front – easy to overlook in the concern to get the thing in the right place when seen from the *side*. To mount boiler fittings, I always use a five-minute epoxy resin adhesive, which gives a few minutes grace to get things 'just

ABOVE *This is why I like cast white metal replacement chimneys and other boiler fittings: you can easily 'roll down' the skirt to get a good fit on the boiler. You can use the same technique on brass (cast or turned) parts, but you will need to anneal the metal (heat it to dull red heat then quench it in cold water) to soften it and make it malleable. Also, you will need to use far more pressure while rolling down, calling for use of a metal or hardwood former of appropriate diameter, rather than doing the job in situ on a plastic boiler.*

BELOW *Use of a square and a small mirror arranged as in the photo enables you to sight a chimney from the side and the front at the same time during gluing operations, giving you a sporting chance of getting the thing on truly vertical! I use five-minute epoxy resin for this job, which gives a decent length of adjustment time.*

so', as well as filling any slight gaps. Although much less often called for when reworking RTR loco bodies, the same approach and techniques can be used to replace unsatisfactory or inappropriate domes or safety valves, and to add optional top feeds or other miscellaneous bits of boiler-top hardware.

Boiler bands

These are still a bone of contention on many plastic-bodied locomotives, as very rarely are they delicate enough to look convincing, and all-too-often veer towards the truly gross. As suggested in the 'refining' section of the last chapter, if a model's boiler bands are over-thick or, as used to be common, of an oddly rounded profile, then I normally opt to lop them off with the scraper for replacement at the detailing stage – which is now – or as part of the painting process. Leaving aside for a moment the small matter of what moulded boiler band removal does for the factory paint finish (that is, often precipitates a total repaint!), the other little practicable problem is – having removed the moulded offerings, what do you replace them with?

In reality, boiler bands are narrow flat steel strips clamped under tension around the boiler barrel and firebox to hold the thin sheet-metal cladding plates in place over the external insulation. Typically, they are around $3/16$in thick by 2–3in wide,

RIGHT *Boiler bands are, in reality, strips of thin, flat metal – often no more than an eighth of an inch thick, as here, on a GWR 'Dukedog' 4-4-0. Most model bands are far too prominent.* Author's collection

which at 4mm:1ft translates to a mere 0.06mm x 0.66mm – 1mm, with 0.06mm being 2½ thou – about the thickness of a piece of thin 'bank' paper or a strip of Sellotape.

Where a model is being repainted anyway, many modellers opt to fit new scale boiler bands from just-such pre-painted paper strip or adhesive tape as part of the painting process. The bands are attached, usually using tacky varnish as an adhesive for the paper variety, after the basic painting is complete, but before any final varnishing/sealing or the application of weathering is carried out. In a fully lined paint scheme, any lining-out of the paper/tape boiler bands is obviously carried out flat on the bench before attachment. Where waterslide transfer lining is being used, the thickness of the transfer backing film is

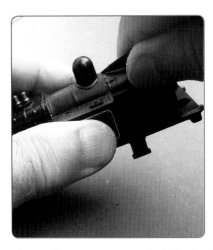
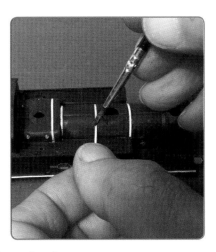

often sufficient to represent the boiler band as well as the painting, which simplifies matters considerably.

That leaves plain bands in situations where it is desirable to fit them before painting or where paintwork is going to be patched or touched-in. Such plain bands can be readily made of metal or styrene strip, paper or adhesive tape. Metal strip does not really make much sense in the context of a plastic body; it's a pig to fix in place and much of what is ostensibly sold for the purpose is woefully oversize – typically, 10thou thick x 1mm+ wide. Styrene is a much better bet, although again, even the thinnest (5thou) Plastikard or Evergreen micro-strip is about twice scale thickness. That said, 5 x 30thou plastic strip generally looks OK and is a breeze to fix with a few drops (small drops at that!) of liquid plastic solvent. This leaves the tape or paper options for those who, like the author, would rather understate detail and texture. My own preferred option is cigarette paper, scalpel-cut to width on a piece of glass and attached by wetting with solvent.

A last refinement in the matter of boiler bands is to model the retaining/tensioning clamps where these are visible – as, for instance, on the top of most Belpaire fireboxes. More usually, they are beneath the boiler, but even there they are often surprisingly prominent when the locomotive is viewed at eye level. Alan Gibson does a neat little brass casting for a typical clamp which is well worth the trouble where the prototype fastening is clearly visible. Cut it into the pre-attached boiler band and fix it with a sparing drop of cyano.

Handrails

Real locomotive handrails come in three basic formats: rails held in stanchions (often referred to as handrail knobs by modellers); vertical handrail pillars, usually set in cab doorways or on tender-fronts, and grabs. These last are lighter and shorter rails turned down through 90° at each end like an office staple and set directly into the platework of the loco superstructure. These rail types vary in size, with main boiler or cabside rails mounted in stanchions usually falling in the range 1¼in to 1½in in diameter. Pillar rails are often of tapered form, typically going from something over 2in at the base to around 1½in at the top. Where parallel-sided pillars are fitted, they are usually a bit heftier than normal rails – around 1¾in in diameter. Short footplate, cab/bunker or boiler-top grab-rails held in stanchions are usually of a similar size to main rails, but

ABOVE *Replacing boiler bands on a plastic body: I remove them in the same way as join lines and other blemishes, with the scraper. They are reinstated using fine strips of cigarette paper fixed by being soaked (sparingly) with plastic solvent. Excess strip is trimmed using a truly sharp scalpel while the solvent is still setting, to get the ends well snugged down. Clamps are added as appropriate with scraps of fine Microrod (as here), or brass castings.*

small, knobless grabs in 'staple' form are usually of smaller diameter, typically an inch.

If you are going to be strict about scale fidelity, then only the latest and most refined of RTR locomotives possess handrails that are truly fine enough to match these

BELOW *The most common (and demanding to model) form of prototype handrail: along both sides of the boiler and around the front of the smokebox as a continuous rail. Note the differing lengths of the smokebox and boiler-side stanchions. Once again, this is the GW 'Dukedog'. Author's collection*

prototypical dimensions. The normal 4mm 'true scale' convention is to make main handrails held in stanchions from nickel-silver wire of 0.45mm diameter, which scales out at 1³/₈ in. This is the size for which modern turned handrail knobs are drilled. Tapered pillar cabside/tender front handrails are always a bit of a problem, as they ideally need to be turned – not an easy proposition. Fortunately, they are rare on post-Victorian locos. Parallel-sided pillars are much easier – 0.6mm nickel-silver wire is usually fine. For the smaller elbow-ended grabs, 0.33mm wire scales out exactly at the required inch.

Very few RTR productions hit this degree of fine-scale conformity, but the best of them get very close. The boiler/cab doorway handrails on the Bachmann '45xx' for instance, are 0.5mm diameter – which is only a whisker over true scale. However, presumably in the cause of production expediency and robustness, the horizontal cabside and bunker elbow-end grabs are made in the same wire, which makes them just a tad clunky. The side is also let down slightly by the boiler-top grab, which is a one-piece plastic moulding rather than wire-in-stanchions and consequently is considerably oversize at 0.7mm diameter. It also lacks the crispness of a wire rail, being slightly bowed.

While we're picking nits, the other slight disappointment on this loco – in common with almost all RTR models, even the very best of them – is that the handrail stanchions themselves are a little on the well-fed side, both in the matter of head size and shank diameter. But given the robustness requirement and the demands of mass-production, this is hardly to be wondered at. It is important to bear in mind that we are talking hand-applied factory detail here, albeit accomplished by a skilled workforce aided by sophisticated jigs and tools – work that only the really competent modeller could realistically better. This means that only the most fastidious of us are going to find the not-inconsiderable task of handrail replacement worthwhile.

However, go back a few years to RTR models introduced from the later 1970s up until about 2003 (quite a few of which are still in the catalogues), and things become a good deal less refined. Look at the boiler handrails carried by many early Mainline and Airfix productions and you're back in 'footballs on a gas pipe' territory, with chunky wire held in stanchions that look like refugees from a larger scale. Secondary grabs and rails, on the other hand, are often represented by little more than a narrow moulded ridge, if they're represented at all.

Cab doorway and tender-front pillars are often moulded as flat strip rather than round bar, and such 'applied' secondary rails as there might be tend to be flimsy plastic mouldings rather than crisp wire in turned stanchions. Dig down a further layer into the history of the plastic-bodied RTR locomotive, and you're back to the era when handrails were moulded-on as a rounded ridge, with or without any representation of the stanchions, or formed of grossly oversized wire held in chunky split-pins. Robust and expedient maybe, but realistic? I don't think so… It goes without saying that where realism is a requirement, all of these less-than-satisfactory handrails call for removal and replacement.

Replacing duff handrails
Disposing of unwanted moulded-on rails and smoothing the surface of the mouldings has already been described in the 'refining' notes in the previous chapter. Doing away with chunky wire and oversized stanchions is usually a matter of a few moments' controlled brutality with pliers and snips. When extracting turned stanchions from their sockets, I ease them out by carefully levering with the jaw-tips of the fine snipe-nosed pliers, used behind the head and twisted gently from side to side. The object is to apply vertical force without 'waggling' the turnings too much, as that tends to distort the socket-hole. If you number any 'S' scale modellers among your acquaintance, by the by, then put those oversized 4mm scale stanchions aside for them. One scale's 'slightly oversize' is often the next-scale-up's 'just right'…

The big problem left by the removal of over-beefy handrail hardware is usually a row of socket-holes in the moulded body of a size through which a scale-sized stanchion turning will happily pass in its entirety – base, shank and head! Such excessive orifices need to be either plugged and re-drilled to suit the smaller diameter shanks of the replacement stanchions, or be sleeved-up to fit the replacement shanks. If you opt to fill and re-drill (usually much the easier option), then in my experience, paste-type filler is *not* the answer. When you come to make your new hole then nine times out of ten the filler just breaks away and you're back to the original gaping chasm.

My preferred answer to this problem is to find some plastic rod of a suitable diameter to plug the hole, opting for a larger diameter and enlarging the hole to suit where I can't find a size to make a good fit in the existing opening. I push the rod

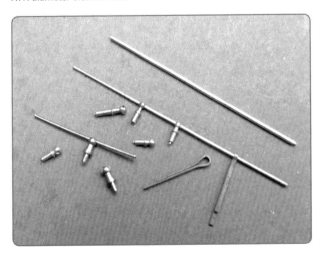

LEFT *Faced with over-sized handrail stanchion mounting holes, I drill them out to 1mm diameter and plug them with 1mm Microrod solvent welded and heat-fused in place. Once firmly set, this is carved off flush on the outside and carefully re-drilled for the new, scale stanchions. I usually elect to drill under-size and open the holes out with a fine taper brooch.*

through the hole so about 1mm sticks out at the rear inside the body, snipping it off flush on the outside before chemically welding it in place using a potent solvent cement like Plastic Weld. Then, to notch up my belt while buttoning my braces, I take the trusty baby Antex soldering iron and, using the back of the tip, melt that protruding millimetre of rod and fuse it well into the rear of the moulding, to add a heat-weld to the chemical one.

It is best to let such a plastic plug harden for at least 24 hours before you drill your new holes – a task to be undertaken with due delicacy; this is *not* a job for a Dremel! Sharp drills used carefully under finger power in a pin-vice or Archimedean drill, lubricated with washing-up liquid and withdrawn frequently to clear the flutes, is the way to go. Start with a small (usually 0.7mm) pilot-hole then open out in stages to the final diameter using drills going up in 0.2mm steps or delicate twiddles with a sharp taper brooch. Obviously, you want to keep the holes perpendicular to the boiler circumference or tank/bunker/tender-side, but you'll be cleverer than me if you get them all dead plumb. For this reason – and to avoid any need for force when fitting the new hardware – I aim to make my socket-holes a slightly slack fit for the replacement stanchions, to allow a bit of room for manoeuvre in the cause of accurate alignment.

Handrail hardware

Now is possibly the time to give some consideration to the components we are going to be using to replace the discarded RTR ironmongery or carved-off plastic. I've already mentioned the normal wire diameters used in 4mm scale: 0.45mm/1³/₈in for main rails, 0.6mm for pillars and 0.33mm/1in for subsidiary elbow-end grab rails. Straight-drawn 12in lengths of these diameters are readily available in nice hard brass or nickel-silver wire, as is 0.5mm for those wishing to match RTR rails of this size. Most of the turned stanchions offered for 4mm scale are drilled to suit 0.45mm, but a quick twiddle with a fine taper brooch will readily adapt them to the slightly larger size.

Handrail stanchions are available at scale size or in somewhat beefed-up form and come in three basic lengths, unsurprisingly classified as short, medium and long. The differing lengths are needed to maintain straight handrail alignments on taper boilers and those boilers where the smokebox and/or firebox are set out from the line of the boiler barrel proper. The handrail held in fixed-length stanchions that dives in and out along the boiler-side like the rocky road to Kathmandu is another one of those old modelling chestnuts that has no counterpart in reality.

The most readily available and comprehensive range of scale-sized turned stanchions is that from Alan Gibson, and that is what I generally use. They have a 0.95mm diameter head and are drilled to take 0.45mm wire. Markits also offer a good selection of turnings, including the original Romford/K's design of handrail knob that Noah used on the Ark. This has a massive 1.5mm head and is a definite football, designed to be strung on 23 SWG (0.61mm) gas-pipe. But Markits' 'scale' stanchions have a 1mm head diameter drilled to take 0.5mm wire and are available in the three lengths with fairly stout taper shank. They make a good match for the type of stanchions used on many modern RTR locos, which can be very useful in the cause of consistency.

When considering 4mm scale model handrail stanchions – especially where non-standard shank lengths or odd-diameter

BELOW *Handrail hardware. At the top is a length of 0.6mm NS wire for making pillars, and below that some standard fine-scale 0.45mm NS handrail wire threaded with short and medium Gibson scale-sized stanchions, and a closed-down ¹/₃₂in split pin. A medium-length Markits stanchion, a short Gibson and an open split-pin form the next row, and at bottom left we have an old Romford 'football' and a couple of Mainline RTR-fit stanchions, one threaded on to typical RTR-diameter 0.5mm wire.*

handrails are involved – don't overlook that classic old-time solution, the closed-down split pin. These were the standard fit in the days before 'turned knobs' – and remained the choice of the discerning modeller unconvinced by brass footballs. A $^1/_{32}$in steel or brass split pin closed down tight on to appropriate-diameter wire gives a stanchion head that is very close to scale, while allowing any length of shank that might be appropriate. They are also nicely robust and amenable to tweaking to get the final handrail alignment 'just so'. The lack of a base flange is only apparent on the closest inspection, and by no means all prototype handrail stanchions had such a fitment anyway.

When it comes to larger-than-normal diameter handrails – usually those housing internal linkages or doubling as pipework, as on the many locos fitted with the MR/LMS design of boiler-mounted vacuum brake ejector – then the split-pin based stanchion is often the only way to go. Oh yes, one last attribute of the humble split-pin; a box of 250 will cost you about the same as a packet of 10 turned stanchions…

Shaping and installing handrails

Forming a typical boiler handrail that combines the rails down both sides of the boiler with the section across the smokebox front, into a single length of wire is definitely one of the trickier operations in model steam locomotive detailing. Such a rail has to be made accurate in three dimensions and kept symmetrical in form, as well as incorporating curves of several different radii and being free of kinks. The prototype 'cheats' in this regard as such a rail is in reality typically made in several sections, usually jointed within the handrail stanchions on the smokebox side. You can get away with this approach in 7mm scale, but the head of a 4mm handrail stanchion is just too tiny to make a viable joint.

The really tricky part of the job is forming the curved portion of the rail on the smokebox front and aligning it with the main boiler-side rails. To get the various bends in the right place, a simple template is useful. If you have a decent scale drawing of the engine in question, a photocopy of the front elevation accurately sized for 4mm scale can form a perfectly workable bending guide for the handrail. Cut out the relevant section of the photocopy and stick it to a piece of flat, stiff card. Where a drawing isn't available, it is usually possible to make a simple card template by working directly off of the model. Cut the card to sit on a convenient datum like the front footplating, and measure/mark the cardinal points of the rail: the position of the top central stanchion, the horizontal centreline of the main rails, the point where the curve around the perimeter of the smokebox door meets this centreline, and – most critically – the extremities of the short horizontal portions of the smokebox-front rail where it returns along the boiler-side.

Handrail bending

When making a one-piece handrail, the first essential is to make sure you start with a piece of wire that is going to be long enough to do the whole job. Nothing is more vexatious than making a corking job of shaping the rail neatly around

the smokebox, only to find it comes up a couple of millimetres short along the boiler-side! To actually form the rail, the usual expedient is to start at the mid-point – generally, the central stanchion on the smokebox front above the door. The first job is to form the curve around the perimeter of the door, which is best accomplished by using the finger-tips in the quest for a smooth, symmetrical curve. If you can find a piece of dowelling slightly under the required diameter to use as a former, that is always helpful. You need it to be a millimetre or two undersize to accommodate the slight degree of spring in the handrail wire.

Once the main smokebox front radius is formed, the short horizontal segments of rail on either side that link to the main handrail alignments along the boiler-sides, can be put in, using the tips of tapered round-jaw pliers to get a neat, small radius where these horizontals join the main curve. Use the template to locate these bends as accurately as possible, as their position is crucial to the overall handrail alignment. Once you have these bends in, check that the rail is all in the same plane by laying it on a flat surface; tweak as required to get it lying true. Once you're happy with the shape of this part of the rail, don't forget to thread on a short handrail stanchion for that top central position, as you won't be able to do this once you've made the return bends that take the handrail around the front corners of the smokebox.

Getting these 'return bends' in exactly the right place is the most critical part of the job, the point at which our template really earns its keep. I like to carry out a double-check by fitting sections of plain handrail wire held in two or three stanchions along the boiler-side such that they project out beyond the smokebox front, using these wires to confirm the positions of the bends marked on the template. Once I'm happy these are accurately plotted, I use a fine-line permanent market to transfer the bend-points to the part-formed handrail as an aid to making the actual bends. These right-angle handrail corners are normally of very small radius, calling for the very tips of the round-nose pliers or, more usually, the regular flat-jaw snipe-nosed pliers. Before you make the second bend, do just check that the centre-top stanchion is still in place on the curved smokebox-front segment of the wire; the corner bend will be too tight to thread it around afterwards!

Fixing boiler handrails

The last stage is to tweak the front corner bends with the snipe-noses to get the rails down each side of the boiler nicely parallel, and to ensure that the smokebox-front portion of the rail sits truly vertical when the handrails are in place. Then it is a case of threading on the appropriate combination of handrail stanchions to each side-rail before trimming the rear of the rails where they meet the side tank-front or cab-front (assuming they are not locating into socket-holes at these junctures). This trimming is a job I like to do in two bites; an initial chomp to leave the rails a millimetre or two over length, then a final accurate snip with the flush-cutting nippers as the rails are actually installed.

I always prefer to thread the stanchions on to the rail and enter them in the holes in the boiler side as I locate the rails in

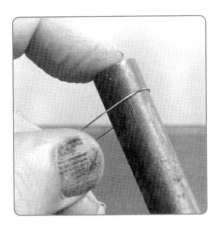
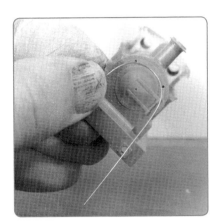

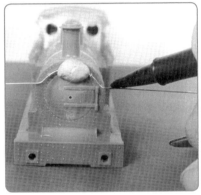

ABOVE *Forming and fitting a one-piece boiler handrail; one of the trickier jobs in model locomotive construction. The curve around the smokebox door is made first, then the horizontal sections leading out to the elbow returns into the boiler-side rails are formed. The elbow position is marked with a felt pen, but before the return bends are made the smokebox-front handrail stanchion(s) must be threaded on! With the return bends made, the boiler-side stanchions are threaded on and the rails trimmed to final length at the rear. Lastly, the stanchions are secured in place – with gel cyano in the case of a plastic body like this, although the merest touch of the soldering-iron was used to secure the handrails into the stanchions.*

place, rather than pre-fixing the stanchions and then trying to thread the rails through them. I always essay a complete 'trial fit' before attempting to permanently install handrails as in 40-plus years of trying, I've never yet managed to produce a set of rails that did not call for a spot of adjustment!

On a plastic body, I find it far easier to get everything nicely in alignment when I can tweak the alignment of stanchions or fiddle their fit in the holes as needed. Once I'm happy with the sit of the rails, I fix them by easing the stanchions out slightly against the spring of the wire and adding a drop of gap-filling cyano to the exposed shank before easing the rail back into place. Start at the smokebox front corners and work aft down each side in turn.

The last job is to 'lock' the rails in place in the stanchions so they can't move fore-or-aft or slide out. You don't need to do this at every stanchion; two a side is enough. I go for the smokebox-side one nearest the front corner, and the last but one at the rear of the boiler side. You can either fix the rails

with a drop of cyano or be bold and add a dab of flux followed by a swift touch with a tiny droplet of 145° solder atip the trusty Antex.

Short rails and grabs

Short rails held in stanchions are a simpler form of the main boiler handrails, so call for no further comment as they are made in the same way from the same bits. Elbow-ended 'staple' grabs, on the other hand, are a totally different proposition, as they have to be accurately bent to shape and secured directly in the moulded plastic footplate, cabside, bunker, or whatever. This can be accomplished in one of two ways: the rails can be set into holes pre-drilled in the plastic mouldings and held with cyano, or they can be melted in using the small instrument soldering iron. The former method calls for considerable accuracy both in regard to the matching of the hole locations to the tails of the grab-rails and also the fit of the wire diameter into the actual hole. This wants to be as tight as possible, the ideal being a force fit, which is the way Bachmann *et al* do it back in Dongguan (and probably the reason they use oversize wire).

However, drilling an accurate 0.33mm hole in a plastic moulding is not an easy proposition. For a start, finding a 0.33mm drill-bit is far from easy, and even if you do manage to run one down it will be expensive, and very fragile. As small drills just *love* to bind in plastic, it is all-too-probable that it will snap sooner rather than later! Also, the amount of force you can apply to a 0.33mm-diameter wire grab to push it into a tight-fitting socket is somewhat limited. It is horribly easy to end up with a kinked or misshapen grab. The usual compromise, therefore, is to drill the holes at 0.4mm, which is

ABOVE *When faced with doing anything to a location as awkward as a bunker rear, the first problem is to find some way of holding the model so you can get at it. This picture shows how I often arrange things, using a loco cradle and a piece of stripwood to get the engine with its bottom in the air. Here, I'm using a 0.5mm drill to centre-pop the handrail location at one end.*

ABOVE AND BELOW *Melting-in a grab-iron. The first picture shows the asymmetric form of the grab, with one tail longer than the other. The long tail goes in first, located in the centre-pop at one end, as in the second view, which shows the soldering iron (an Antex CS 15W) being touched-on to melt the long tail part-way into position. The third photo shows the card spacer being used to locate the grab while it is finally melted into place with the spacer in place to protect the bunker surface and preventing the grab sinking. It is surprising just how much chivvying-around you can do to get it sitting just so, as in the final picture. Any molten plastic forced out by the melting operation will form a raised collar around the base of the grab, which can be readily cut off with the tip of a scalpel.*

a rather slack fit, and rely on a gap-filling cyano to glue the grab in place. This is not a particularly satisfactory arrangement as rails fixed in this way are somewhat prone to come adrift and either fall out, or get pushed in flat against the tank-side, or whatever. The oversize hole also looks a bit odd, as there is no equivalent on the full-size animal.

Melting the tails of the grabs into place overcomes all these problems and is nowhere as dodgy a proposition as it sounds. The trick is to make the two tails of unequal length by a millimetre or two, which means you initially only have to worry about locating one end (the longer tail) of the grab accurately. I drill a tiny centre-pop mark to aid this, as shown in the illustrations. Only once this initial location is established do you need to worry about where the other tail goes, after which it is a case of heating each end of the grab in turn to ease the tails gently into place. A simple card spacer of appropriate thickness is all you need to get the grab set out at the correct distance from the loco and nicely parallel with the underlying surface. The result is a grab that sits and looks both prototypical and true to scale, while being adequately robust.

Plumbing

Injectors and water-feeds, steam pipes various, manifolds, valves, unions and connections of all sorts, vacuum brake ejectors and air pumps, compressed air lines, lubricators and oil-ways, even electric cable conduits – the average steam locomotive is festooned with a veritable plethora of variegated plumbing. Furthermore, this tangled skein of pipework – oft-repaired, altered and added-to – is one aspect of the prototype that can almost be guaranteed to vary from engine to engine, so modelling it accurately is a clear signature for a portrait model of a particular engine.

Replicating pipework in miniature is very akin to handrail modelling. Indeed, as already noted, in reality many locomotive handrails also served as pipe runs. On older RTR models, pipes – like handrails – were frequently reproduced as raised rounded ridges, or at least they were when they were reproduced at all. More often than not, of course, a great deal of such detail was simply ignored and omitted. Only the best of contemporary RTR models can lay claim to a full suite of plumbing, much of it in the form of fine push-fit mouldings in flexible plastic. These look OK and resist handling well, but the nature of the material used – which has a very smooth and shiny surface to which paint is reluctant to adhere – makes them a little unrealistic and difficult to weather and

RIGHT *There's a surprising amount of plumbing on even a clean-limbed British loco, never mind one of those pipe-festooned foreign jobs. This is the vacuum ejector and lubricator pipework on a BR standard Class 4 2-6-4T.*

blend in with the basic paintwork. And, of course, the limitations of the manufacturing process mean that only one pipework configuration can usually be reproduced, which may or may not match the particular prototype you happen to be modelling.

All of this means that pipework modelling is an important area of the detailing process. Fortunately, it is also a relatively straightforward proposition. The basic material is, of course, wire in a variety of diameters – together with washers, small BA nuts and odd scraps of brass tube, strip and sheet. Plus, such appropriate detail castings – ejectors, injectors, clack valves, lubricators and so on – as might be available from commercial sources. The exact size and type of wire needed will vary from prototype to prototype; long, straight runs of pipework – such as boiler-side vacuum-ejector or blower pipes – are best modelled in straight-drawn hard brass wire of appropriate diameter, whereas the more sinuous pipery is better made in a softer wire such as copper.

Locomotive plumbing ranges in size from fine-bore lubrication tubing of ³⁄₈in or less diameter up through high-pressure air or steam-feeds to blowers, pumps, generators and so on at 1–1¾in up to water and vacuum pipes at 2½–3in. (These are all inside diameters, so the pipes are a bit more on the outside.)

For 4mm modelling, the common wire sizes for pipework are as follows. Lubricator lines, 36–40 SWG/0.193–0.122mm copper – respectively, domestic 5-amp fuse wire or a single strand from ordinary 7/40 layout wiring flex. For the pressure-feed steam/air lines, 30/26/23 SWG gauge copper or 0.33/0.45/0.6mm hard-drawn brass wire. Large-diameter water and vacuum plumbing calls for 22/21/20/19 SWG copper, or 0.7/0.8/0.9/1.0mm straight brass. Flanged joints are normally represented by turned brass spacing washers – as sold for crankpins, valve gears and so on – while screwed unions can be convincingly (if expensively!) modelled using small (12–16BA) brass nuts. Common, straightforward sleeved joints and elbows can, fortunately, can be confected far more cheaply, using wraps of the fine 40SWG copper wire.

Fabricating and fixing plain pipework

Basically, making plain model pipework comes down to forming the appropriate bits of wire to shape, adding joint and valve detail, trimming to an exact fit (no gaps in real pipes!) and fixing it in place. A simple straight pipe – such as a blower feed or vacuum ejector exhaust (both of which usually run straight down the boiler-side from the cab to side of the smokebox in line with the chimney centre) can be made simply from appropriate straight-drawn brass wire. Typically this is 0.6/0.7mm for the blower and 0.8/0.9mm for the exhaust, with a 90° elbow bent into the smokebox end. The blower pipe – being a live steam feed – will normally have a screwed union to the elbow, represented by a 14BA nut; the exhaust pipe can have a screwed union or a sleeve, the latter represented by a double-turn of the 40-gauge wire and a trace of solder, as in the sketch. Where the pipe passes into the smokebox there is normally a flange, modelled with a suitable-sized (14 or 12BA) washer.

Fixing such a plain pipe is a case of drilling a suitable hole for each end and making and fitting an appropriate number of pipe brackets. These serve much the same function as handrail stanchions, but are usually much simpler and plainer. Once again, the humble ¹⁄₃₂in split-pin already commended as a handrail stanchion can be pressed into service to represent heftier brackets

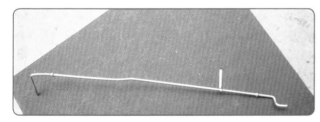

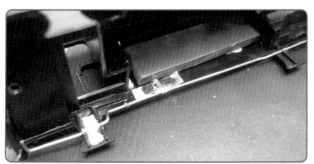

LEFT AND BELOW *Making and fitting a bit of plain pipework – like the steam-heat pipe that runs along the nearside of the example 'Jinty' – is a straightforward exercise in bending a bit of 0.8mm brass wire and adding a couple of dummy joints from twisted wire, and the odd mounting bracket from fine strip. Fixing the finished pipe to the loco called for a combination of melting-in (behind front step) and gluing. I used cyano reinforced with patches of cyano-soaked tissue – a surprisingly robust form of joint.*

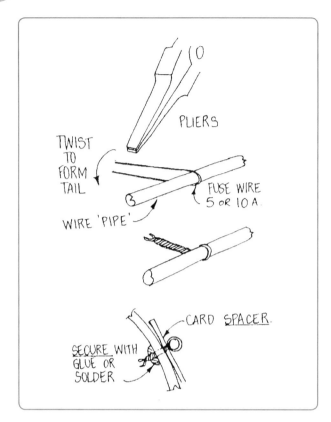

on larger pipes, closed-down as needed with the snipe-nosed pliers. Lighter brackets and fittings on smaller pipes I make from fine (40 SWG) copper wire or very fine strip (30 SWG wire, hammered flat), depending on the prototype arrangement.

For a typical narrow bracket I make a single turn of the 40 SWG round the pipe and twist the ends tightly together to make a shank or spigot to locate it into a suitable hole drilled in the boiler side. This shank is reinforced and the bracket fixed in place on the pipe with a smear of flux and a sparing wipe with the soldering iron. The pipe is secured to the model with gel cyano or epoxy in the bracket-mounting holes and at each end.

Complex pipework

The real fun in model locomotive plumbing comes with those tangles where different pipe-runs meet and either pass each other by, or join together at a 'T', manifold (a casting to which a number of pipes of common purpose are joined), or some valve or fitting. Either way, fabricating such a rat's nest is usually an exercise in 3-D modelling, best executed in nicely malleable copper wires so that the various bends can be easily formed, and the whole assembly tweaked readily into final alignment during installation. Before worrying about that stage, however, we first have to solder together all the bits of wire, tube, washers, nuts and so on forming the pipework and related fittings – a real bit of modelling!

The key to success when conducting such shenanigans with the soldering iron is to be able to hold all the bits and

ABOVE *Fixing pipework with twisted-wire brackets.*

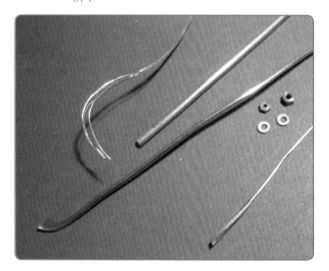

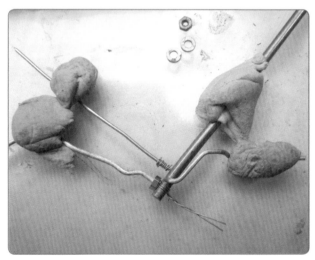

ABOVE AND RIGHT *Fabricating an injector, typical of more complex pipework. Materials include wire of various sizes, fine brass tube, fine strip, plus small BA nuts and washers. The bits are bent to shape and then held in the correct alignment by being Blu-Tacked to a piece of plate glass. They are then soldered together to give the result in the last picture, a fair approximation of the exhaust-steam ejector on an N class Mogul.*

pieces firmly in alignment while the various joints are made. This calls for a nice flat base (I use a small handbag mirror) and a good supply of Blu-Tack. I aim to get as many pieces of my putative pipe anchored to the base as possible with generous blobs of the sticky putty, leaving nice long tails on each piece to enable me to put extra bends in as needed to get all the pipes into the right relationship. Even so, it is rare to be able to hold all the necessary components in place at one go and conduct the soldering in a single instalment, so it will almost certainly be necessary to protect existing joins from stray heat as additions are made. For this purpose, little wads of wet tissue (loo-roll is best) are surprisingly effective. Keep the tissue as soggy as possible and mould it tightly around the joint you need to protect. Even so, you don't want to hang around when making 'successor' joints; a clean workpiece, a modest dollop of Powerflow and a clean, well-tinned bit are the order of the day.

Rivets

Adding rivets as details to a moulded-plastic loco body is usually called for under one of two headings. Reinstatement of rivets damaged during refining or replacement operations, and adding extra rivet detail where the manufacturer has left it off, or where a particular prototype locomotive had additional or alternative riveting arrangements. I used to use one of two manual techniques for this work. For larger/ more-prominent rivet- or bolt-heads, I adopted the plastic-sheet wagon-builder's favourite ploy of attaching tiny cubes (10 x 10 x 10thou) of styrene sheet material with solvent cement, while for smaller and subtler encrustations, I melted short lengths of fine copper wire into the moulding and then snipped these off just above the surface with the flush-cutting nippers and rounded the stub off with fine abrasive paper. Neither technique gives a perfect match for a nice, neat moulded-on rivet head, but the wire variant, particularly, can be surprisingly effective at reinstating the odd rivet that has gone AWOL.

However, nowadays there is a simple and far more effective alternative for such retro-riveting work, in the form of

ABOVE These are 3-D decal rivets by Micro-Mark, applied like any other waterslide transfer and hence almost infinitely adjustable. The only snag is that I am not aware of a UK stockist, so you have to get them direct from the USA by mail order. One pack – about $15 – is pretty much a lifetime's supply.

waterslide rivet decals. These have been developed by Micro-Mark in the USA (www.MicroMark.com) and are such a simple and effective idea that you wonder why no-one thought of it years ago! The rivets come on sheets containing a good selection of head sizes and spacings, which should enable you to match almost any pre-existing model or prototype riveting.

Micro-Mark's rivets are applied just like any other form of craft waterslide transfer: cut the desired items from the sheet with a sharp craft-knife, working close to give the minimum of extra backing film around the rivets. Then simply soak the decals in warm water until the film releases and slide/chivvy your rivets into place. Once you have the dear little pustules properly positioned, 'snug them down' with a decal-setting solution like Micro-Sol or Carrs Transfix, which will ensure close adhesion and lose the edges of the (very thin) backing film. Adhesion of these transfers is excellent on metal or plastic and on curved or irregular-shaped surfaces. They are the absolute bee's knees for adding rivet detail to plastic loco bodies and, once painted, look just as if moulded-on.

Lamp-irons

These used to be the acme of aspiration in the good old days of 'super-detailing', but nowadays are taken as a given on modern RTR locos. However, they are one of the few areas where the expediencies of production and the need to allow for handling mitigate against a true-scale item. A full-sized lamp-iron is normally made from flat metal strip about 3in wide and little more than half an inch thick. That scales out at 1mm x 8thou at 4mm/1ft – and 8thou strip is pretty delicate stuff in anybody's book! Most etched kits give you brackets 10–12thou thick, while traditional DIY loco builders often opted for brackets made from 1mm x 15thou 'boiler-band strip' material. Even the best RTR iterations are considerably thicker than that. The lamp-irons on the Bachmann '45xx' that I've been using as my guinea-pig are 23thou thick, and they are amongst the most delicate I've yet come across. That said,

BELOW Reinstating or adding rivets the old way: tiny .010in cubes of Plastikard Microstrip applied with the tip of a fine brush and held with a dab of Mek-Pak.

they are just about acceptable to my eyes, but the clunky 30thou thick affairs on the same maker's J39 and SR N are definite candidates for replacement.

The lamp-irons on the tender rears of these engines (and many other comparable RTR models) are also decidedly lacking in realism, being either moulded-on half-relief affairs, or simplified and undersized pieces of strip: too thick, but too short. Either way, they are also prime candidates for replacement with properly formed brackets made from suitable strip and cyano-fixed or, preferably, melted into place.

Moulded-on lamp brackets also featured on the smokeboxes of many older RTR models, while footplate brackets were notable only for their absence, which at least relieved one of the irksome chore of carving them off, something that is regrettably necessary with the tender-rear offerings (fairly straightforward) and smokebox afflictions (often tricky). The removal technique is just as described in the last chapter for other unwanted moulded-on details.

Forming model lamp-irons

Making replacement or new-fit lamp-irons is an exercise in accurate bending of suitable metal strip, in which capacity, half-hard brass about 10thou thick is to be preferred to hard brass or nickel-silver. This is because many lamp-irons, most notably, smokebox-front and tender-rear varieties incorporating a lamp 'shelf', call for the strip to be folded into crisp 180° bends, a requirement that can all-too-often result in fatigue fracture if attempted in too hard a metal. Slightly pliable lamp-irons will also bend rather than breaking off if subjected to occasional handling damage, which is much the better option.

The key tools for lamp-iron production are our best snipe-nose pliers and the flush-cutting shears, plus a fine (second-cut) flat Swiss file. How you make the actual irons depends on how you are going to fix them in place. If they are going to be held with cyano, then the complete iron can be formed,

trimmed and finished and then positioned with tweezers for installation. But if you're going to melt the brackets into place, then it is a good idea to leave yourself a nice long tail to hold the thing with, while you're plying the soldering iron, trimming them to final length once they are in place.

Actually producing the irons is just like producing the real thing – basically an exercise in forming nice crisp bends in strip metal; the difference is we use precision pliers and work 'cold' rather than heating the metal to red heat and belting it over an anvil with a great big hammer! Bending lamp-irons to shape with pliers means that the various bends will be slightly radiused, which is just as they should be.

Prototype lamp-irons come in a variety of shapes and sizes – see the illustrations – with the GWR (of course!) doing their own thing and tacking them on the loco sideways. Most lamp-iron configurations are straightforward enough to bend up from our flat strip – except for GWR tender/bunker-rear 'shelf' brackets, where the side placement creates a bit of a problem as it requires the strip from which the bracket is made to incorporate a horizontal right-angled bend 'in the flat'. This is something the full-sized blacksmith can accomplish a great deal more easily than Joe Modeller with his pliers. You can buy detailing frets incorporating L-shaped 'blanks' to facilitate the manufacture of such brackets, or you can compromise slightly on the exact shape by adopting the system shown in my sketch, and fold the strip over onto itself to create the required bend, which leaves a not-quite-right corner with a 45° angled edge rather than a curve.

If you're making 'finished' irons for mounting with tweezers, don't forget to radius the top corners with your fine file; the lamp-iron with absolute square corners is found only on model locomotives! If you have left a handling tail on your irons, this radiusing will have to be done once they are secured in place – see below. Some companies fitted lamp-irons with circular-arc tops, calling for rather more work with the file or the use of suitably shaped etched blanks. Appropriate blanks will also be needed for a few odd-shaped brackets, such as the inverted 'T' pattern favoured by the LSWR and many Scottish railways.

BELOW *A shelf lamp-iron for a smokebox door or tender/bunker rear – bent to shape from .010in brass strip. The short leg on the right has been cropped to a point to form the melt-in tongue by which the bracket will be mounted on the model. The actual lamp-iron is left long to give a handle during fixing and is cropped to length once the bracket is in place.*

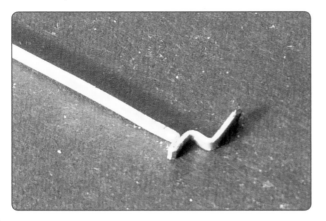

BELOW *GWR offset lamp irons.*

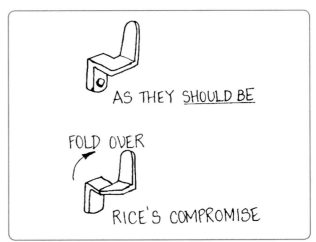

AS THEY SHOULD BE

FOLD OVER

RICE'S COMPROMISE

Fitting lamp-irons

Prototype lamp-irons are arranged to have a fixing 'land' arranged to sit flat on the mounting surface, to which they are then secured by riveting. On an all-metal model, such a bracket can be spot-soldered in place, but this convenient and mechanically strong mounting technique is obviously not suitable for a moulded plastic superstructure. No matter how super your 'superglue', just gluing the irons in place 'flat' on to the body moulding is not a workably robust method in my experience. At the very least you need to reinforce the join with a little 0.45mm wire spigot, which calls for some tricky drilling work to provide the necessary hole in the lamp-iron – best attempted before the iron is bent to shape. A corresponding hole is drilled at the mounting location on the body moulding, and a short length of spigot wire glued into it with a spot of gel cyano. Any excess should be cleaned away from the mounting surface with tissue to ensure the bracket sits flat. I let the glue holding the spigot cure hard before attempting to fit the actual lamp-iron. This is offered up and positioned with the fine tweezers and secured with the tiniest drop of thin cyano applied on the tip of a fine piece of wire. This is very much a case of 'less is more'… Once the glue has cured hard, the excess spigot wire is snipped off with the flush-cutting shears, just slightly proud of the lamp-iron foot, and it will give a very good impression of the prototype's securing rivet.

However, even when spigotted on as described above, glue-fitted lamp-irons are still somewhat delicate and prone to handling damage. A far more robust mounting can be made by incorporating an extra bend into the lamp-iron foot to provide a locating tongue that can be fitted into an appropriate slot in the body moulding, the arrangement used by most RTR makers. For factory-fitted models, the required slot is obviously incorporated when the moulding is made and the iron installed (usually force-fitted) during the assembly process. If over-thick factory-fit lamp-irons are being replaced with something a little more delicate, then it makes obvious sense to reuse the original mounting slots. However, steps will have to be made to take up the slack in the fit of the new irons in the old holes. Often, all that is required in this regard is to put a further 180° fold into the locating tongue to produce a double-thickness of metal. This can be push-fitted and held with a dab of gel cyano.

The problem comes when the lamp-iron needs to be fitted to a plastic body bereft of pre-formed mounting slots. Actually drilling such a slot to make it a good fit for a brass-strip lamp iron is a very ticklish proposition – which is where the melt-in technique comes into its own, as it automatically produces its

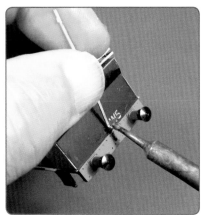

ABOVE *The melt-in fixing of lamp-irons on the plastic body of the 'Jinty', which is much as for grab-irons, with a drilled dimple to aid location. After fixing the irons are trimmed to length, have their corners rounded off if appropriate, are finally aligned, and are set truly upright.*

own slot to a very close tolerance. It really is surprisingly simple to fit lamp-irons in this way. If you're worried about the potential for disaster, try a few practice runs on some plastic sheet or a scrap plastic body moulding of some sort. The main drawback – if that is not too strong a word – is the need to leave a decent-length handling tail on the lamp-iron itself, which means it will need to be trimmed to final length and the top corners radiused after it has been fixed in place, which is not actually as difficult as it might appear.

The illustrations show the order of business: cutting the tip of the locating tongue to a point, and drilling a little location dimple helps ensure the bracket finishes up in the right place. Then it is held by the tail and simply pushed gently into place with the tip of the small soldering-iron. I do this in several short stages with pauses in between, to ensure that the bracket does not get too hot. Usually, the basic melt-in mounting provides a secure enough fixing. However, where it is possible to gain access to the rear side of the mounting surface, which is usually no problem on loco footplates and tender rears, but not quite so easy on smokeboxes and bunkers, I make the melt-in mounting tongue long enough to come right through the thickness of the moulding by a millimetre or so. This allows the excess to be bent over inside the model as an additional securing measure.

To facilitate trimming to length and corner radiusing, the bracket is bent to protrude by around 45°, being straightened and aligned to its final position once this has been done. As an aid the trimming and rounding operation, a pair of tiny 'nicks' can be filed in either side of the strip at the bracket-top location when the lamp-iron is formed. The last job in the fitting process is to use the tip of a sharp craft-knife to carve away any slight lip raised on the surface of the moulding, adjacent to the tongue by the plastic displaced during the melt-in process.

Note that in the (common) case of 'solid' bunker/tender rear moulded lamp-brackets being replaced with strip, the original prototypical cosmetic mounting detail – the actual mounting land and its securing rivets – can usually be retained. Only the portion of the bracket above this needs to be carved away and the replacement formed with the melt-in tongue arranged at the lamp shelf level, rather than at the foot . This is a simple ploy which looks surprisingly effective.

Smokebox door handles

These are an essential fitment on any steam locomotive not possessing a dog-clipped door (one held shut by a series of screwed clamps set around the perimeter) – a system that, in Britain, was commonly found on Midland Railway locomotives from the Deeley period onwards, together with their LMS successors. It was also seen on Maunsell locomotives on the SECR and SR. For efficient steaming, the prototype needs to maintain a near-vacuum in the smokebox, which means the door has to clamped tight shut to give a good seal. Dog-clips are the best way of achieving this – but come smokebox-cleaning time (at least once a day), a half-dozen or more clamps had to be undone by spanner before the door could be opened – a time-consuming process. So most railways adopted the door secured with a central dart and a single screw clamp, which did not produce as effective a seal, but was far, far quicker to open and close.

The actual dart was of arrowhead form and was fitted on the inner end of a short shaft passing through a reinforced boss in the centre of the smokebox door. This shaft had two lever handles (or a single inner lever and a hand-wheel on some engines) mounted on the outer end, the outer handle or hand-wheel being effectively a clamping nut running on a screw thread forming the outer end of the shaft. To secure the door, the dart was set in a horizontal position using the inner handle, which was loosely fastened to the shaft in line with the dart, and located through a slot in a substantial securing bar that spanned the inside of the smokebox opening horizontally at the mid-point. The handle was then rotated through 90° – normally downwards – to bring the dart into the vertical position to lock the door. The whole shebang was then clamped in place and the door-sealing compression applied by screwing the outer lever handle or hand-wheel vigorously down the threaded portion of the shaft to bear hard on the inner handle and door boss. This pulled the dart tight against the rear of the securing bar and squeezed the door firmly into place.

In terms of our models, what we see of this arrangement is the outer part of the shaft and the two lever handles (or single handle and hand-wheel) plus, usually, the raised circular reinforcing boss or flange where the shaft passes through the centre of the smokebox door. Characteristically, these lever handles were quite slender – little more than an inch in diameter – but often of surprising length, especially the outer clamping handle, which could easily extend to 18in or so. At 4mm/1ft scale this makes, perforce, for a somewhat delicate little assembly, so the usual compromise on most RTR engines has been to mould all or part of it (usually the inner lever and boss) integrally with the smokebox door.

Older models have an all-solid representation, with more recent offerings running to a free-standing outer handle. In reality, of course, both handles stood some way proud of the door, but in plastic such a refinement is somewhat flimsy and few RTR makers – even today – essay such an arrangement. Hornby's M7 and Thompson L1 are among the few honourable exceptions. In truth, plastic moulding is not the ideal way to produce this sort of detail, so an upgrade to an aftermarket lost-wax cast or turned brass replacement is often a worthwhile refinement, even on quite recent models. On older models with solid smokebox door handles, it is a visual necessity. As always, photographic reference is needed to show what you're aiming for, while it is a good idea to look hard at the replacement offerings. There are quite a few chunky and oversized specimens floating about that look considerably less convincing than the plastic originals!

Actually replacing moulded-on smokebox door handles is not a particularly daunting proposition. As usual, carving off the original is the difficult bit – accomplished as already described for removing other plastic approximations such as handrails and pipework. The door boss is normally provided as part of the replacement assembly, so that has to go as well while you're at it. Working *across* the

LEFT AND BELOW *The ins and outs of the smokebox door dart fastening. The dart locates in a narrow slot in the locking bar, which means that the inner positioning handle is always close to vertical, as on the left.*

ABOVE *Here is a nice fine set of turned-brass smokebox door dart handles by Alan Gibson, fitted to my NER E1 0-6-0T.*

door lessens the likelihood of lopping an unintentional chunk out of the door hinge straps, and the use of angle-ended rubbing sticks is the best way of smoothing the door centre.

Before you smooth off too much of the original, don't forget to pick up the door centre position and drill a hole for the shank of the replacement handle assembly. Fitting the replacement is a case of gluing the shank of the new part(s) in place and, in the case of the turned-brass variety, securing the handles in an appropriate disposition. In which case, you need to ensure the inner handle is vertical (or very nearly so), otherwise your dart won't be 'locked'. In clockwise terms, this handle is almost invariably pointing to the six o'clock position. By contrast, the outer handle can theoretically be anywhere round the clockface, depending on how tight the door has been clamped and how worn the dart is. Although, that said, most seem to end up somewhere between a bit over seven and round about three o'clock.

Bufferbeams

There is no doubt that a fully and correctly detailed front bufferbeam, with a decent set of authentic buffers, a scale screw or three-link coupling and properly modelled brake and steam-heat connections, gives any model loco a definite lift in realism and prototype character, as it is very much part of the 'face' of the engine. On tank locomotives, the rear beam is equally prominent and calls for the same treatment, and although tender rear beams are generally less in the public eye, I still find it worth taking some trouble over them, especially on general-purpose 0-6-0s and other locos likely to do much tender-first running.

The first step in creating a convincing bufferbeam on any model loco – RTR or kit-built – is to discard, reject and generally do away with that crashing eyesore, the tension-lock coupling. Hornby-Dublo banished auto-couplers from the front ends of their express passenger power way back in 1937, and we should at least do the same – although hopefully the cosmetic hook-and-link we will be fitting in its place will be somewhat more refined than the Dublo effort!

For practical purposes on all other engines needing to couple with tension-lock fitted stock, a simple and far-less-obtrusive loop of fine wire set at the appropriate height fore and aft will work just as well, while permitting a full and proper set of bufferbeam fittings to be modelled. I bend such loops to shape from 0.45mm hard brass or nickel-silver wire and either melt them into place in the lower edge of the bufferbeam, using the technique already described, or solder them to the frames or spacers of a replacement chassis.

Buffer upgrades

Buffers of the appropriate type realistically modelled and mounted are obviously a prime requisite for a convincing

BELOW LEFT AND RIGHT *Buffers are a weak area on many older RTR models, like the Mainline/Bachmann J72. What you get is on the left in the first picture, what you should have is on the right! Upgrading typically involves providing a Plastikard or sheet-metal overlay for the bufferbeam, as Andy McCallum has done on his model in the second view.*

bufferbeam. While the latest offerings from the big RTR makers come equipped with authentic, functional (usually sprung) buffers located on the correct centres and set at the right ride height, such rectitude is new-won. Many less-recent RTR locos – plenty of second-generation models included – came with buffers that neither looked the part nor functioned effectively. Fitting a decent set of turned buffers, preferably sprung, in place of inadequate original equipment is one of the oldest detail upgrades in the whole loco-modelling book.

Nowadays, there is a wide choice of suitable aftermarket replacements available from Gibson, Markits, Maygib, Slaters *et al*, covering all the more common patterns and even quite a few of the distinctive pre-Grouping styles. So finding something suitable is not usually too much of a problem. However, as so often is the case, on older prototypes the only sure guide to authenticity is a photo of your chosen subject engine, as buffers were one of those fitments that got replaced or changed and different locomotives from within one common class may have been equipped with any one of a number of different patterns at different times. I have even come across locos with odd buffers, i.e. not all of the same type!

Removing unsatisfactory buffers from RTR models is either very easy – in that they are a simple push-fit turning or moulding that can be pulled out and discarded – or a pig of a job, where they are moulded integrally with the buffer-beam. In which case, sawing or carving them off usually does for the rest of the buffer-beam detail! Where this happens, the best approach is to simply file the whole buffer-beam smooth and re-instate the missing detail by other means, preferably working to a good photographic reference as the exact disposition of rivets and fittings about the bufferbeam is another feature that varied from engine to engine.

An overlay in shim metal or thin plastic sheet is often a good way of producing a nicely detailed bufferbeam, as the rivets can be simply and crisply embossed with a rivet-punch or scriber. The Micro-mark transfer rivets already mentioned also work well in this context, while a few of the replacement loco chassis kits – like the Mainly Trains J72 illustrated as an example – include photo-etched bufferbeam overlays on the frets.

Fitting new sprung buffers is usually straightforward enough, being simply a matter of drilling suitable size holes in the right position and gluing the shanks of the replacement buffers in place. It is normally possible to pick up the appropriate locations from the remains of the sawn-off

originals, but where this is not certain – or where you are not convinced the RTR buffers were correctly located in the first place (not unknown!) – then it is best to go from first principles and set the buffers out from the loco centreline. This is, of course, the draw-hook position. Real buffers are on 5ft 9in centres, an inconvenient 23mm at 4mm scale, or 11.5mm either side of the hook. Life would have been a lot easier if they had settled on a round 6ft for the buffer centres!

If you are using a bufferbeam overlay as suggested above, then it is often far easier to set everything out on this then use it as a template to position the necessary holes in the actual beam. Fixing buffers is a job I prefer to accomplish with a smear of five-minute epoxy rather than risking cyano, which can all-too-easily get where it is not wanted and gum everything solid! Where replacement sprung buffers come in unassembled form I prefer to fit the buffer housings and any beam overlays and other detail (see next section) first, then prime and paint the whole bufferbeam before fitting the buffer heads and springs as a final operation. A drop of light oil in the buffer housings before the heads are installed is a useful insurance against corrosion and gumming-up of the buffer action.

Cosmetic couplings

Doing away with the unsightly tension-lock in favour of an unobtrusive wire loop enables us to fit our models with cosmetic reproductions of the prototype's coupling arrangements – a draw-hook and either a twin-shackle screw-coupling or a three-link chain. The latter is only encountered on shunters and unfitted goods engines, so normally it is the screw shackle we are dealing with. Nowadays, most RTR makers give you a fairly decent reproduction of the hook, but just about nobody provides the actual coupling, so this will need sourcing elsewhere.

For very many years, the standard fit has been a somewhat-chunky ready-made screw coupling available from a number of sources. This was originally intended for functional use on layouts employing manual coupling systems, being in

BELOW Etched fold-up screw couplings like these Roxey offerings both look good and function well in a practical role if needed. They are not too fiddly to assemble and can be treated chemically with a 'blackening solution' to give a good base colour for weathering. Prototypical link or screw couplings make a huge difference to the whole 'face' of a model locomotive.

consequence very considerably oversize both in hook and link. As we are only expecting our coupling to do cosmetic duty, we can opt for something a bit closer to scale and more visually refined – although not, perhaps, going as far as the other extreme: Exactoscale's DIY dead-to-scale, fully working affair. Quite exquisite, but experienced watchmakers only need apply…

That leaves two middle-of-the-road choices: Springside's neat lost-wax-brass cast dummy screw-coupling, nicely to scale, robust and easy to install, but rigid in the hanging-straight-down position – and hence unsuited to many locomotives, as a glance at a few prototype pictures will suggest. This leaves one of the DIY fold-up etched screw-couplings, available from a number of sources. My own preference is for the version offered by Roxey Mouldings, which seems to me to strike a good compromise between scale size/appearance, ease of assembly and installation, and robustness. Branchlines offer something very similar.

These flexible screw-couplings can be hooked off to the side, doubled on to the draw-hook, or laid over an angled or stand-off shield protecting the ATC gear, where this was fitted (see prototype photos illustrating this section). They can also be used functionally at a pinch, which can be useful for double-heading. Such etched couplings are not too tricky to make, as the picture here shows. I give them a dunk in chemical blackening solution and paint/weather them finally once they are in place, usually as a force-fit in the slot left after removing the RTR hook moulding helped by a spot of epoxy if needed.

Bufferbeam connections

Modern RTR locos may have decent sprung buffers and a goodly sprinkling of rivets about the bufferbeam, but precious few of them can boast a convincing set of vacuum/steam-heat hoses – or 'bags', as these flexible connections were traditionally referred to by generations of railwaymen. Model bufferbeam hose connections have long been a *bête noir* of mine, as they so rarely resemble the real thing. For very many years – several generations, even – there has been on the market a 'universal' wire-wound upright loco vacuum standard. They came with Jamieson kits way back in the early 1950s, while Eames, W&H Models or Hamblings would flog you a pair for five pence in old money (plus $^1/_2$d purchase tax!).

This off-the-peg fitting was standard fare throughout my youth – not to mention adolescence, maturity and dotage – being universally stuck on to any and every 'detailed' locomotive, irrespective of the prototype arrangements. It turned up on locos which should have sported low-mounted vacuum connections, on Westinghouse air-braked engines and, in many cases, on locomotives that did not in reality possess the vacuum brake at all! Quite frequently, one came across it mounted such that would have been impossible to open the smokebox door of the hapless loco. Hardly ever did it convince, as even when it was appropriate in form, it was devoid of almost all prototype detail and the wire-winding was of a stoutness that would have rendered it as flexible as a granite gatepost. But blow me, if this exact same item doesn't *still* turn up on modern models of otherwise-impeccable scale

ABOVE *The front end of a steam loco is an important element of its character, so getting this as correct as possible on our model is well worth the effort. The right shape and location of the vacuum and steam-heat connections and details like the AWS shoe shield behind the coupling are essential if it is to look convincing.* Author's collection

pedigree! Ptah! And that's before one comes on to consider the equally prominent steam-heat hoses called for on any locomotive with passenger-hauling pretensions. They are usually only remarkable by their absence!

In this day and age, you would expect there to be a plethora of hyper-detailed hi-tech aftermarket hosiery to stick about your bufferbeams; but by and large, this isn't so. There is a modest selection of white metal-cast hoses – but these are way too flimsy for a loco that has to earn its keep on the layout, which only leaves a scanty handful of lost-wax brass offerings and those tired old wire-wound efforts to choose from. The basic problem is, of course, that the prototype exhibits wide variation in the shape and positioning of this bufferbeam pipery, which is often very distinctive in form – as I hope the selection of prototype pictures appended in the course of this narrative will suggest. This non-conformity means that 'dedicated' castings would be needed for many loco types – not really a practical commercial proposition for any but the most popular of prototypes.

The prototype

Real vacuum connections are traditionally made of rubberised canvas hosing of about 2½in internal diameter, reinforced externally with a steel wire coil to stop it collapsing in on itself under atmospheric pressure. The rigid metal pipework forming the rest of the vacuum brake system is of similar bore, giving a 3in or so external size. It is often very visible running along the footplate valencing.

Air-brake hoses, by contrast, were of small-bore (usually 1in) thick-walled rubber tubing without wire reinforcement. The associated metal pipework was also on the skinny side and an isolating cock in the brake standard was a normal fitment, so the uncoupled hoses could be left hanging. Vacuum bags are sealed-off when not coupled-up by being parked firmly on the dummy – a fixed connection provided at the base of the vacuum standard. Any loss of vacuum from the hose would result in the brakes leaking 'on', so a vacuum hose with the uncoupled end flapping about in the breeze – as seen on all-too-many models – would, in reality, have resulted in a full emergency brake application!

Steam-heat bags are of similar reinforced construction to the vacuum connections; the pressure of the steam in the train-heating circuit was relatively low, while condensation in the pipework could produce a partial vacuum in certain circumstances. The rigid steam pipework, while being of similar diameter to the vacuum lines, was often lagged – so looked larger. An isolating cock was always fitted at the end of the fixed steam pipework where the bag was joined on.

It is worth pointing out that some railways, notably the GWR and BR (Western Region), removed the steam-heat hoses during the summer months, so all you had was the fixed pipework ending in the shut-off cock, and a bolting flange. It still wants modelling, though! While vacuum or air-brake standards were normally mounted on or above the bufferbeam, the steam-heat connections were almost invariably below the beam with the bag hanging down, usually supported when not in use by a hook and chain.

DIY bufferbeam hoses

Fortunately, making a set of bufferbeam hoses that are accurate to prototype and sufficiently well detailed to look convincing is not a particularly difficult modelling proposition. It involves no more than some bending and twisting of wire and a spot of simple soldering. I always make the bags and their associated fixed pipework as an integrated assembly; the vacuum standard obviously unconnected to anything else is a hoary old modelling chestnut! Giving yourself the attached pipework to hang on to also makes it a lot easier to wind the braiding and mount the completed assembly firmly in place. As with all such detailing projects, the first essential is a good photo that clearly shows the prototype arrangements, as I find this sort of modelling is very much a case of 'going by eye'. Obviously, what you make has got to fit its allotted space on the model, but no amount of measurement will get you the subtle, often three-dimensional, curve of a parked vacuum hose or a dangling steam-heat bag.

The basic materials are wires of various diameters, usually 0.8mm–0.9mm brass or copper for the metal pipework and the core of the flexible hose and 36 or 40 SWG copper filament for the braiding which represents the reinforcing wire coil. The fine copper filament is sourced as already described in the pipework notes above. The method is shown in the little sequence of photos here. I start by forming one end of a length of core wire to the shape of the flexible hose. If using straight-drawn brass wire for your core, it may be found helpful to anneal the end of the wire you're going to bend (i.e. soften by heating to a dull red and then quenching in cold water), particularly if the curve is of tight radius or is a complex three-dimensional shape.

The tapered round-nosed pliers are the tool for this job, as we are after a smooth, flowing shape devoid of kinks. Once you're happy you have a nice shapely curve to your 'bag', the next job is to add the reinforcing coil. This is done before bending any sharp corners or angles into the pipework, as the trick is to wind your coil on a nice unencumbered straight section of the core wire then slide it along to the curved hose portion once you have it all tidy and closed up. Take a length of the filament wire about 4in or so long and wind it as tightly as you can around the core, aiming to keep the coils nicely close-packed, but being careful that they do not overlap. Don't worry if the resulting coil is a bit uneven and 'gappy' in the matter of coil spacing, as it is a simple matter to push the turns up tight after they have been wound.

Once you have wound enough coil to sheath the length of your bag with a bit to spare, cut off the surplus filament (which won't be much as it is surprising how much 40-gauge it takes to wind a half-inch or so of coil), and push the finished braiding along the wire and on to the curve of the flexible connection. Get the top of the coil in the right position for the top of the bag, and secure it in place with a dot of flux and a tiny drop of solder. Trim off any excess coil at the free end of the hose and repeat the spot-soldering operation. That is all you need to retain the coil in place. I have never found the need to flood the whole thing in solder as some folk do.

Once the basic flexible hose is in place, the rest of the fixed pipework can be bent to shape to match the prototype configuration and to fit the model. The objective is to make the whole thing look like continuous plumbing, so gaps and loose ends are to be avoided. The last job is to add the incidental details: the coupling and dummy at the vacuum connection end, the clamp where the hose joins the fixed pipework, and any unions or securing brackets on the latter. The illustrations show how I represent these features with a turn or two of filament or a scrap of strip, once again all secured with the merest trace of solder.

Real vacuum or steam plumbing is usually secured to the bufferbeam or footplate with a clamp or strap-type pipe brackets, made as already described for general pipework. Very often, you can use these mountings for their prototype purpose, gluing the trimmed-down tails of the split-pins or wire wrappings into holes drilled in the loco body moulding – a job for which I once again prefer quick-setting epoxy adhesive to cyano-acrylate. I usually give my completed pipework and hoses a quick blast of sprat primer before mounting it on the model for final painting and blending-in.

Steam-heat connections are made in exactly the same way as vacuum hoses, the differences coming in the detail. The lever-handle shut-off cock on the bag connection, and the suspension chain or cable is used to support the uncoupled, parked hose. Again, the pictures show my approach to these details.

A rather different proposition is the skinny plumbing and small-but-smooth hoses of the Westinghouse air-brake. Here, the core wire is 0.6mm diameter, and the hoses are represented by short lengths of fine PVC wire sleeving. Unfortunately, normal layout-wire is too beefy for this purpose. What I use is stripped from old single-strand GPO telephone wire, but

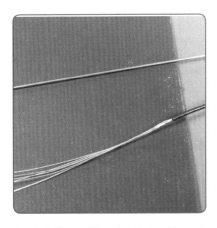
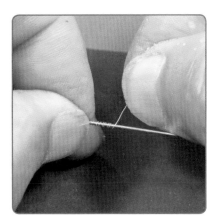
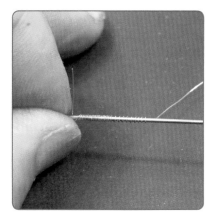

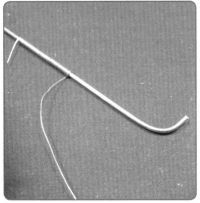
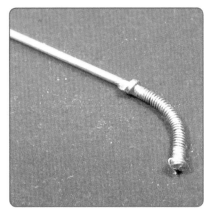

Fabricating a vacuum standard by winding 40-gauge wire around a core of brass or copper wire about 0.8mm in diameter. The coil is wound relatively loosely then closed up, as in the second picture. It is also wound near the end of a straight length of core wire, then pushed along on to a curve of appropriate form for the required connection, and soldered in place, as in the fifth picture. This is much easier than trying to wind a curved coil.

Note the doubled-end coils at each extremity, representing the clamp at the inner end and the connection fitting at the outer. The standard is then bent to shape and extra detail – pipe joins, mounting brackets, the dummy on which the end of the hose is parked – are added. The finished item, together with the accompanying steam-heat bag, is seen mounted on the rear bufferbeam of the 'Jinty'.

electronics suppliers like All Components (see Sources index) will sell you ultra-fine flex which yields suitable-diameter sheathing. Once again, the curve of the flexible portion is formed first before a suitable length of sleeving is fed over it. It is usually a tight fit on 0.6mm wire, and warming the whole issue with a hair-dryer makes the PVC more flexible and amenable. The shut-off cock and other details are fabricated in the same manner as on the other pipework.

Cab interiors

Back in the bad old days, RTR model locomotive cab interiors were graced with nothing more comely than a brutish square block of magnet, and a lot of unlikely daylight where the floor should have been. Nowadays, they are so completely and finely detailed that you can practically read the boiler pressure off the dial of the steam gauge! In the latter case, there is not much you need to do bar adding a convincing crew – a procedure covered among the 'finishing touches' described in Chapter 8.

However, models based on older body mouldings will often call for rather more work, especially where a replacement chassis and modern drivetrain have left empty a footplate once blighted by an unseemly mechanism. A typical example of this situation is the old Mainline/Bachmann J72, which came from the factory with the cab crammed to the roof with split-frame pancake, but is devoid of a cab floor, lower cab front and cab rear/bunker front – let alone anything resembling interior detail – when mated with a modern chassis.

Other popular models exhibiting a similar void when re-powered include the Airfix LNER N2, GWR '14xx' and '61xx', the Hornby-Dublo/Wrenn R1, and the Mainline '56xx',

'57xx' pannier tank, '63xx' Mogul, and 2251 'Collett Goods'. The last-named duo are something of an isolated case as most RTR tender locomotives since the Triang 'Britannia' and B12 of the early 1960s have kept the motor out of the cab and provided at least rudimentary backhead detail – one of the few benefits of the move to tender drive mechanisms.

'Full cab fittings' was a proud boast and five-star kudos-point earner back in the days of Chapter 1, and there is no doubt that decent cab detail really lifts a model tender locomotive, especially one with a low tender and an open cab like the Hornby T9 illustrated. The better kits often gave you a pretty spiffy set of cab fittings, but scratch-building a fully detailed cab interior is a lot of work where such goodies are lacking.

Fortunately, there is a pretty reasonable selection of boiler backheads (more properly termed 'backplates'), reversers and other cab details available as aftermarket castings, so you can usually buy something close enough to convince. In the context of an RTR-based tank locomotive with a closed cab, going to town with a full-house detailed cab interior is often somewhat OTT anyway, as most of it can't be seen from any normal viewing distance. Dancing daylight where there should be a solid floor, on the other hand, is painfully obvious from the same standpoint so at the very least, I like to make sure that the basic cab structure – back, front and floor – is all there, which usually comes down to a simple fabrication job in sheet plastic, preferably black. That and a crew are often all you need to make such a locomotive look convincing from a

BELOW A loco like the T9, with its skimpy cab and low tender, demands a well-detailed footplate. Fortunately, Hornby oblige, aided by a spot of extra paintwork and some subtle weathering by Philip Hall.

BELOW A lot of older RTR tank locomotives lack any cab interior at all, not even having a floor. The least we can do is to give the crew something to stand on, together with providing the more visible fittings such as the brake handle and reverser lever. This is Andy McCallum's J72, which sports a very well-fitted cab – visible, as befits a shunter, through open cab doors.

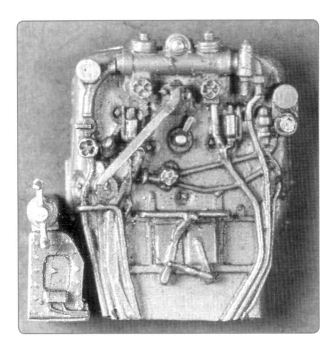

ABOVE *Well-detailed cast boiler backplates and other cab fittings are available from a number of trade sources. This is my old Riceworks set for Stanier taper-boiler engines, which has been available from London Road Models. Similar fittings are listed by Gibson, Brassmasters and Comet.*

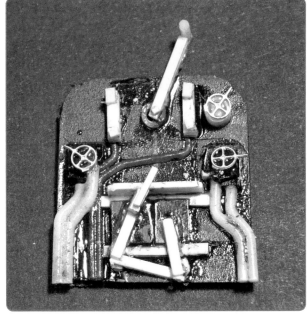

ABOVE *The DIY super-slim backplate I knocked up from Plastikard for my 'Jinty' – easy to install after painting, through the removable section of the cab floor. The etched hand-wheels are from a Mainly Trains cab detailing fret; the rest is Microstrip and Microrod.*

couple of feet away. Usually, the only fitting you actually need to represent is the handbrake handle, which is often prominent in the cab doorway or cut-out.

Only where the model needs to be able to sustain closer examination is a greater array of cab interior detail actually called for on a tank engine – and even then it need not necessarily be complete. If any part of the cab space is going to be invaded by the loco's drivetrain, it is the central area of the lower cab front, roughly where the firehole door should be. Given that this part of the backplate is normally sited deep between the rear portions of the side-tanks where they extend back into the cab, it hardly shouts at you if it is not there. It is the detail on the upper portion of the boiler backplate – the regulator handle, gauge glasses, brake valve and steam manifold – that really catches the eye. So if you have to saw off the bottom of your backplate casting to miss the gearbox, it's no great loss. By the time the crew have taken up station on the footplate, you will never know it isn't there!

How you go about installing a detailed cab interior in an RTR tank locomotive body moulding depends very much on one factor: 'Can you get the cab roof off?' In a goodly number of popular examples – including the J72, '56xx', '57xx' and '14xx' – the answer is 'yes' – which means you can go in from the top to install the cab architecture (tanks, bunker-front and so on) on your plastic sheet floor, along with the actual cab fittings and the all-important crew. Where this isn't possible, as on the Wrenn R1 or Airfix '61xx', then the cab interior is best built up as a complete sub-assembly based on the floor and installed from below as a finished and painted unit. In fact, this is an approach that has much to commend it in many

cases, even where top access is available, as it is often much easier to build up and paint things like bunker fronts or the side tank rears 'on the bench' rather than in-situ.

The various illustrations should give an idea of what's involved in producing a typical cab interior. The basic structural material is plastic sheet, preferably black, and the job is essentially a simple exercise in plastic fabrication.

I often use this same built-on-the-floor approach when confecting cab interiors for tender locomotives. Given their somewhat greater visibility – especially on general-purpose locos with low tenders, such as the GWR 'Dean Goods', '63xx' Mogul and 2251 – then these cabs generally need to be more completely detailed than is the case with tank engines. Fortunately, very good backplate and reverser castings are available from a number of sources for GW taper-boiler Belpaire firebox engines.

GWR cab controls were highly standardised, so the same basic sets of castings suit a wide range of prototypes. As with the tank loco, the basic cab interior is built as a sheet-plastic module complete with any internal splashers, sand/tool boxes or raised floor areas, with the cast details glued in place with cyano or epoxy. The fall-plate (see over) can also form part of the same module. The whole thing can be painted and the crew installed before the module is fitted to the model.

Often, I make such sub-assemblies a push-fit rather than attaching them permanently, as it can be handy to be able to whip them out for repair or access. In many cases, though, the manufacturer has done at least the basic cab interior detailing job for you; as with most tender-mechanism engines. The Airfix/Hornby 'Dean Goods', for example, has a well-detailed moulded-plastic boiler backplate which, with a spot of careful titivating and painting, looks just fine. The same is true of the majority of more recent RTR tender locos, some of which have very detailed cabs that can be made to look pretty stunning– although painting fine cab detail in situ like this is a somewhat trickier proposition than painting the same thing 'on the bench'. On the latest generation of 'super-duper' RTR, this delicate work is done for you at the factory; where it isn't, some relevant detail-painting techniques are described in Chapter 8.

Fall-plates

Missing from virtually every RTR and a fair proportion of hand-built model tender locomotives is any representation of the fall-plate, a vital fitment on any steam locomotive other than late-LMS Ivatt designs, something Southern by Bulleid, or a BR Standard. The fall-plate is the hinged steel flap that usually formed a rearward extension of the cab floor and bridged the gap to the tender platform, like a gangplank on a ship. A few engines had fall-plates hinged to the tender, but loco-mounting was the more usual arrangement.

With a handful of notable exceptions (the larger GER 0-6-0s, 'Claud Hamilton' 4-4-0s and B12 4-6-0s), only the late-steam-era designs mentioned above did away with this moveable 'drawbridge' arrangement in favour of a fixed rearward extension of the cab floor which was overlapped by a short rigid 'shovelling plate' built forward from the front of the tender body. This could thus be brought to the extreme fore end of the tender underframe without needing to leave room for the platform of the traditional tender. This arrangement lends itself readily to modelling, as the overlap does not impede the independent movement of the loco and tender which is needed to get around sharper-than-scale curves, and is not tied to a particular loco-tender gap.

A functioning hinged fall-plate is a somewhat sterner proposition, while even a simplified fixed representation brings problems of its own where track inequalities have to be negotiated, as it inhibits the independent movement of the loco and tender. Either is a vast improvement on an un-prototypical yawning chasm, however! The first thing to admit is that no 4mm loco fitted with anything approaching a scale fall-plate is going to get around train-set curves. As a general rule, the 30in minimum radius I advocated in the previous chapter is about the limit for fall-plates, which need the loco-tender coupling distance to be somewhere near scale if they are going to permit adequate side-swing, let alone look convincing. The fact is that the bigger the loco-tender gap, the longer the fall-plate will need to be to bridge it, and the longer the fall-plate is the more it interferes with the loco-tender articulation. So a little experimentation to determine the minimum comfortable tender coupling distance is well worthwhile. You will be surprised how close you can go and still get around that ruling thirty inches!

Having come up with a suitable drawbar or other tender-coupling arrangement, we can set about contriving our fall-plate. I have never been a fan of fixed fall-plates, which are not only less realistic but more prone to impede the independent riding of the loco and tender. So I make mine as

prototypical moveable flaps, hinged at the rear of the cab floor. This is far easier to do where the latter is a removable item, as suggested above in connection with the built-up cab interior modules. So, even where the RTR maker provides a nicely detailed backhead and so on, I still find it worthwhile to make an 'overlay floor' simply to facilitate the provision of a flexible fall-plate, as it is much simpler than trying to hinge the latter off the back of the loco body moulding proper.

While it is possible to replicate the prototype's loop-and-bar pivoting arrangements, it is far quicker and easier – as well as more robust – to cheat and use a fabric hinge fashioned from a small piece of ordinary gauze bandage. As can be seen from the illustration, the job is very simple. The fall-plate itself is cut from suitable sheet material – either thin plastic or sheet metal or, where appropriate, etched brass diamond-pattern chequer-plate – and trimmed and filed to the finished shape, not forgetting any necessary cut-outs to clear tender brake standards and so on. The plate is also curved to shape to match the gently humped form usual on the real thing. To give a bit more room for side-swing where curves are tight, the fall-plate can also be made a millimetre or two narrower than full scale width without it being too noticeable.

To hinge the plate, a piece of gauze big enough to cover the entire underside of the cab floor plus the fall-plate (with a bit to spare to allow adjustment) is cut, and glued firmly to the underside of the floor with a contact cement like Bostik 1 or UHU, leaving a nice flap along the rear to take the fall-plate. This can now be similarly stuck to the gauze, leaving a

BELOW *My method of making a hinged fall-plate uses gauze bandage as a hinge, stuck to a Plastikard fall-plate and cab floor with UHU. Crude, but effective!*

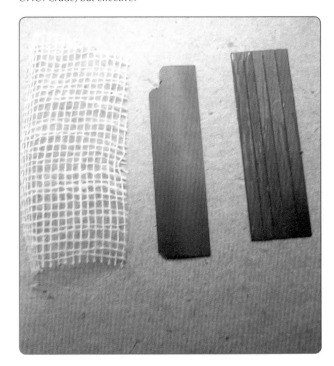

narrow gap between plate and floor to ensure free vertical movement. Once the glue has dried, any excess gauze is trimmed away, the crew glued in place on the cab floor, and the whole sub-assembly painted before being fitted to the loco. Again, I usually leave this loose as it is often easier to couple up the loco and tender with the floor/fall-plate tilted up out if the way, or even completely removed (especially when there are loco-tender electrical connections to make). It can be slid into place once all is well.

Dragbeam details

Or rather, the details visible in the gap between the loco drag-beam and the tender draw-beam. To all intents and purposes at 4mm scale, this comes down to a series of hose connections, two to six in number. Most prominent are the two vital water-hoses that carry the boiler feed-water to the locomotive's injectors which – Bulleid and BR Standard locomotives apart – are usually mounted one each side. (OVSB and BR put them both on the RHS of the engine as a combined fitment). These water-hoses are normally the outermost connections, sited just inside the loco and tender steps and so are normally quite visible. If you model nothing else in this area, adding these hoses will add a degree of verisimilitude to your model as the prototype literally never went anywhere without them!

The remaining connections lurk more in the middle of the loco–tender gap and are consequently less visible. These include the steam-heat connection – if any – and the various brake lines: the steam-brake connection between loco and tender and, where applicable, the vacuum or air-brake train lines. A full-house set of six hoses comes on a dual-brake-fitted passenger loco: two water hoses, steam brake, steam heat, vacuum train line, and Westinghouse train line. Coupling that lot up in the narrow loco–tender gap on a dark night must have been fun!

Fortunately, so far as our model goes, we can make our hoses as permanently coupled pairs firmly attached to either the loco or the tender, whichever is more convenient and best suits the loco–tender coupling arrangements used on that particular model. I normally opt to reproduce what I can see in a normal photographic view of the loco, which usually comes down to the water hoses and perhaps the steam-heat and vacuum brake lines, which were also often mounted close behind the loco/tender steps for ease of access. The actual hoses – including the water-hoses, which had to resist the suction produced by the injectors – were of the same wire-wound rubberised canvas form as for normal vacuum brake/steam-heat bufferbeam connections, and are consequently modelled in exactly the same way. The free end of

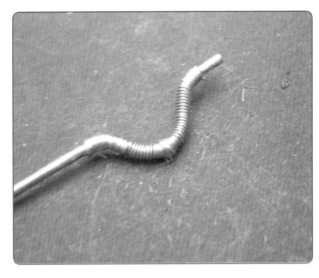

ABOVE *Tender water connections are made in the same way as vacuum or steam-heat fittings, with the core bent to an appropriate shape to represent the coupled hose, and an extra turn at the mid-point to represent the coupling.*

each hose is arranged to terminate far enough up behind the dragbox or draw-beam to be unseen, making sure that it does not impede the independent riding and articulation of the loco and tender. The illustrations should show this final piece of basic detailing work.

BELOW *The telling difference that details such as the fall-plate, cab doors and water-hoses make to the N class Mogul is evident here. There is more on achieving this 'look' – which definitely make the loco and its tender appear 'all of a piece' – in the notes on the Mogul makeover in Chapter 9.*

8 FINISHING TOUCHES

Having built or modified our mechanism and refined, reworked and detailed our loco body, we now have to heal the scars with a lick of paint, complete with lettering and lining as appropriate. All then to be toned-down and unified with some subtle weathering and finished off with some delicate post-paint detail touches: cab glazing, the addition of a crew to the footplate, and a convincing coal-load to the bunker or tender, the installation of cab tarpaulins, fire-irons, coal-watering hoses and the like. Also, there is the provision of the appropriate lamps and/or head-code discs without which no real loco could ever turn a wheel on a running line. A good paint and final-detailing job can often elevate a model of humble origins into a league above its status while, as we all know, the best of models is all too easily ruined by a duff paint job.

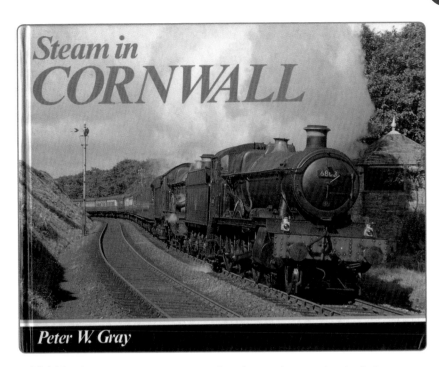

ABOVE *Accurate colour photography came along just in time to record the closing decade of the traditional steam railway. Colour albums – such as Peter Gray's superb record of the Cornish railways as I remember them from childhood – are an invaluable reference source for modelling, as well as providing inspiration by the spade-full.*

The aim of my own attempts at painting and finishing have always been directed at achieving a 'natural' look that blends the model locomotive into its surroundings on the layout, rather than an 'in-your-face' showcase paint job. This is an approach that calls for subtle and muted colours, a finish no shinier than eggshell and often tending towards the matt, and an absence of impossibly bright-and-shiny polished metal or other obtrusive embellishments.

Lining and lettering transfers also need to be toned-down to blend in with the overall colour values. Even when I'm finishing a 'clean' engine, I still aim for the same restraint in gloss and colouration as it needs to take its place naturally in the scene – although as I predominantly model the 1950s-era BR scene – reproducing a truly 'spit-and-polish' finish is not exactly a preoccupation! Nevertheless, I do try to vary the state of the paintwork of the various locos in my stud to reflect their time 'out of works' as everything in the last degree of decrepitude is no more convincing than a collection of locomotives all bulled-up brighter than a colour-sergeant's buttons. In which regard, I must express my admiration for the restraint and realistic colouration and finish of many current RTR locos, especially those by Hornby; the T9 and M7, in particular, hit just the right note and form a useful benchmark. Although would that I could, produce lining as good as that!

Some thoughts on realistic colour

Before setting out on the 'how' of finishing models, I feel it is no bad idea to arrive at a clear understanding of just what we are trying to achieve. In the context of a book sailing under the 'realistic' banner, this must surely be the replication of the

OPPOSITE *Bachmann's GWR '45xx' is a very good model just as it comes, and only calls for a few subtle tweaks – many of them accomplished with a paintbrush – to make a truly realistic addition to the stud.*

actual colouration of the working steam loco, rather than some idealised representation of what it *should* theoretically have looked like. As with so much in realistic railway modelling, the key to this lies in observation, in taking a good look at the real thing and then trying to come up with something to match what you see. This very rarely comes down to merely opening a tin of paint conveniently labelled 'chassis frame black' or whatever; a bit of mix-and-match trial-and-error is usually more like it!

The trouble is, of course, that nowadays there's nowhere you can go to observe the full-sized steam railway going about its business in everyday garb, like the prototype I became so familiar with in my youth. The various 'heritage' railways – even those that attempt some degree of authenticity in what they present – are impossibly clean-and-shiny by comparison. I suppose I must count myself fortunate in that mine was the last generation to be able to call on such direct acquaintance with the working steam railway. Those of lesser years are perforce heavily dependent on photos and movie footage, particularly where this is shot in colour.

Fortunately, given that in the later 1950s and 1960s colour photography – at that period, still relatively in its infancy – was a costly and demanding pastime, there are a surprising number of invaluable images available. We modellers have a lot to be thankful for in the colour archives left to us by photographers like Ivo Peters, R.C. 'Dick' Riley and Peter Gray. A study of their portraits of working steam – as beautifully reproduced in some of the excellent colour albums now available – are without doubt the best reference source for realistic model locomotive finishing. So comprehensive is this photographic coverage that there is almost certainly a volume covering your favoured prototype area and subject.

'Real' colour

With one not-particularly shining green exception, all of the 15 or so locomotives that populate my various 1950s-era BR layouts are black – but no two of them are the same shade. Furthermore, the various black parts of each black engine are by no means of common hue; these 'black bits' are in fact, not black at all, but rather dark shades of a range of other colours: deep charcoal blue-greys, mostly, or warm sooty browns – to miss-quote Henry Ford (who apparently never actually said it anyway!) 'You can have any colour black you like, so long as it's not actually black'. For true black is, in effect, the total *absence* of colour and is found nowhere in the natural world that light falls. A 'dead black' object is just that: dead. To endow our model locomotives with a lifelike finish we need to be cognisant of how the real thing actually looked and a good deal more subtle with our choice of colour.

Studying a photo of an in-service steam locomotive – in colour or black and white – will soon suggest that even a plain black engine (a description which, when you come to think about it, covers the majority of British motive power since the

early 1900s), is by no means uniform in shade and finish. The exact colours of the footplate and framing, smokebox, cab roof and tender top are all usually at variance with each other as well as with the actual 'livery' black. And that's before you consider the chassis, which will be different again and far from uniform in shade within itself. It is just such subtle but significant variation in colouring that I set out to try to replicate on my models, by mixing paints discretely for each area of the loco as I go along.

By concocting a fresh brew of 'black' every time I paint a smokebox or a cab roof, rather than using a 'standard' smokebox or cab-roof shade, I can create the endless subtle variety of colouration that characterised the prototype. What such a process amounts to in practice is mixing small batches of black paint 'let down' with varying additions of earth brown, brick red, grey and silver. You might regard such a process as more properly being part of 'weathering' the model, rather than an integral part of the basic paint job. I tend not to draw such distinctions because to me it is all a part of creating a realistic finish, and in that context, why paint something plain black then 'weather' it to a different shade when you can go straight to the final 'weathered colour' in one hit?

The other thing about painting a model locomotive realistically for use on a layout (as opposed to going for an

LEFT *All-black engines don't come much plainer than this 1950s-era ex-GER J15 – yet even in a monochrome photo like this, it is quite evident that the colouration is far from uniform. The loco and tender underframes, cab roof and smokebox all exhibit markedly different tonal values.* Author's collection

BELOW *Here is my attempt to replicate the variegations evident on No 65465 in the photo above, on my own model of sister-J15 No 65454, as running at much the same period. Weathering aside, there are five distinct shades of 'black' in this paint-job.*

up-front 'showcase' finish) is that a large part of the objective is to make the thing blend in with the colour values of the layout as a whole. In which context, it is important to remember that looking at a 4mm scale model from two or three feet away is the equivalent of looking at the real thing from a distance of 75 yards or so. In nature, the closer you are to something the stronger, brighter and shinier its colours appear; the converse of this is that something viewed from 75 yards away will have lost a distinct proportion of these qualities. So what we actually need to reproduce are the colours and degree of 'shine' that match those of the prototype seen through say 75 yards of atmosphere – which isn't as clear and transparent as you might think!

I have to say that the better RTR paint jobs among the contemporary crop take this colour degradation into account, being suitably restrained in their colouration and finish and consequently needing little, if any 'toning down' to blend in with a well-observed and modelled scene. But 'twas not ever thus and some of Hornby's tender-drive offerings of a few years ago were more in-your-face than a Technicolour punk hairdo when it came to the bright-and-shiny stakes. Where needed, I tame such excesses of finish with thin washes of matt colour or an overspray of tinted matt varnish, as described under the weathering and varnishing notes below.

The basic paint job

In the context of the sort of RTR-based modelling espoused in this book, the painting requirement can range from a spot of minor touching-up of a factory finish to a complete 'bare plastic' paint job. In the latter case, the task is no different from undertaking a full paint job on any other model locomotive, whatever its origins. This is a subject that has been well-covered in a number of excellent books and DVD programmes produced by far greater experts than I, a selection of which are listed in the Bibliography. These tracts describe in detail the established 'proper' approach to the task, using enamel or cellulose paints applied by airbrush to obtain a smooth and even paint finish, with lining carried out by hand using a draughtsman's ruling pen or a purpose-made lining pen, together with ultra-fine sable brushes with about three hairs apiece.

This is all a pretty skilled business and takes a fair bit of learning, a lot of patience and a steady hand. Even in my prime, I was never any great shakes as a pukka loco painter *à la mode*, and these days the even greater shakes of Dr Parkinson's 'trembling palsy' certainly haven't improved my proficiency with the ruling pen and three-hair brushes. I have also never got on too well with that invention of the devil, the airbrush – a device which, in my hands, stutters and splatters and drips and breaks wind without carrying any paint. That is, when it is not flooding the place like a fire-hose!

In spite of such handicaps, I find I can still manage to turn in a paint job adequate for my modest purposes (no showcase!) by using aerosol sprays to apply any necessary overall priming and basic livery colours, then going over to brush-painting for all the secondary colours and detail work. Brushes also figure large in the various weathering techniques

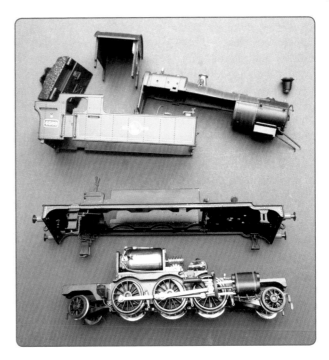

ABOVE *Painting a model is usually made a great deal easier if it comes apart, as does the Bachmann '45xx' so readily. Two screws and half-a-dozen plastic latches are all it takes to get to this state, when everything is nice and easy to get at with paintbrush or airbrush. Putting it back together is surprisingly straightforward.*

described in a page or two. To line and letter the finished result, I find a cocktail of transfers to be the best bet, with pen lining a last resort! If I use an airbrush at all, it is to drift on the occasional coat of matt or satin varnish – often tinted – to tone down paintwork or to seal an overall finish.

Preparation

Before painting any model by any means, a certain amount of preliminary spadework has to be done in the matter of filling any remaining cracks and blemishes, smoothing away any tool-marks, and feathering the edges of any remnants of the factory finish if it's a repaint rather than a bare-plastic job. The other essential task is, of course, to make sure the model is clean, free of file-dust and other detritus and devoid of any *trace* of grease. The best way to ensure this essential cleanliness is to give the model a good bath in warm, soapy water – but not, please, using a washing-up liquid or similar that claims to be 'kind to your hands'. The lanolin such potions usually contain, whatever it may do for your silky skin, won't do anything at all for the adhesion of your paint. Something far more astringent – such as a general-purpose cleaner meant for floors and the like – is a much better bet for paint preparation. I get by with Flash liquid mixed a bit stronger than recommended on the bottle, but I hear great things of the lethal-sounding Cillit Bang.

No matter what the method of painting, it is usually very much easier to accomplish when the model can be broken down into a number of sub-assemblies/separate components. This is something that I have long contrived on kit-built and scratch-built models, but now I find a lot of recent RTR locos come apart in much the same way. They are usually held together by push-fit plastic latches and self-tapping screws. Taking the trouble to disassemble a model allows each part to be painted/weathered separately, which can save a lot of masking-up where the model is being sprayed. It often makes components needing painting a lot more accessible. Even if you are only picking out detail and adding a little colour variegation, as I was doing on the Bachmann '45xx' that figures in this chapter, the effort of dismantling the model as in the picture, was well worthwhile. It also gave me a great deal of respect for Bachmann's design team; the way the loco breaks down is very well-thought-out and logical.

Priming

The primary purpose of a primer is to improve the adhesion of the finish coats of paint by providing a stable and secure base layer securely bonded to the surface being painted. Some primers – often described as 'surfacing' or 'Hi-Build' primers – are also designed to fill any minor blemishes or porosity and produce a smooth substrate for the top coats. These are usually bad news in model terms, as they contain a lot of filling medium and are designed to form a thick coat that doesn't do a lot for our delicate detail! You can buy aerosols of dedicated model primers from the likes of Humbrol or Tamiya, but I have always got on perfectly well with the normal grey or red-oxide general-purpose primers sold by car accessory shops and ironmongers.

For some reason, the red-oxide often seems to produce a slightly finer finish than the grey, so that's what I generally use. It is suitable for black or dark green locos and ideal under LMS crimson, but not so good under lighter colours like LNER Apple Green or Caledonian Railway Perth Blue, in which cases the grey is a better bet. These primers adhere well to both metal and plastic and the larger size aerosol cans, in which they typically come, seem to give a finer and more consistent spray – although shaking them vigorously for the recommended two minutes is a bit of a work-out! But more on all that in the spraying notes below.

In the case of a model based on a moulded plastic body, adhesion of the finish paints to the basic structure is not usually an issue. It is the metal detail fittings – particularly parts formed of brass and nickel-silver wire or strip – that are usually reluctant to take and retain paint, as anyone who has ever had a go at painting an etched kit will tell you. There are three possible painting approaches to this problem: spray-prime the whole model anyway; brush-prime the relevant metal parts only, or spray-prime (and even completely finish-paint) such metal details *before* fitment to the plastic body, as suggested in connection with bufferbeam hoses and other pipework in the previous chapter.

Spray-priming the whole model is obviously only advisable where a bare-plastic paint job or a total repaint is in prospect. In these cases, though, such overall priming has the added benefit of giving a uniform base colour over which to apply the finish coats. Where the factory finish is being retained and it is simply a matter of patch-painting to make good blemishes and colour newly added detail, then careful brush priming of

ABOVE *So long as you avoid Hi-Build surfacing primers, then normal off-the-shelf aerosol cans of primer serve for most modelling needs. Only where you are trying to paint an etched-kit or scratch-built model in brass or nickel-silver do you need an etch primer, which offers better adhesion on such bare metals.*

any bare metal will suffice. As a brush-on primer, you can either use the aerosol type – by spraying a quantity into a suitable container (aluminium foil cake case or similar), and dipping your brush in – or by buying a tinlet of dedicated brushing primer from Humbrol or Precision Paints.

There is a fourth method for finishing metal detail, which is to take a leaf out of the RTR makers' book and treat handrails, lamp-irons and the like with a chemical 'blackening agent'. This combines with the surface of the metal to produce a coating that ranges in colour from a deep purplish-brown to a medium blue-grey. However, it won't 'take' on solder or cast metals, so is not really suited to solder-assembled pipework or similar fabricated detail. Such hit-or-miss colouring on a handrail or similar can also looks a touch odd sometimes, as you can't really control the shade. But as the blackened surface also accepts paint reasonably well, certainly better than bare metal, you could regard it as an alternative form of priming – with the added benefit that, if the odd bit of paint does rub off, you're not left with bright-and-shiny metal showing through.

Aerosol painting

Over the years, I have found Aerosol paints vary considerably in their quality and characteristics – most notably in the matter of drying times and the fineness of their pigments and their consequent tendencies to produce an 'orange peel' finish. For many years, I got on very nicely with the spray cans of cellulose car touch-up paint you used to find on the rack at Halfords. Suitably shaken, these gave a very smooth – if

ABOVE *One of the most useful of the commonly available aerosol paints: Halford's Satin Black. This makes a very good livery black for all those engines that ran in this colour scheme, which, post-1923, was the vast majority! Or is that a 'lack-of-colour' scheme? As well as paint, you will also need thinners – not for thinning per se, but for clean-up work and removal of unwanted paint.*

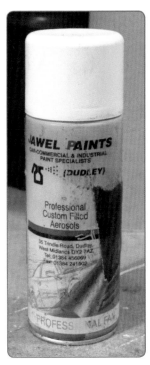

ABOVE *Authentic railway colours in aerosol form are available in dedicated ranges like Precision Paints or Spray Away, the latter only 'while stocks last'. Where no suitable colour is available, you can get paint custom-mixed and supplied in aerosol format by a specialist, who will work from a colour sample.*

somewhat glossy – finish using only a thin coat which did not clog detail, while the wide range of available colours meant you could almost always find something appropriate.

These days, cars are no longer painted with cellulose enamels and touch-up sprays, where you can still find them, are usually 'Hi-build' synthetics of some sort. These produce a smooth gloss finish all right – but, as with the surfacing primers, only in the form of a relatively thick layer that does detail on a small-scale model no favours at all. The other problem is that the sort of colours they paint modern cars have very little application in the field of steam-era railway modelling. How one yearns for Land Rover Arden Green – a dead ringer for GWR 1928 loco green, or Vauxhall's Carmine Red, a very passable LMS Crimson Lake.

All is not lost, however. You can currently get high-grade cellulose enamel aerosol sprays in a pretty wide selection of dedicated railway colours in the Spray-Away range sold by the ubiquitous Mr Waterman's Just Like the Real Thing emporium (see Sources index). These come as large (400ml) cans, albeit not cheaply; £16 a pop, as I write this. Admittedly, one tin paints a fair few 4mm scale locos and the large can size gives a more consistent spray action, but if your taste in loco liveries is catholic then you could soon find yourself with a fair bit of money tied up in paint! Fortunately, for cheapskate BR modellers like Rice, one can of dull black answers most needs...

In which cause, the matt black car paint beloved of the go-faster brigade can also serve, although it is a little on the 'intense' side for anything other than a relatively ex-works

finish. For pre-Grouping liveries and other shades not listed by Spray-Away, there is a further source of high-grade cellulose in just about any colour. This is to go to a specialist paint supplier offering a computerised matching service and have a small batch of colour mixed to special order to a suitable sample, such as a good colour photograph.

Such photographic reference isn't possible, of course, for liveries pre-dating colour photography, in which case the usual source is a printed colour patch in a livery register – although do bear in mind that such samples are very much 'up front' in colour values. Getting the paint supplier to tone the shade down by a notch or two (which the computer systems allow) is usually the best bet. It is usually possible to have such a one-off paint mix supplied in an aerosol – but once again, it won't come cheap; £20–£25, typically. This is still cheaper than paying for a professional paint job, though! You can find such paint specialists in trade directories or online, or they often advertise in the pages of classic car magazines.

Spraying with aerosols

There is not too much to say about this, really as it is more or less a case of 'do what it says on the tin'. Shaking the ball bearing around for the full two minutes like a demented maraca-player is a bit of a bore, but such extended agitation really is the only way of making sure the paint is fully mixed, thus avoiding spits and splats or floods of solvent. Warming the tin of paint slightly beforehand with a hair-dryer helps ease the mixing process; it also aids paint flow and drying.

ABOVE Painting models using aerosols does not demand much in the way of dedicated facilities if you do as Andrew Duncan is doing here, and conduct operations out in the garden on a nice sunny day. Several locos were being painted in one go, here seen at the priming stages.

Failing the availability of a purpose-built spray booth with extraction, always spray in a well-ventilated location – in front of an open window or, preferably, out-of-doors on a nice sunny day, as in the picture hereabouts. Where spray drift is a problem, a decent-sized cardboard box turned on its side makes an effective extemporised booth. If you do have to use an aerosol in a confined space where there is likely to be any sort of build-up of fumes, then a mask with an active filtering

BELOW A GW Mogul – built by Andrew Duncan from a Mitchell kit – with a basic paint job in GWR loco green and black, about as far as you can usually get using aerosols. The loco was made to come apart into a number of sub-assemblies to aid this process and do away with the need for extensive masking-up. The chassis was sprayed under power, as described.

system is a wise precaution. Tool merchants like Screwfix sell them, as do many paint suppliers. While I'm striking a cautionary note, don't forget that the solvents in all these cellulose and synthetic paints are highly flammable – so cast an eye about for any untoward sources of ignition before whipping up a storm of vapour.

Obviously, before cutting loose on your prize model with the aerosol – be it humble primer or hi-falutin' top-coat – it is wise to make a trial pass or two on a test object, to check that the paint is fully mixed and emerging as a fine and consistent spray (and that it is actually the right colour; voice of experience…). Such a test-shot will also give you an idea of the best spraying distance and pass rate for that particular aerosol as well as how well the paint covers and thus how many passes you will need to make.

As with the paint mixing, a little warming of the model and its environs with the hair-dryer can aid the flow and help the paint take, as well as ensuring speedy drying. However, be careful not to get the model too warm before spraying, as this can lead to the paint drying on contact, which is apt to lead to a grainy, orange peel finish. Good painting technique also sees each pass with the spray commence to one side of the model or the other, so that any splats or stutters don't finish up as part of the paint job. By the time the paint-stream hits the work-piece it should be flowing cleanly and evenly. The object is to avoid any excessive build-up of paint while ensuring even, opaque coverage. The basic maxim with spraying paint is that you can always make another quick pass to build up a thin patch – but if you've been heavy-handed and flooded the job, there's not a lot you can do about it!

Chassis painting

Painting a loco body is one thing; painting a chassis is another ballgame altogether! Given that you have to paint a lot of moving parts without gumming them up solid or getting paint on the motor commutators, or other electrically sensitive areas, it would seem that a fairly finicky approach is called for. Some folk paint the wheels and frames separately before assembly, or colour all the individual parts as they go

along, but I will confess I have never had any joy with that method. When I'm in full chassis-building mode I like to motor along without having to keep stopping and bother with paintbrushes, while the finish of the pre-painted bits always seems to suffer as construction proceeds.

Of the other alternatives, I did once try carefully brush-painting a completed chassis, but all that did was take an age, ruin a perfectly good brush, and miss a lot of parts I needed to reach. So for many years now I have taken the completely opposite approach and sprayed my chassis with aerosol primers and matt-black topcoats while they are under power, with the wheels turning steadily at modest speed. It sounds heathen – but it works, and the mechanism seems none the worse for the experience.

To spray-paint a mechanism under power, the chassis is first given a thorough clean with meths and a stiff hogs-hair paintbrush to get rid of any crud, grease and flux residue, and then dried with the invaluable hair-dryer. The motor and gearbox are then protected by a paper shroud and the axle bearings and rods/valve gear pivots lightly oiled. A pair of wander-leads are arranged to supply the motor with the modest handful of volts required. I use an ordinary 4.5V lantern battery as a power source; we don't want any great speed. A small hand vice is clamped to a frame spacer to act as a suitable handle, and I am ready to go spraying. I don't bother trying to protect areas – wheel-tyres, coupling rods and so on – that need to finish up paint-free as I find it easy enough to clean away any unwanted paint, post-spraying with a drop of solvent and a cotton bud.

Actually, spraying a running chassis is much the same as spraying a loco body, except that a rapid succession of light, quick passes is more effective at avoiding the 'unpainted spoke shadow' effect on the frames behind the wheels without resulting in excessive paint build-up on the wheel faces. I start with a light coat of oxide primer followed by basic matt black.

As soon as the chassis and wheels have a reasonable and even coating of paint, I stop spraying. With the chassis still running and while the paint is fresh and 'green', I apply solvent-wetted cotton bud(s) carefully to the wheel treads and clean them of paint. Cellulose thinners is the usual cleaning agent, but Butanone (liquid plastic cement) also works well.

If your pick-ups bear on the *backs* of the wheel-tyres, don't forget to clean paint off those as well. The last job is to disconnect the power and apply the same cotton bud and thinner treatment carefully to the rods and valve gear. Shiny valve gear not being in my lexicon of realistic loco finishes, I don't clean the paint and primer right off. Rather, I aim to leave a thin film to act as a 'key' for weathering colours applied later. The basic spray-finish of the chassis is only a starting-point for the final paint job, of course.

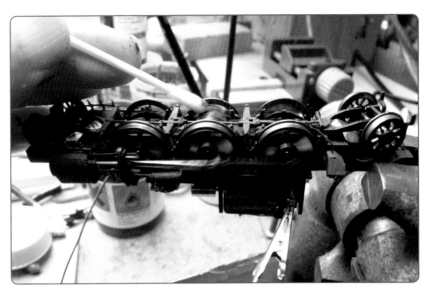

ABOVE *Cleaning up a chassis under power after painting comes to the same thing, whether the chassis has been sprayed from scratch or, as here, is a factory-painted RTR chassis that has been subjected to a brush-applied colour variegation job. Cotton buds, thinner and a modicum of volts are the essentials.*

There is a lot of secondary painting to do – most notably, where wheels or cylinders are a livery colour rather than black – as well as the whole subtle business of weathering, covered in the notes following. When you have done all that, the last chassis-painting job is to remove the motor shroud and wander-leads and test the chassis on the track to ensure it still runs. You will probably find you need to do a bit more cleaning around the pick-ups and wheel-rims before it settles down. A bit of careful tyre-burnishing with a fine fibreglass brush won't go amiss; quite apart from helping to ensure good pick-up, if there is one part of the anatomy of a real locomotive that *should* be bright-and-shiny, the wheel-treads/flanges is it!

Brush painting

Back in the days of my youth, when airbrushes were rarer and more exotic than Ming vases and aerosol cans barely invented, we all used to brush-paint our models. With a bit of practice and due care, it was quite possible to end up with a perfectly decent blemish-free paint job devoid of runs, blobs or brush-marks. To read many a modern tract on painting, however, you would think it was impossible to apply paint by such primitive means. Far better, apparently, to spend long, fiddling hours masking-up so as to be able spray every last drop of every last colour with your hi-tech airbrush! Not to mention the tedium of trying to clean the dratted contraption properly between each change of colour.

Tish! say I; it is far quicker and just as effective to use traditional hairy brushes for all but the basic colour coats of the livery – the more so as it is a methodology that facilitates the flexible, observation-based approach to colour outlined in the 'realistic colour' notes that prefaced this section. So these days, even though I do spray the priming and base colour coats of my locos, I still use brushes for all the secondary colours, for detail painting and weathering, and for the touching up or patch-painting of existing RTR finishes.

As paint for brushing, I have always been a fan of Humbrol's acrylic – finding it easy to use and mix, with generally good covering power and rapid drying. It goes on smoothly from a brush and is not prone to leaving brush-marks. If you do have them, then you're using the paint too thick. Being water-based, acrylics are readily thinned when required – while more water and the occasional drop of soap is all that is required to keep brushes in good order. No solvents and therefore no fumes! Acrylic paint also lends itself to weathering techniques like stippling and dry-brushing.

What it is absolutely no good at all for, at least in my experience, is lining through a ruling pen – a task for which oil-based enamel is vastly superior. Nowadays, the Humbrol range of shades is huge and includes all sorts of interesting metallic and weathering paints. The dedicated 'railway colours' are currently only available in acrylic, with the perceptive exceptions of 'lining orange' and 'signal red' – both essential lining colours, still listed as enamels. Someone at Humbrol is evidently a loco painter! Otherwise, if you're wedded to enamels or are in need of more obscure or pre-Grouping livery shades, the Precision Paints oil-based enamel range is both comprehensive and of excellent quality. This is what I use for airbrushing liveries when I go down that route, and if you're careful about thorough mixing and thinning to get the right creamy consistency, then it goes on nicely enough with a brush.

As for the brushes themselves, the received wisdom has been that only the finest artist's watercolour sable brushes will do for model work – a costly and delicate option that I find quite unjustified. For many years since, I have found the new generation of synthetic-bristle watercolour brushes to be just as good as a château-bottled sable for all general painting

BELOW *Brush-painting is a major technique in my armoury, for patch-painting/touching up/variegating, and detail painting on both spray-painted or factory finishes. Here are my preferred paints and implements: Humbrol acrylics for most jobs, but enamels for metallic colours and lining. Brushes are all moderately priced synthetic-bristle types, these days just as good as expensive sables for this type of work. A modest selection of round-point watercolour brushes in sizes No 0–3 covers most jobs. The scruffy quarter-inch flat specimen at bottom right is used for dry-brush weathering techniques.*

jobs; only for the finest lining and lettering work do I find the 'natural' product in the sub-0 sizes to be superior. As a result, 99 per cent of all my painting is achieved with a handful of ordinary round-point watercolour synthetics in sizes from 0–3 plus a circa 6mm-wide 'flat'. The brands I prefer are either Daler's Dalon or Windsor and Newton's Prolene. These are widely stocked by art supply shops and chains like The Range, as well as being available from several online sources.

You can set yourself up with an adequate selection of such brushes to tackle most jobs for the price of a couple of pukka sables. They are robust and easy to care for, especially if you're assiduous about cleaning them thoroughly and *promptly* after use and put them away teased to a point and stored 'with their heads in the air'. What you definitely don't want with any paintbrush is paint drying in the root of the bristles close to the ferrule, although some build-up there is inevitable over time. If a synthetic brush does start to loose flexibility from this cause, an *occasional* dip or two in a bottle of Butanone plastic solvent and a thorough wiping with kitchen towel will restore matters and prolong brush life. That said, given the modest price of these brushes, once a particular specimen is past its best it is not too painful to retire it from the front rank into that of the 'weathering/scenic' platoon, used for rough painting, stippling, dry-brushing and so on. There, they can join a few cheap-and-cheerful flat-bristle hogs-hair brushes about a quarter-inch wide, and a couple of slightly larger round-bristle specimens. Outlets like The Range sell sets of ten or so such brushes in a plastic wallet at only a pound or two.

'Wet' painting

This is the basic brush-painting technique for adding secondary or 'weathering' colours to the main livery and picking out small detail, as well as patch-painting and touching-in 'factory' paintwork. As the title implies, 'wet' painting is the straightforward flowing-on of liquid paint to obtain a smooth, even covering coat. As with all painting methods, the key thing is to mix the paint to the right consistency for the technique being used – which, in this case – is normally somewhere between that of 'single' and 'double' pouring cream. The exact proportion of pigment-to-varnish/carrier will depend on the density of the pigment involved and the base-colour over which it is being applied. Where a colour lacks opacity – which some do – then the required shade may need to be built up as several thin coats rather than a single thicker one. Where you find you need to use such a 'fugitive' colour, it is worth considering applying an undercoat of a base colour more sympathetic to the topcoat, just as you would do in normal domestic decorating.

'Stir the contents thoroughly', the directions on the side of the tin always tell you. This is something I *never* do with either acrylic or oil-based enamel, preferring to dip quantities of pigment and carrier separately and mix my paint in a separate container. This enables me to control the consistency of the mix to suit my own purposes, whereas if you mix the whole tin-full you're stuck with the proportions provided by the paint-maker. While it is easy enough to thin a mix that is too stodgy, if it comes out too translucent or too runny, there is not a lot you can do about it!

Starting with a nice dollop of near-neat pigment trawled

from the bottom of the unmixed tin and then adding carrier and thinner as required gives you a great deal of say in the outcome. External mixing like this also, of course, greatly facilitates the mixing of the sort of irregular 'adjusted' shades that I advocated back in the colour notes. One last benefit of 'external' paint-mixing is that it can also extend the shelf-life of model paints – especially enamels, which often seem to start going off and gelling once they have been fully mixed. Whereas the worst that usually happens with unmixed paint stored for any length of time is that the top of the varnish layer skins over – an impediment that is easily removed.

Transfers

Leaving aside Micro-Mark's ingenious waterslide rivets, transfers generally have two functions in finishing RTR-based models: applying lettering/numbers/heraldry, and lining out. These two operations are rather different propositions, and in my experience a transfer-type that suits one may not be ideal for the other. We have a choice of three basic transfer processes available to us: Dryprint/rub-down (Pressfix) and varnish/spirit fix (Methfix) transfers, or waterslide decals (the rest). The essential difference between transfers and decals is that a true transfer leaves the backing-sheet or carrier behind when it is applied, whereas a decal remains on the backing film, which is transferred with the image onto the surface of the model.

In terms of use, they all have strengths and drawbacks: dry-prints are relatively easy to position and apply (provided they haven't dried-out in storage and 'gone off'), but are non-adjustable once they're on the model, and can be fragile. Spirit-fix transfers are a pig to position due to the obscured backing paper and can smudge, whereas decals, while being easy to position and adjust, are stuck with that backing film – which can be obtrusive and hard to disguise.

As is so often the case in modelling, there is no universal 'right answer' when it comes to transfers. Given that applying lettering/heraldry and lining-out are two very different tasks, then perhaps it is not too surprising that a transfer process that suits the one does not necessarily prove the best bet for the other. Not all locos are lined anyway (very few of my BR stud are!) but virtually every engine carries numbering, together with ownership lettering and crests or BR totems – both forms of heraldic device. Here, I very much prefer a true transfer, as I have always found the outline of the carrier film of a waterslide decal difficult to hide and often surprisingly obtrusive, especially on a weathered/patinated model.

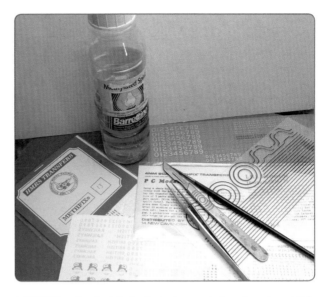

ABOVE *Transfers for lettering/insignia come in three formats: spirit-fix Methfix; rub-down Pressfix, and waterslide decals. Lining transfers usually came in the last two. For insignia, my own preference has long been the spirit-fix type, and the picture shows the solvent, ordinary methylated spirit, together with the implements needed for their application. The same tools – scalpel, square-ended tweezers and a fine 'chivvying' brush – also serve for waterslide transfers.*

Modern waterslides use a much thinner carrier film than used to be the case, which has improved matters, while the use of a decal-setting solution like Transfix or the American Micro-Sol can help thin and blend the edges of the film. But given the choice, I always opt to avoid the problem, by using a 'direct' transfer for lettering – for which my own preference has always been Methfix. There is nothing wrong with rub-downs, but I have always got on better with the less-than-instant 'fix' of the spirit transfer, which gives you a modicum of adjustment, and is a lot easier to remove if you make an utter pig's ear of things – always a consideration in my case!

When it comes to lining, however, I find that facility for repeated adjustment is the key requirement, which is where a

BELOW *This GW Collett 'Hall', which Andrew Duncan and I modified from the old Wills body kit fitted to a Comet chassis, was aerosol painted with Railmatch enamel and lined with Fox waterslide transfers.*

good waterslide decal wins hands down. Spirit-fix transfers are far too fragile for a job like this and so are not usually supplied in lining format, which leaves pressure-fix transfers as the only alternative. These days, I find that the need for initial precision is a bit of a stumbling block with rub-down lining. It is all-too-easy to get a length of line slightly askew – but none too easy to adjust matters once you have! Using decals, a few drops of water and a small paintbrush enable you to go on fiddling and tweaking your lining pretty much until the cows come home. Although, that said, getting a decent length of straight lining truly straight and kink-free is not the easiest trick in the book. With waterslide lining, the issue of backing film is not such a problem, as it is relatively easy to trim the lining outline closely with a scalpel when cutting it from the sheet and hence restrict the carrier film to the actual area of the lining. There, it is pretty well undetectable, especially if you use a decal-setting solution to 'snug the edges down' and ensure that the decal lies truly flat. I do find the colours and finish of the waterslide lining I use (Fox Transfers) to be decidedly on the 'bright and shiny' side, calling for a little toning-down with colour-wash and/or tinted matt or semi-matt varnishes, as detailed below.

ABOVE *This is what I mean by a 'patinated' finish on a model loco; just enough toning-down and weathering of the finish to suggest that the loco has seen some service without looking as though it is fit only for the scrapyard. Subtle is the watchword… This example is my old scratch-built ex-GER E4, parts of which date back to 1967. The model was sprayed with a matt-black aerosol and then worked on with acrylics.*

Weathering

Or, as *mon ancien ami* M. Gérard Huet (*modèlist extraordinaire*) would term it: *un peu de patination*. For that is truly what we are after, that subtle degradation of the original ex-works finish, that suggests age and use. 'Weathering', on the other hand, all too often seems to be taken to mean the total subsuming of the paintwork in a riot of rampant rust, liberal limescale, all-pervading soot, thick-caked mud, and oozing oil leaks. To my eye, such antics are more suggestive of caricature than realistic finishing. All right, during the dark days of the Second World War, many locos did work in a very dirty and run-down condition, but by 1948 or so, a very creditable recovery in standards had taken place.

Likewise, at the very end of steam in the later 1960s, a number of the handful of surviving steam locomotives did degenerate to an execrable state. But the vast majority of such locomotives worked out their days in pretty reasonable condition. Indeed, many a steamer went to the breaker's yard with a shine still on the paint and in first-class mechanical order. In my recollection, the average BR loco in the 1950s and early 1960s ran in a workaday state of finish that, while being by no means 'bulled-up', was generally clean enough to enable numbers to be easily read and the machinery to be properly maintained. Imperfections there were a-plenty, of course – dents and dings, patches welded on to tender tanks, the odd minor rust-patch, or repainted repair. But streaming leaks and machinery totally caked in oil-bound dirt or corrosion? Such things had to be attended to forthwith if the

locomotive was to be reliable in service and were nowhere near as prevalent as some folk seem to think.

Traditionally, of course, model railway locomotive studs have suffered from exactly the opposite problem, where every engine right down to the humblest shunting tank ran around looking as if it had just been specially 'bulled up' to work the royal train! What we are after is a happy medium between these two extremes – a state which the term 'patination' seems to me to describe nicely. As with all realistic modelling, it is best to work from a prototypical starting-point, so whenever I'm weathering an engine I like to base my efforts firmly on a photo or photos. If this is not of the actual 'subject' loco, then it is at least a member (or several members) of the same class. That way, I can get an idea of where dirt normally built up or 'rain washing' occurred on that particular type – a valuable basis from which to work.

Weathering a model locomotive effectively is a subtle business that can make use of a wide range of techniques. If you're new to this sort of work, rather than taking the plunge on some prize and much-worked-upon project loco, it is well worth acquiring a gash loco body of some description, just to use as a guinea-pig for experimenting with painting and weathering techniques. The Mainline J72 moulding, which figures as an example at several points in this deathless narrative, came off eBay for 99p! There have also been some excellent books written, and 'how-to' DVDs covering a variety of techniques and, expounded by far greater exponents of the art than I. A selection of such titles is listed in the Bibliography, and I would suggest that at least one of these is a worthwhile addition to any modelling library.

What follows in the next few paragraphs is only my personal approach to the task – which, largely, eschews any clever stuff with the airbrush (apparently seen by many as *the* essential weathering tool), in favour of the restrained use of the humble hairy variety. The basic recipe includes a bit of mild 'distressing' or toning-down of the basic finish, a few dabs of brush-applied paint, a trace of powder pigment and maybe a finishing/sealing coat of tinted matt or dull-eggshell varnish, which is the only task for which I find the airbrush at all useful.

I have to admit that there is one other element of the finish of many of my locos, that is purely accidental and results from actual *Anno Domini*, in that quite a few of them have been running on my various layouts for several decades now. (The oldest still in original paint just passed its 40th birthday!) Prolonged exposure to natural daylight, repeated handling, the occasional dusting with a stiff paintbrush and the odd bit of touching-up or repair have imparted a sort of 'natural patina' to the underlying paintwork that has a surprising veracity!

Brush weathering

This approach to the business of adding age and wear to a pristine paint-job uses five basic techniques: normal wet-brush painting, burnishing, colour washing with dilute paint, dry-brushing of relief detail, and the brush-application of weathering pigments or chalks. The brushes used are a soft glassfibre burnisher, a few small flat, and a round-bristle cheap-and-cheerful hogs-hair brushes, and a modest selection of good-quality synthetic-bristle artist's watercolour brushes. These are exactly the same ones as used for secondary and detail painting, and already listed in the brush-painting notes above.

The paints used are likewise the same Humbrol acrylics I preferred for other secondary painting tasks. For weathering work, I use a small palette of basic colours mixed as needed to produce the range of shades appropriate to the task in hand.

This basic selection comprises seven matt colours and a solitary touch of gloss. The numbers are Humbrol's colour codes: 11 silver, 24 yellow, 27 grey, 29 earth, 33 black, 34 white, and 70 brick red, with any necessary shine being imparted by a dash of No 30, clear gloss.

In my weathering method quite a lot of the process is integral with the basic paint job – especially where a loco is being painted from scratch – in that I carefully choose and mix secondary paint colours that are in themselves weathered shades, as already described in the notes above on colour and basic brush-painting technique. When I'm patinating a factory-applied finish I apply the same approach, over-painting the uniform black areas normal on RTR paintwork with my variegated selection of off-blacks for smokebox, footplating, cab roof, frames, wheels and so on. Just this stage alone usually makes a considerable difference to the realism of the model as a whole, as well as individualising the model and distinguishing it from the ranks of the RTR clones.

Toning washes

A wash is simply a very thin coat of very dilute paint flowed quickly and smoothly over base colours and lettering/lining with the object of toning them down and subduing over-bright bits.

BELOW *Toning-down a 'fresh' paint job – in this case, the factory finish of a Bachmann '45xx' – involves the application of a suitably dilute mix of dark grey-brown acrylic paint, almost all of which is immediately wiped off with a tissue, leaving the merest film of paint on the surface of the model. (Practice on a scrap model or a wagon first, just to get the hang of things.) The aim is to just take the 'sting' out of the colours; the comparison with the out-of-the-box model shows the effect.*

It is the brushed equivalent of a 'drift coat' of fine overspray applied with an airbrush. My usual toning-down shade is a darkish grey with a brown tinge, just a trace of the acrylic paint in a very wet mix with plenty of water. You can always use several successive washes to build up the required degree of 'cut-back', whereas if you overdo things on the paint front it is difficult to remove the excess. I apply washes with the quarter-inch flat watercolour brush, using as little of the paint mix on the brush as I can get away with. A quick blast with the ever-useful hair-dryer will dry a thin wash coat in a few seconds, when you can judge whether you have achieved the desired effect, or whether a subsequent coat is needed.

Burnishing

While a lot of the patinating process on a model locomotive is about replicating the degradation of once-shiny paintwork and the build-up of dirt and pollution on various surfaces, as with the patina acquired by antique objects in general, this dulling down is not the only characteristic of the process of wear and tear. Some parts of the object, by contrast, may acquire a polish or lustre due to abrasion, handling, repeated water-washing, or from actual cleaning and/or polishing.

Locomotives that might overall be summed-up as 'shabby' still usually boasted a few more-or-less shiny bits: cab handrails, smokebox dart handles, many cab fittings, often the boiler-top and steam domes, and odd places like toolbox lids.

All these could exhibit varying degrees of lustre, often somewhat greater than the near-matt finish of my basic livery black, where this has come from an aerosol. Just as the colours on different parts of a loco varied, so did the degree of lustre. While an over-spray of varnish is the usual method of adding gloss to matt paintwork, this is hard to apply on a localised basis – so I take an alternative approach and add the necessary degree of shine by buffing up the paint with a stiff brush, usually just a cheap hogs-hair paintbrush. Sometimes I resort to a glassfibre propelling-pencil type burnisher used soft e.g., with the actual glassfibre bristles well-extended. It is surprising just what a difference a little gentle polishing with such implements can make in subtly lifting a matt finish and adding a little 'manual handling' shine to handrails, levers and the like, as well as delineating clean areas of the paintwork. Polishing with brushes is a very controllable way of adding these subtle variations in finish.

Dry-brushing

This is possibly the best known of all brush-applied weathering techniques. Used subtly, it can highlight detail and bring out textures; overdone, it can make the model look as if it got in the way of a bunch of rabid paint-ball enthusiasts. As with so many aspects of weathering, it is very much a case of building up the desired effect in small increments rather than going in with all brushes blazing. The first requirement for successful dry-brushing is the right paint-mix, which in itself wants to be 'dry' – plenty of pigment dipped from the bottom of the paint-pot mixed with very little varnish or solvent, to give a consistency approaching paste.

This stiff paint is applied with a stiffish paintbrush – either a well-worn or clogged watercolour brush or, more usually, a small flat hogs-hair brush. The brush is dipped in the mix, then drawn across a piece of kitchen-towel to remove all but a trace of paint. The colour is applied to the model by stroking the brush lightly across the detail you're aiming to highlight so that just a trace of colour is left on the surface at each pass, building up the desired effect by repeated passes. By using a mix of different colours (that photo reference again!), some very subtle

ABOVE AND BELOW Brush burnishing: the 4mm. scale equivalent of a wipe over with an oily rag. The 'smokebox black' I used on the '45xx' dried pretty well dead matt, so to give it just a hint of sheen I burnished it lightly with a soft glassfibre brush. The effect is very subtle and difficult to photograph, but it makes the loco look as if it has got dirty and has then been cleaned, rather than being newly painted. Be sure to get rid of all the little bits of glassfibre bristle afterwards.

BELOW Dry-brushing highlights on to the texture of detail – in this case, the '45xx's injector pipework. Acrylic paint in a stiff mix, with only a trace on the brush, is the secret of subtle dry-brush work. It is easy to overdo it.

and convincing effects can be achieved, particularly on detail like pipework and fittings, injectors, loco brake gear, and chassis detail generally, riveted bufferbeams, and tender-tops.

Powder weathering

The last brush-applied weathering technique is the use of fine powder pigments brushed into place with a soft brush – a job for which slightly 'tired' watercolour brushes are ideal. The weathering powders can either be bought as such, Carr's being the main source, or you can produce your own by rubbing artist's pastel crayons on coarse abrasive paper. These are available from good art shops in a vast range of shades.

Powder weathering is particularly effective at replicating track dirt flung up from the ballast and building up on the loco chassis and beneath overhanging surfaces like footplate edges, cab steps and buffer shanks, as well as accumulating on areas like bufferbeam faces (especially tender rear beams), and on tender underframes generally. To reproduce these effects, I apply the powder to the model working in the direction from which the dirt would have come. The actual powder is picked up on the tip of the brush and lightly dusted into place, once again aiming to build up the final effect gradually, any surplus being flicked off with the brush or blown away.

As with all weathering techniques, a bit of trial-and-error testing on your trial body is a good idea as some of the Carr's pigments (notably the rust shades) can be surprisingly fierce and need to be applied very sparingly. The powders are retained either by the overall final coat of varnish (see below) or, where this is not being applied, by a quick, gentle dusting of artist's fixative (the sort sold for charcoal and pencil rather than the watercolour variety) drifted on to the powdered areas by spraying across them at a slight angle, rather than pointing the aerosol straight at the powder, which is all-too-easily blown away.

Varnishing

The first thing to say about varnishing locos is that I rarely do it. Very few of my BR locos are so treated, as varnishing, by its very nature, has a unifying effect in the matter of the overall lustre of the finish, which, as just described above, is what I have been at considerable pains to vary! Where I do varnish paintwork – as when unifying transfer lining with underlying livery colour – I do so at an intermediate stage, before applying secondary, detail and weathering colours, rather than as the final overall finishing coat, as so often proscribed.

To me, the varying degrees of gloss exhibited by the different surfaces and materials of which the prototype is made up, need to be faithfully represented in the finish of the model in the cause of realism. Things like cab glazing and coal, for instance, don't look half as convincing after a coat of spray varnish as they do 'raw'. For the very limited amount of varnishing I do undertake, I have for a long time had good results with Ronseal satin polyurethane let down for airbrushing with a drop of white spirit. A small tin will last you a lifetime… If no airbrush is available, then an aerosol can of clear satin cellulose from Spray Away is a good bet for a reasonably lustrous effect. For a duller finish I have found

ABOVE *Powder weathering using pastel dust or ground pigment is another weathering technique it's all-too-easy to overdo this too, but at least you can wash it off with soapy water and have another go! I mix my powders in a cake-case and apply them with the same brush I use for dry-brush work. As always, I work closely to my photo-reference, in this case a superb Peter Gray study of the real No 4569 on a Wadebridge–Bodmin train in 1960.*

artist's watercolour fixative – effectively, a spirit-based matt varnish – a useful alternative. You can also buy spray cans of oil-based varnish in different degrees of gloss from paint-makers like Precision, although I can't claim any familiarity with them.

Cab glazing

I have put glazing after painting, weathering and varnishing because that is when I do it, pretty much as the final finishing job, as if anything about a loco wants to be clear and crisp it is the glazing. However dirty the rest of a loco might have been, the spectacle glasses were always cleaned – for obvious reasons! Real glass always somehow presents a different surface – smoother, flatter and far more reflective – from all the other materials integral to a locomotive's structure, with which it forms a definite textural contrast.

I try to keep this differentiation on the model by using a hard-and-flat glazing material, usually thin (about 0.7mm/30 thou) clear moulded plastic cut from Ferrero Rocher chocolate boxes or, best of all, precision-cast clear acrylic sheet of a similar thickness, which can be bought from Charvo in Yorkshire (see Sources index). I prefer these materials to the much thinner rolled clear styrene sheet usually sold for glazing models

because they have a flatter, crisper surface and a greater clarity, which makes them more akin to glass. Being moulded, they also cut and file more cleanly than the rolled sheet. While 0.7mm is obviously way more than scale thickness, it is still quite a bit less than most RTR moulded glazing and still gives a substantial enough edge to allow a reasonably secure bond when stuck into place with solvent or cyano.

Real loco-cab glazing is almost always flush with the outside face of the cab, or very nearly so, which, with a typical moulded-plastic RTR body, means it is going to be a case of carefully cutting and filing a tight-fitting glazing insert for each window opening, and cementing it in place with the correct degree of set-back. Taking the trouble to accurately cut and fit decent glazing is one of those fiddly and tedious jobs that no-one much likes to do, but which is well worth the effort if you persevere.

How much of this hair-shirt glazing work you will need to do depends to a large extent on the origins of the basic model. Older RTR locos normally 'came without', so glazing always was a DIY job. Modern RTR, by contrast, usually comes with moulded glassware that is a great deal better than nothing, even if, to my eye at least, it lacks the reflectivity and close flush-fit of the real thing and often suffers from a thick and chunky look (mainly because it *is* thick and chunky!). A few recent RTR models do possess moulded-insert glazing that is clear and crisp enough to convince, but usually such inserts have a texture to the finish and an obtrusively rounded edge to the moulding that, in my eyes, makes the trouble of replacement worthwhile – at least for the larger cab-side windows, where such flaws are more noticeable. Getting a truly square edge where the glazing meets the window-frame is one of those little touches that really lift a model.

To make cab glazing, I lay my piece of Charvo, or choccy-box plastic, over the opening it is hopefully going to grace and trace the required outline with a fine-line permanent marker, erring slightly on the over-size side. I then cut this blank out by scoring-and-snapping if it is straightforwardly rectangular, or with a piercing saw for more complex shapes. The blank is offered up to the window opening and then carefully filed and sanded to a final accurate fit with needle files and an abrasive rubbing stick or block – a job that comes down to

pure trial and error. This is where the persistence comes in, several attempts often being needed to get a usable set of glazing. Or they are when I'm driving the file!

Once a satisfactory fit is obtained, the 'glass' is secured with a trace of solvent (Butanone) or cyano – applied from the *inside* of the model if at all possible. That way, if any wayward adhesive should mar the surface of the glazing, the chances are it will do so on the inner face where it is less noticeable. As I write this, I learn of the introduction of laser-cut flush-glazing kits – such as have long been available in the USA – to suit British RTR models, which is very good news. For locos, the first introductions have come from Shawplan, covering sundry diesels and, unsurprisingly, the Bachmann '57xx' 0-6-0PT, with many more promised. Not cheap, but worth the expenditure in terms of quality of fit and the saving of effort. Details are in the Sources index.

The crew

I have lost count of the number of layouts I have seen obviously inspired by the apocryphal tale of the *Mary Celeste*, where locomotive footplates are as bereft of crew as were ever the decks of that doomed vessel. True, there are sundry recorded instances of ill-tended steam locos setting off on their own account sans crew and going on a little rampage, usually to the severe detriment of sundry sets of level crossing gates or the odd buffer-stop. But such antics are frowned upon on the better-regulated railways – which, of course, all ours are! This means every engine will be tended by at least two stout fellows, whose presence on the model is as vital as that of the boiler or driving wheels. The crew-less loco trundling down the track is a complete anachronism and one of the oldest chestnuts in the whole railway-modelling game – even if it is only marginally senior to that other well-worn blooper, the fireman frozen in mid-swing upon the tender-front, his shovel hovering in perpetuity twixt tender and firedoor. Few things this side of a face on the smokebox door look less realistic…

Nowadays, there is a very good selection of miniature figures suitable for footplate duty, either intended as such or rendered eligible by suitability of pose or garb. It is usually no problem to find or adapt a suitable duo for any engine, avoiding any further howlers such as the seated driver with right arm raised regulator-wards installed on a GW loco – driven, of course from the right. In the normal course of events, the driver stays in his allotted look-out position – be that right or left – and hence nicely handy for regulator, reverser and brake, even if not necessarily hands on. If anybody is going to wander about the footplate or face widdershins, it is the fireman.

On an express-passenger engine that invariably runs chimney-first, one would expect to find both crew members keeping a forward look-out, but on locos that spend much of their time running backwards, I like to position my crew-members such that one is facing each way. That way, there is always somebody looking where the engine is going. I generally use cast-white metal figures from Alan Gibson, Monty's or Phoenix – usually nicely proportioned and detailed without the overdone textures some other cast figures exhibit.

ABOVE *Vital appendages! Unless your loco is dead and cold on shed, then it will need to be crewed. In my quest for individuality and realism, I set great store by the provision of convincing footplate figures in natural repose – no hovering shovels for me. On locos likely to do much tender-first running, I also make sure that one crew member is placed to look in that direction. Note also the crew's impedimenta – fire-irons in the appropriate stowage on the tender, and the fireman's bike atop the coal.*

Footplate figures are often very visible and well repay careful painting and detailing. I prime the castings with spray primer and brush-paint them carefully with matt acrylics, endeavouring to endow them with distinctive facial characteristics to impart both realism and individuality. Traditionally, enginemen's footplate garb consisted of one of two basic outfits (or often, a combination of the two). The first rig was a lightweight jacket worn with either trousers or full overalls, all made in heavy cotton fabric that started life a dull light blue in shade, tending to a pale bluish-grey with repeated laundering. The alternative was a heavy wool serge uniform jacket and trousers in a dark blue or charcoal-grey. Either outfit was completed with black steel-toed work-boots and a grease-top or uniform flat cap. Most drivers wore a formal shirt and tie beneath their jackets; firemen were more casual, often sporting open-necked shirts and neck-scarves. Traditionally, the neck-scarves were red, which meant that an improvised danger flag was always on hand.

Which basic clothing was worn depended upon the prevailing weather conditions; if your layout is set on the traditional blazing hot day in high summer, your crew won't thank you for decking them out in full winter serge! Once painted, the finished figures have the soles of their boots filed flat and are held in place by being planted in a wee dollop of a contact cement such as Bostik 1.

While about the crew, don't forget their implements and accoutrements. The fireman needs his fire-irons – dart, pricker, long riddling iron and long and short shovels, often stowed on the tender or side-tank top, or across the bunker rear. I make these from fine wire and shim. Then there is the matter of the lubricating oil stores can and long-spouted 'poorie'. To keep the oil warm and fluid, these often resided on the shelf above the fire-door (where there was one). Also stowed close to the fire-door was the vital quart-sized tea can, while the crew's snap bags – containing their day's rations – often hung from convenient cab fittings. All little touches can be added, again as illustrated. One or two of my locos also sport the fireman's bicycle (from the Wills Scenic Series) on the tender-top – a common sight in East Anglia, certainly.

Coaling-up

No steam loco is going to get very far without an adequate supply of fuel, and given that the average middle-ranking steamer burned 30-odd lb of the stuff every mile, that supply needed to be substantial. A goodly proportion of the model locos I have seen over the years have had not so much as a lump aboard – in stark contrast to those whose tenders were piled mountainously with enough coal to get to Mars! Neither extreme can be considered realistic, I think you'll agree. For a convincing depiction of a working steam loco going about its daily business we generally need to coal our locos in a part-depleted state, to suggest that some proportion at least of the fuel has been consumed since the loco came off shed. The layout on which every loco is running around with tender or bunker brimful always strikes a slightly jarring note in my eye! Far more convincing is the common situation where each coal load exhibits the characteristic – if variable – dip in the front in the case of a tender coal-space, or the tank loco in which the coal level has dropped somewhat from the upper rim of the bunker side-sheets. Modelling coal loads accurately demands that we replicate this state of affairs.

Unfortunately, the majority of RTR steam locos come 'coal included', a more-or-less (usually less!) convincing representation often being moulded integrally with the tender or bunker-top. Of course, almost inevitably these moulded approximations seem to represent a full load – or impossible overload, in the case of one or two tender-drive specimens like the Airfix 'Dean Goods' and original Hornby '28xx', heaped to the heavens to make room for the motor. More recent RTR

BELOW *Although by no means the worst example around, the coal in the Maunsell 3,500-gallon tender of Bachmann's SR Mogul is not particularly convincing and, as usual, represents a pretty full load. Unfortunately, the tender body mounting is by way of a plastic support column moulded integrally with the underside of the coal, limiting what you can reasonably do about it.*

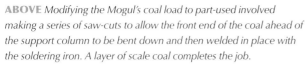

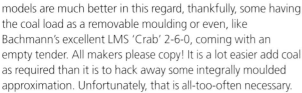

ABOVE *Modifying the Mogul's coal load to part-used involved making a series of saw-cuts to allow the front end of the coal ahead of the support column to be bent down and then welded in place with the soldering iron. A layer of scale coal completes the job.*

models are much better in this regard, thankfully, some having the coal load as a removable moulding or even, like Bachmann's excellent LMS 'Crab' 2-6-0, coming with an empty tender. All makers please copy! It is a lot easier add coal as required than it is to hack away some integrally moulded approximation. Unfortunately, that is all-too-often necessary.

It is not only the overall shape of the moulded loads that needs attention but as depictions of a pile of loose coal they are often a long way from convincing, almost invariably figuring on the 'to be improved' list. The frustrating thing is that building a truly realistic coal load is a simple, speedy and satisfying task. The raw material is the real thing, coal being one of those materials that is so fine-grained in its structure that – crushed and sieved to a suitable size – it can effectively make a model of itself. If you don't want to be bothered bashing the living daylights out of a full-size lump and sieving the results through a small kitchen colander with holes around 3mm in diameter, then you can buy little bags of ready-marmalised coal from most of the scenic material suppliers.

Real loco coal varied in size from slack (small lumps of less than 3in or so mixed with granular coal and dust – every fireman's nightmare!) up to large lumps, which could be a foot or so long by about six inches round, usually calling for use of the coal-hammer. It all depended on the coal type/ source and the way the coal had been handled and loaded. Mechanical coaling plants tended to break up any large

lumps, for instance. If you were being really pedantic, I suppose you could research the correct diet for your locos, but if you aim for the middle of the size range (3–6in lumps) you won't go far wrong – hence my advocacy of a 3mm hole as a suitable sieving-size for 4mm scale coal. This will weed out anything above about a scale 8 inches in any dimension.

Such 'scale' coal looks so much more realistic than the moulded stuff that many people are tempted to just stick a layer

BELOW *Removing the moulded coal load from the bunker of a tank locomotive can often be quite tricky. Here's how I tackled the '45xx', which has the bunker front/coal load/bunker rear coping plate as a separate moulding. The bunker rear coping was carefully sawn off with a piercing saw, cleaned up and cemented to the bunker rear, The coal was then cut off the bunker front before the latter was clipped back into place.*

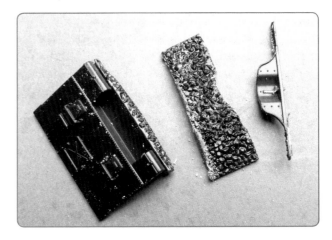

on top of the existing plastic coal load. Unfortunately, this tends to compound the over-full tender/bunker look, so I find it worthwhile to get rid of the plastic coal entirely and install a false floor of black plastic sheet in the bunker or coal space at an appropriate height on which to build my desired coal load. The illustrations alongside and in the final examples chapter show what is typically involved in removing a moulded-in-place coal load and constructing such a dummy floor.

To build a new coal load, I first make the basic shape I am after from modelling clay or putty (Plasticine, Blu-Tack, DAS Pronto, or Milliput), allowing for a decently thick covering of scale-sized coal. This solid core is then painted flat black prior to receiving a generous coating of contact adhesive (UHU is best as it comes in a tube with a fine nozzle), followed by an initial layer of crushed coal which is lightly pressed into place and allowed to dry. I then add further accretions of coal to get the final load configuration. This loose coal is retained by *sparingly* dribbling in a thin cyano-acrylate adhesive, which penetrates

the granules by capillary action and, when it sets, retains the load securely. Do go easy with the CA – it is amazing where it will get if you dribble a tad too much! You can repeat this CA/loose coal routine as needed to complete the coal load – not forgetting the inevitable overspill on to the rear of the tender-top aft of the rear coal plate. I often find that such a crushed-coal load – which is usually far cleaner and dust/slack free than a real tender-full – looks a bit too bright and shiny as it comes. A sprinkling of real coal dust or 'coal black' weathering powder followed by a quick blast of artist's matt charcoal fixative usually does the toning-down trick.

Lamps

No loco in the steam era ever turned a wheel on a running line without displaying the correct identifying code of oil-lit headlamps or, in some cases during daylight hours, indicator discs, on its leading end. These headcode markers were demountable, being carried on brackets (lamp-irons) located at predetermined positions. The lamps showed a white light at night and, latterly at least, the daytime discs and the lamp bodies were also painted white. The actual code was generated by the number of lamps/discs displayed – normally from 1 to 4 – and the particular combination of brackets they occupied.

The prime purpose of the basic four-lamp code was to indicate to signalmen and other relevant officials the class of train being worked. In some cases, most notably on the

BELOW Coaling up the bunker of the '45xx'. The basic shape of the load is built up with little wads of glue-soaked tissue, which are then painted matt black. The main layer of coal goes on to a generous coat of Bostik 1 or UHU, and is then adjusted/built-up with additional coal placed loose, and held with a trickle of cyano. The result is a partially depleted bunker – far more typical than the usual brimful heap.

ABOVE *The four lamp positions of the 'standard' headlamp code are only ever all occupied for a royal train, or a train conveying a visiting head of state. This is LNER No 8783, an ex-GER 'Super Claud' 4-4-0 – one of two such engines kept for royal comings and goings from Sandringham.* Author's collection

BELOW *The standard headlamp code, extracted from the 1951 BR Rule book. These codes were general, but not universal, local and regional variations being covered in working notices.*

STANDARD LOCOMOTIVE HEADLAMP CODE

 1. Express Passenger Train. Breakdown Train going to clear the line, or Light Engine going to assist disabled train. Empty Coaching-Stock Train timed at express passenger train speed.

 2. Ordinary Passenger Train. Mixed Train. Breakdown Train not going to clear the line. Branch Passenger Train. Rail Motor Train or Railcar.

 3. Express Freight or Ballast Train authorised to run at a maximum speed of 35 m.p.h. Empty Coaching-Stock Train not carrying headlamps for group "1".

 4. Parcels, Newspaper, Fish, Meat, Fruit, Milk, Horse-box, Cattle or Perishable Goods Train composed of vacuum-braked stock with brake-pipe connected to engine. Express Freight Train. Livestock, Perishable or Ballast Train with not less than one-third of the vacuum-braked vehicles connected to the engine.

 5. Freight, Mineral or Ballast Train. Train of empties carrying a through load to destination.

 6. Express Freight, Fish, Meat, Fruit or Cattle Train. Ballast Train not running under group "3" or "4" headlamps. Special Train conveying 36-ton breakdown crane but not proceeding to an accident.

 7. Through Fast Train not running under group "3", "4", or "5" headlamps and carrying a through load.

 8. Light Engine or Light Engines coupled together. Engine and brake-van.

 9. Freight, Mineral, or Ballast Train stopping at intermediate stations.

 10. Ballast, Freight, or Inspection Train requiring to stop in between signal boxes (in the section). Branch Freight Train.

 N.B. Headlamp codes are subject to alteration in the case of "through" trains working over branch lines, and also to minor variations on the different Regions of British Railways.

Southern/BR(S), extra brackets and lamps/discs also indicated the precise route it was to take. This was a legacy from the pre-Grouping era, when each company did more-or-less its own thing in the matter of lamp codes. Some railways with convoluted route structures – most notably the old LBSCR and LSWR – devised headcode arrangements of fearsome complexity involving multi-coloured lamps or discs and doubled lamps stacked one above the other on extra-tall brackets.

Fortunately, in the post-Grouping and BR eras things are much simpler and a standard set of basic four-lamp codes was adopted across the entire railway network. After the 1923 Grouping, where local codes were in use, as on the Southern, these were detailed in the relevant working time-tables or working instructions. In daylight hours, the Southern generally used discs rather than lamps, and one of these discs would normally be inscribed with a number. This denoted the duty number of the rostered turn (see Chapter 4) that the engine was working.

The LNER/BR (E) also used discs, but only in the normal four positions, destination boards being displayed for routing where needed. Where oil lamps were used to indicate the headcode these were normally lit even in daylight, but the real indication was given by the painted body of the lamp – usually coloured white, but snazzily enamelled in red for principle trains of the GWR and BR (W).

It is also notable that on those latter-day LNER and Southern locos equipped with electric lights at the code positions, these were not deemed acceptable as daytime code indicators, and so adjacent lamp-irons were still provided to allow oil-lamps or discs to be displayed. Therefore, even a shiny new B1 4-6-0 or a Bulleid Pacific still needed its due complement of antique ironmongery! None of the BR Standard steam engines had electric lighting, so the humble oil locomotive headlamp – pretty well unchanged in design from its advent in the early 1840s – saw steam out on Britain's railways, and even perched incongruously on the noses of the first generation of diesels!

The basic post-1923 standard lamp positions are: three immediately above the bufferbeam – left, right and centre – plus a central top bracket. On the front of a loco, the lower brackets sit on the footplating while the top bracket is sited either directly in front of the chimney or on the smokebox door beneath it. Astern, the same pattern of brackets is provided on the tender or bunker rear. Southern locos, as noted, sported an extra pair of halfway-high brackets each end: at either side of the smokebox front forward, above the outer bottom brackets aft.

The basic four-position lamp code is given in the diagram alongside. Note that a locomotive running light engine, as well as displaying the appropriate single offside lamp at the leading end, would also carry a tail-lamp showing a red lens indication on its nether end. There is one other light combination not shown here – that used for engines on pilot duties at large stations or goods yards. To avoid the need for constant re-jigging of lights, pilot engines carried a white and a red lamp fore *and* aft, positioned on the outer footplate brackets; white on the right and red on the left, when facing the engine.

Modelling loco lamps is easy enough. There are suitable

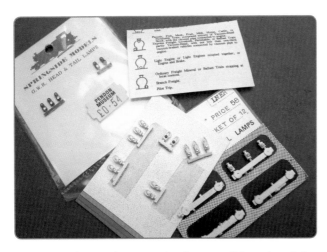

ABOVE *Ready-to-use locomotive headlamps in all the main varieties as used by the 'Big Four' and BR are available, usually with jewelled lenses – although many modellers contend that a bead of epoxy resin looks more convincing than a faceted brilliant. Mounting lamps is always a problem on 4mm scale locos, especially if you want to be able to change the codes.*

ABOVE *My old J15 brings the branch goods tender-first into Cade's Green, correctly displaying the appropriate lamp code on the tender rear. This is my compromise movable lamp mounting method, with the lamp body drilled to sit over the tongue of the bracket, rather than hanging from it. Such lamps are apt to droop a bit and are all-too-easily lost, but at least – given a steady hand and a pair of tweezers – it is possible to display the appropriate code for the train being worked.*

BELOW *The LNER and Southern, and their succeeding BR regions, used headcode discs for daylight indication, as on Beattie well tank No 30586 at 'Trerice'. These discs are much easier to make removable than lamps. The example here is an etching from Roxey Mouldings.*

basic castings available from several sources for DIY finishing, or you can buy some very nice pre-painted examples fitted with reflective jewelled 'brilliants' as lenses from Springside. These are what I use, with the finish toned-down a trifle with my usual dirt wash. If you want to go one better, DCC concepts can even provide you with *working* headlights using sub-miniature LEDs!

For those needing headcode discs there are some very nice etchings also available. Details of all these fitments are listed in the Sources index. The difficulties with both lamps and discs come, of course, in the mounting. On a loco permanently assigned to a particular duty, there is no problem; the appropriate markers are simply stuck on to the relevant lamp-irons and all is well. But on layouts like mine, where locos undertake differing duties, and run-round their trains, then to preserve the operational niceties I need to be able to move my lamps around. I'll confess right now, that I don't always bother, but I like to be able to do so when my 'scale conscience' gets the better of me.

While it *is* possible to replicate the prototypical bracket-and-sleeve lamp-mounting arrangement in 4mm scale – Pendon does so – it is pretty hair-shirt stuff. I opt for a much simpler bodge, where a suitably sized hole (0.8mm or thereabouts) is carefully drilled in the base of the lamp body, deep enough to allow the lamp to fit *over* the lamp-iron. This is, of course, not quite right – the lamp should sit in front of, or beside the bracket, not on top of it. However, the error is only apparent when you look very closely – something it never pays to do with my locos at the best of times!

Headcode discs are a little less heathen; I touch-solder a length of fine brass capillary tube on the lower rear of the disc then cut off the surplus to leave a little bit of tube about 1.5mm long on the back of the disc. This is carefully opened out with small drills and a taper brooch to allow the disc to perch on the lamp-iron. Positively the last word in finishing touches!

9 LOCO EXAMPLES

This is a modest book on a very big subject – and I am all-too-aware that it only scratches the surface of many aspects of the loco-building business. So, following the well-proven premise as to the relative value of words-versus-images, it seemed a good idea to round off all the verbiage by illustrating the various topics and techniques discussed, with a couple of specific examples. These models have been produced using the philosophy and methods described, together with step-by-step pictorial sequences covering many of the techniques advocated.

Example 1: Makeover for a Mogul

Bachmann's model of the Southern (ex-SECR) N class Mogul, while not one of the very latest of RTR productions, is still very much in the current genre. It is dimensionally accurate, pretty well detailed, has an excellent paint finish and a good mechanism that runs and pulls well, even without the help of any traction tyres. The principal variants of the type have all been available at one time or another, with different detailing, alternative tenders and apposite paint schemes to suit the various prototypes. So, all-in-all, a pretty satisfactory model – which aspects of such a paragon could need much attention to bring it up to par and meet the author's benchmark?

The answer is a surprisingly long list, which forms exhibit 1 alongside, taken from the pages of my notebook. The version of the N I was contemplating was a BR late-1950s-era example, fitted with a BR Standard Class 4 chimney, BR ATC gear, and trailing a straight-sided Maunsell 3,500-gallon tender. The particular engine of this configuration Bachmann

offered was No 31843, an Exmouth Junction stalwart and thus ideal for the Launceston MRC's North Cornwall Line 'St Teath' layout, for which the model was originally intended. This at least saved me the task of renumbering – although, as the list shows, that still left plenty to do!

N Class Mogul 31843 - To do list

Check at 82E Exmouth June 1958-60
Photo ref: 31839 (82E)   31843 - Mate SR steam WC P

Loco:
1) Tender coupling - close up, get rid of 'box' under drag beam
2) Fit fall plate/cab floor
3) Seam & gap on smokebox — make good
4) Fit loco brake pull-rods (Missing)
5) Bore out chimney
6) Replace vacuum ejector pipe on boiler
7) Replace front footplate lamp irons ('ornd') Headcode discs
8) Make & fit front vacuum standard + steam-heat connection
9) Fit ATC shoe protection shield
10) Fit front coupler loop, remove tension-lock
11) Fit front screw coupling + stowage hook
12) Cab doors?
13) Fit injectors
14) Loco crew

Tender
1) Loop for loco coupling
2) Get rid of tension-lock, provide loop
3) Make + fit water hoses
4) Make & fit rear vacuum standard + steam heat
5) Lower coal load, re-coal
6) Fire irons
7) Replace rear lamp irons X NOT WORTH IT!

Touch-in + detail paint, weather (lightly)

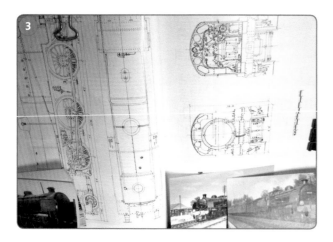

The first job was to assemble some prototype reference, as in the next photo: a decent set of drawings (from a loco profile feature in *RailModel Digest* issue No 5), plus as many pictures of the right variant and group of engines as I could lay my hands on. I had postcard views of Nos 31839, 31844 and 31845, which I reckoned would be a fair guide for No 31843. I was wrong there, of course, as I discovered when I finally tracked down a good clear photo of my target in the pages of the album *More Southern Steam in the West Country* (Fairclough and Wills, published by Bradford Barton in 1975). While the other engines in the group all had their front vacuum standards to the *offside* of the drawhook – which is where Bachmann put it – No 31843 had it on the nearside. Further checking among the ranks of the Ns suggested that the location of this fitting was more or less random, so look out! For the moment, No 31843 is just plain wrong, at least until I pluck up the resolve to move the offending item – or change the number!

Refining

The initial group of jobs to be done on the model came under the 'refining' heading, notably eradicating the visible mould part-line seam along the top of the smokebox and filling in the horrible gap where the smokebox front did not quite meet the main smokebox barrel. This was plugged with high-grade plastic putty, then it and the seam, were sanded smooth with an abrasive rubbing stick (see Chapter 6). There is a finer seam along the boiler top, which I fancy is a cladding plate join in reality, so that was left. The same goes for the top of the firebox, where there is a pronounced join and clamps on the boiler bands.

While I was attacking the smokebox end of things, I set about opening up the internal diameter of the chimney slightly to reduce the visible rim thickness, using a succession of finger-twisted drills in the approved fashion. I must have been a bit heavy-handed with my twiddling, however, as I managed to twist the chimney clean off, to the slight detriment of the skirt. No matter, this mishap actually made it easier to clean up the smokebox mould seam, and the chimney was simply cemented back in place afterwards.

The next task to be tackled was the closing-up of that yawning chasm of a loco-tender gap with a hook-and-bar arrangement that gave an interval that was somewhere nearer

the prototype's 11in spacing. I settled on 5mm (a scale 15in), and thus arranged the loco will happily negotiate a 30in radius curve. Without the cab doors, it would manage 24in if it had to. The Bachmann plastic draw-beam arrangement was binned in favour of a downward-facing draw-hook on the loco (to facilitate the fitting of a fall-plate), and a wide loop on the front of the tender.

The way in which the hook was arranged is shown in photo 6. A short 10BA countersunk-head screw was threaded through the circular draw-gear opening in the engine's drag-beam from the inside, and a 10BA nut screwed down hard to secure it in place. The pin of the hook was then made by bending an 'eye' in the end if a piece of 0.7mm wire, sized to fit over the shank of the screw (a suitably sized split pin will do the same job quite nicely). I found I needed to add a couple of spacing washers behind this hook pin to get the loco-tender spacing right, when a second 10BA nut could be tightened down firmly to hold the hook together. The rest of the 10BA screw was trimmed off flush with this nut, as in photo 6.

The other half of this arrangement consisted of a 0.7mm diameter brass wire loop 16mm wide, set some 3mm in front of the tender draw-beam. This loop was soldered to a small mounting-plate made of thin double-sided glassfibre-cored PCB, as in photo 7, held in place by a pair of quarter-inch long 10BA cheesehead screws self-tapped into the two mounting points provided just behind the draw-beam to take the original Bachmann draw-gear. The draw-loop is

soldered to the upper side of this mounting plate, which locates it hard up against the bottom of the draw-beam (photo 8). The bottom face of the PCB plate is left clear for the mounting of a pair of cosmetic water hoses, made as described in Chapter 7.

Using double-sided PCB for the mounting plate makes it much easier to solder these fittings in place without disturbing the loop, as the heat transfer through the glassfibre core of the PCB is far less than through a piece of brass or nickel of similar thickness. The revised draw-gear and the resulting loco-tender gap can be seen in photo 9. Note that the outer nut of the hook acts as a central buffer bearing against the tender beam when the loco is running tender first.

Fall-plate and cab doors

While I was about the business of the loco-tender gap, I attended to the cosmetic features of this area, starting with the fall-plate. As can be seen from photo 10, I made my Mogul's fall-plate from 10thou Plastikard, hinged to a short, false overlay cab floor with a scrap of gauze bandage as described in Chapter 7. I simply glued the fall-plate and the floor to a suitable piece of gauze with UHU, leaving a narrow gap between the two to allow the fall-plate to hinge upwards (the important direction). My fall-pate was about 2mm narrower than scale to allow for tender swing. I checked this by Blu-Tacking the assembly in place and test-running the loco around the tightest curve on the layout. Once I was satisfied

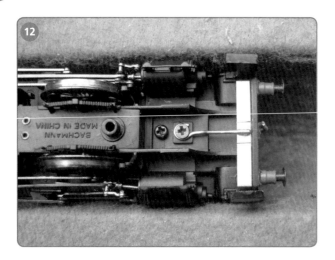

that all was well I painted the fall-plate assembly and glued the cab floor overlay in place with UHU.

The cab doors are made and fitted in a very similar manner. The doors themselves are cut from 10thou Plastikard with Microstrip dummy-hinge detail, while the functional hinges attaching them to the cab sides are little patches of Rizla cigarette paper, which is surprisingly strong, held in place with dabs of cyano. A coat of suitable black paint disguises their presence. I found that to get adequate clearance on curves I needed to make the Mogul's cab doors a fraction short and keep them angled in slightly so that they did not foul the front of the tender sides.

Bufferbeam details

I find that one of the areas of most RTR locos which most repays improvement is the bufferbeams, especially the front beam of tender locos, and No 31843 was no exception. The first job was to ditch the eyesore tension-lock couplings – simple enough, as you just pull them out of their mountings. As already described in Chapter 6, for all practical purposes they can be replaced by an unobtrusive wire loop mounted below the bufferbeam. The loops on my Mogul are anchored on a brass mounting plate screwed to the original plastic mounting block on the tender, and to a PCB mounting strip arranged immediately behind the front bufferbeam on the loco.

This strip is supported by a wire bracket retained by the cylinder block fixing screw – see photo 12. It also provided mounting points for the steam-heat hose, the bracket supporting the AWS shoe shield, and the parking hook for the front screw coupling. Gaps in the PCB surface helped to stop heat travel during sequential soldering operations. To check that this mounting strip did not foul the front pony truck wheels when the loco was 'on its feet' it was placed on a mirror, as in picture 13. Picture 14 shows this mounting strip fully loaded with a steam-heat hose and AWS shield mounts. It's pretty crowded!

While I was about the front end of the loco, I also attended to the matter of the over-sized and clumsy footplate lamp-irons shown in photo 15, where they are compared with the prototype. These veritable tombstones were pulled out with pliers and much more delicate replacements made from 10thou x 0.8mm brass strip, doubled over at the foot.

These doubled feet were located in the original mounting

slots and secured with gel cyano, as in picture 16. I decided that the smokebox lower lamp-irons, although a little crude and over-size, were acceptable. The top lamp-iron is commendably delicate and close to scale as it comes. One wonders why they couldn't all have been like that!

The detailing of the rest of the front bufferbeam started with the vacuum standard, made as detailed in Chapter 7, and located in the mounting holes provided by Bachmann, to the left of the draw-hook. Unfortunately, as already noted above, for No 31843 it should be to the right… The steam-heat hose, however, seems always to have been on the left, so that is where I put it.

If your layout is set in high summer, you could legitimately leave this fitment off as they were often removed outside the 'cold season'. No 31843, in common with most N 2-6-0s in the BR period, was fitted with BR ATC/AWS gear, which had a contact shoe mounted below the front bufferbeam. To avoid this being damaged by the front screw coupling, a hefty steel shield was fitted. I made mine out of Plastikard following the photographs, and secured it to the wire mounting brackets already provided with gel cyano.

The last job was to provide the screw coupling itself, which on these Moguls was an unusual affair having three short shackles in place of the usual two longer ones. I made my version with parts from the Roxey screw coupling etch described in Chapter 7, using the hook, short spindle and two short shackles from the etch, and bending the third wide shackle under the hook from fine wire (see prototype arrangement in photo 15 opposite). All these parts were chemically blackened. A fine wire parking hook was soldered to the PCB mounting strip adjacent to the nearside buffer and the finished coupling secured in place with cyano, in characteristic off-to-the-side-stowage. This makes it strictly non-functional! The completed but unpainted front bufferbeam detail is shown in photo 17.

The front pony truck

An odd (and unhelpful) feature of the front pony truck of the Bachmann N is the considerable side-play allowed between the wheelset and the actual truck. It is difficult to comprehend the need for such side-play on a swivelling truck, as all it does is look odd and allow the truck to shimmy excessively as the loco runs along the track. Accordingly, I added spacing washers to take up this play and centralise the truck between the wheels, as illustrated in photos 18 and 19.

Ancillary pipe-work

Bufferbeam plumbing aside, I found there were a couple of other bits of pipe-work to attend to on No 31843. The first was to replace the vacuum ejector pipe that runs along the offside of the boiler, which Bachmann make as a moulding in springy plastic. As is so often the case with such flexible plastic parts, my ejector pipe has assumed a graceful but unlikely-looking curve and generally lacked crispness, so I decided to make a straighter substitute in 0.9mm brass wire. I carefully removed the moulded pipe, which locates into holes in the cab-front at the rear end and in the smokebox side at the front, with two intermediate spigots in the firebox and boiler

sides. These, of course, broke off and had to be carefully drilled out, but the pipe came away cleanly at either end.

Using the discarded plastic pipe as a template, the replacement was carefully bent to shape from straight-drawn hard brass wire (from Alan Gibson), and the joints were represented by twists of 40-gauge wire as suggested in Chapter 7. New mounting spigots were made from fine split-pins closed down on to the wire, and the flange where the pipe enters the smokebox was made from a 12BA washer. No 31843 had a round flange here rather than the diamond-shaped version modelled by Bachmann, which was carved off. The completed pipe was secured with cyano, and is seen in picture 20.

Photo 21 shows the other piece of plumbing made for No 31843, the injectors – which Bachmann omit, which is about the only significant detail completely missing from the N, leaving aside fall-plates and cab doors. The fabrication of

these injectors from wire of various sorts and sizes, fine tube and small BA nuts featured in Chapter 7, so I am only illustrating the finished item here. They are located in place behind the cab steps, where they are held with Araldite. Note that these tricky little animals are different on either side, this being the fireman's side (exhaust steam) fitting.

Tender

Apart from the draw-gear modifications already described, I didn't find a great deal to do to the Mogul's tender. Added detail included the water-hoses at the front end – clearly visible in the heading shot of the completed loco; these were aligned to look as if they connected to the injectors, which is where they go in reality. At the rear of the tender, the bufferbeam gained vacuum standard and steam-heat connections as well as the wire coupler loop. I wasn't too struck with the rear lamp-irons, but decided that modification was not worthwhile, while I haven't so far provided a rear screw coupling. My main beef was with the coal load, which – as usual – was too flat and too full. The way this was modified to a 'part full' configuration is shown in Chapter 8. Last touches were re-coaling (including spillage) and a set of fire-irons on the rack.

Example 2: The Cockney Sparrow

The good old house sparrow is the most ubiquitous of British birds: anonymous, familiar, found just about everywhere, seemingly identical. If you had to pick a British steam locomotive that shared those same characteristics, then the subject of this little essay would be a strong contender. The LMS 'standard' general-purpose 3F 0-6-0 tank – 'Jinty' to

generations of enthusiasts – could be found in every corner of the sprawling LMS system, from Blandford Forum to Blair Atholl or King's Lynn to Llanfairpwllgwyngyllgogerychwyrndrobwllllantysiliogogogoch, and all points between.

At 412 examples, the 'Jinty' was the second largest class of main-line six-coupled tank engine in Britain after the GWR '57XX' pannier, to which it was closely comparable in terms of size, power and purpose. Standard and seemingly identical they may have been, but like the sparrows. The LMS 'Jinties' were a breed of individualists, full of quirks and oddities and entertaining little diversions. As is so often the case, when you start to focus on a particular individual you find a surprising number of deviations from what is supposed to be the norm.

The 'Cockney' tag in my title is occasioned by the layout for which this engine was wanted. 'Paradise Fields' is a small, 1950s-era P4 'shunting plank' based on a cramped urban goods depot set firmly in the heart of London's East End, within spitting distance of Spitalfields. Although basically former Great Eastern territory, this area is also threaded by former North London and London, Tilbury & Southend routes, which generated considerable goods exchange traffic and inter-depot trip working. So a 'Midland' engine was needed to work this traffic, and for a job like that at any time from the mid-1920s until the end of steam, by far the most likely contender would be – a 'Jinty'. But not just any old 'Jinty', mind; what I wanted was a true 'London Jinty', an engine from either the Tilbury or North London sections.

Here, for once, I had a stroke of luck. My first move, as always, was to accumulate a good selection of prototype reference material – which included the 'Profile' of the class published in the October 1994 edition of 'Morill' (*Modelling Railways Illustrated*), a well-illustrated feature including not one but two on-shed photos, one of each side, of 3F No 47306. The pictures were taken a year or two apart, the earlier in 1956 at Plaistow, the main London shed of the 'Tilbury'; the later in 1958 at Stratford, the main GE depot – to

which the engine had been reallocated in March 1958 during a rationalisation of steam facilities in East London.

This was enough of a cockney provenance for me! No 47306 has obviously been 'in shops' between the two pictures, as it has a different boiler and fittings in the later photo and has been repainted. I determined that this later picture – a lovely Dick Riley broadside colour view – would be my key reference, and that my model would conform as far as possible with this.

Cognoscenti of the breed will by now be muttering to themselves: "Ah! 47306, eh? That's a very early 'Jinty', one of the first 50 built by Hunslet." An engine, in other words, lacking the 'keyhole' sandbox filler opening in the side tanks, generally reckoned a signature feature of the species. Hornby's current body moulding, of course, boasts a very neat keyhole – unlike the earlier Margate versions of the model, into the virgin side-tanks of which, conscientious modellers of my vintage used to carve their own keyholes.

So it was just a little ironic that my problem was going to be getting rid of same and supplying the tank-top filler arrangement that preceded it! Not to mention reworking the cab roof rain strips and sundry other minor features… For No 47306 had another distinction, in that it was an example of the comparatively uncommon sub-species 'passenger Jinty' – a legacy of its original deployment on North London line suburban traffic.

This meant it possessed, in addition to the vacuum brake, screw (rather than lever) reverse, steam-heating apparatus, screw couplings, destination board brackets, and cab doors – most of which accoutrements it seems still to have possessed in the 1956 picture. In the later photo, it still has steam-heat but the destination board brackets have gone and there is no sign of any cab doors. This is significant; many 'shunting' 'Jinties' ran without doors at all, and even where fitted they were invariably fastened in the open position to facilitate easy footplate access. This is a drawback to the Bachmann body

moulding, which is modelled with cab doors in the closed position – something that is not easy to alter as Tim Shackleton found out when he re-worked a Bachmann 'Jinty' for *MRJ* issue 160. The Hornby body, by contrast, favours open doors, which is what I wanted for No 47306.

Ingredients for a model

Nowadays, the would-be 'Jinty' modeller in 4mm scale has a number of possible starting points. The most obvious and straightforward of these is the Bachmann RTR version, a relatively recent production that is on the modern mark mechanically and aesthetically. Hornby also offer an RTR 'Jinty', a considerably older and less-refined model with a rather outdated mechanism, while etched-brass/composite (resin boiler) kits figure in the London Road Models and Gibson ranges. The kit versions come complete with modern etched-frame chassis and offer alternative boiler mountings, coal rails and other details.

For a straightforward 00 model of the most common prototype variants, the Bachmann offering is undoubtedly the easiest way to go. Cab doors apart, the worst thing you will come up against is a change of chimney and/or dome and some fiddling about with vacuum/steam-heat pipes and coal rails. Brassmasters sell a detailing kit offering a selection of

alternative parts covering the more usual variations, although this does not come cheap. EM and P4 modellers can adapt the Bachmann chassis using conversion wheelsets from Alan Gibson or Ultrascale, although as is often the case, this is a bit of an aesthetic compromise, as the frames finish up a long way inside the wheels and the sandboxes end up looking rather odd.

The alternative is to mount either the Bachmann or Hornby moulded body on an aftermarket chassis kit by Comet or High Level. The Bachmann body is obviously the better bet but, as usual, is very hard to find as a spare and somewhat costly when you do. The Hornby moulding, although less refined, is fundamentally accurate and quite well detailed. It is also readily and cheaply available, either new as a spare, or second-hand in the form of a dud complete loco. At the cost of a bit of extra work, it forms a perfectly viable starting point for an authentic 'Jinty'. Using a kit chassis in combination with an RTR body enables you to incorporate a bespoke mechanical specification, with refinements like suspension and multi-stage gear trains.

As a refined mechanism with excellent slow-running qualities was a prime requirement for all the locos on 'Paradise Fields', that was the way I went with No 47306. The chassis I had to hand was Comet's no-frills affair, used in conjunction with a Mashima 1425 motor and a High Level Roadrunner Plus gearbox of 54:1 reduction ratio. Wheels are Gibson's, to P4 standards, and the suspension components are from London Road Models. I like to spread my patronage about, but on reflection the High Level chassis – which includes the gearbox – might have been the more economical option! It is also better-detailed than the Comet version, although, as we shall see, neither of them gives you a set of sandboxes – something no self-respecting 'Jinty' would be seen without!

Body not so beautiful

As for the body, Hornby's effort was the pragmatic choice – obtained as a new spare from an eBay supplier for £11. In the context of this book, it also offered more scope for demonstrating a variety of RTR-body reworking techniques as well as favouring open cab doorways. Apart from the obvious infilling below the boiler and the odd compromise by which the cab-doorway handrails are represented, Hornby have endowed their 'Jinty' with a dome that is not only quite unlike any of the patterns commonly fitted to the prototype, but lacks any skirt detail.

The bunker coal load and coal rails are also a touch unconvincing, while lamp-irons and tank-front steps and handrails are missing. But overall, the character of the prototype is quite well caught. Detail fittings for the 'Jinty' are widely available from several sources – although not, alas, the missing sandboxes. I used a Stanier-pattern chimney and twin Ross-pop-on-saddles from London Road Models and an Alan Gibson Deeley-pattern dome. Other bought-in components included etched screw couplings from Roxey, and turned brass wash-out plugs and a handful of short pattern handrail knobs from Gibson. All the rest was wire of various sizes, together with strip and sheet materials in both plastic and metal.

The job list

I will spare you the homespun pencil list and simply take an illustrated tour around the engine's anatomy, listing what needed to be done (in italics) and, where it is not obvious or covered in the preceding chapters, describing how I actually did it. It was sobering to realise, as I reread my notes while writing this, that I logged no fewer than 128 separate and discrete operations in turning the Hornby body and Comet chassis into an accurate model of No 47306! Although I have detailed the various cutting-away/discarding and making-good tasks under the appropriate sub-headings, in practice, I carried out all such work in a single operation, at the end of which my sparrow had hardly any feathers!

Chassis

Build from Comet chassis kit, compensated and to P4 standards, adjusting length to suit Hornby body.

I'm glad to report that No 47306's chassis caused no untoward problems in construction and the finished job runs as sweetly and slowly as could be desired. Many of the nuts and bolts of screwing this highly typical RTR replacement mechanism together were covered in Chapter 5, so at this juncture, I am only going to look at those aspects of the job not discussed there, starting with the preparation and erection of the frames.

Although Comet's frame design accommodates conventional hornblock suspension components as an option, it is biased

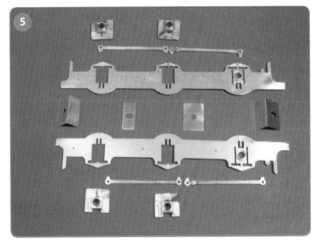

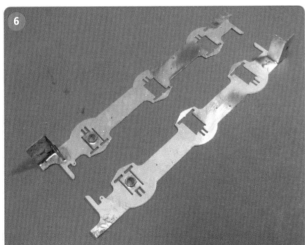

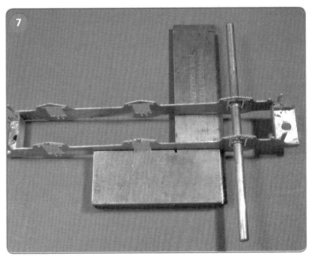

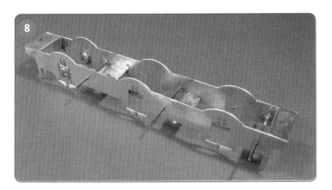

toward the use of coil springs rather than three-point equalisation with a beam – which means that there is no provision for a beam pivot. It is thus necessary to provide suitable pivot holes, located close to the upper edge of the frames midway between the leading pair of axles, as in the first picture of the sequence.

The second photo is a reminder of the basic chassis components – frames (trimmed for length to match the Hornby body) with matching rods, L-section spacers, turned-bush fixed axle bearings and, of course, the hornblock assemblies – by London Road Models, in this instance. The third shot shows the first stage in erecting the frames – soldering the two main end spacers in place, one to each mainframe. This is done to even out the heating of the frames during final assembly. Making one joint per frame rather than two joints on the same side helps avoid excessive heat build-up in one side of the chassis, leading to distortion problems (usually 'going banana') when the assembly cools down.

The frames were aligned – using a length of 1/8in rod and a square, as described in Chapter 5 – and tack-jointed together. Once I was sure all was tickety-boo, the joints were fully flowed and the intermediate spacers were installed. I also installed the brake top-pivot cross-rods at this juncture – which is useful chassis bracing. The centre portion of the rearmost rod was later cut away to clear the drivetrain. The last job was to try-fit the chassis to the Hornby body, and a few passes of the 6in flat file were needed at the fore end to adjust the fit between the bufferbeams.

The installation of the compensation components, wheeling-up and quartering, together with the assembly and installation of the Mashima/High Level drivetrain and the wiper pick-ups, were all covered in Chapter 5. Picture 10 shows the mechanically complete chassis undergoing bench testing and running in, which left only the cosmetic aspects of

the running gear to consider. To avoid clearance problems, the brake gear had been fitted before the pick-ups were installed, so the main task was to provide sanding gear – something omitted from both the Comet and High Level chassis kits. My solution was to fabricate sandboxes from Plastikard, using two layers of 60thou strip (a length of 0.060in x 0.150in and 0.060in square in each layer) laminated to a front face of .015in black sheet to make a suitable 0.210in x 0.135in (5mm x 3.5mm) section from which to cut the individual sandboxes. These were trimmed to length and shape with a craft knife, as in picture 12, and 0.45mm wire sand pipes were melted in.

The glands where the pipes entered the sandboxes were represented with some of the little turned-brass collars that Alan Gibson sells as retainers for his sprung wagon and coach buffers, and the completed sandboxes were glued in place on the frames using five-minute Araldite to give a margin of adjustment (in spite of which, I managed to get one box skewed and had to carve it off and refix it).

Photo 15 shows the more-or-less finished chassis, missing only wheel balance weights and paint. The rear sandbox on this side had to be cut off and refitted as it was none too upright!

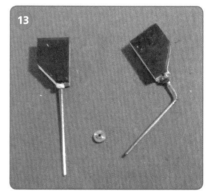

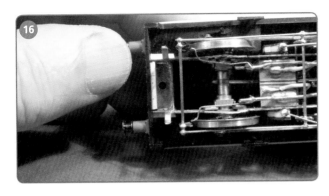

Body/chassis mounting
Fit locating guides and lip behind front bufferbeam to retain front of chassis. Build Plastikard bunker bottom to locate rear of chassis, with laminated Plastikard block above bunker floor to take self-tapping screw to anchor body.

Photos 16 and 17 give an idea of what this involved: locating 'fences' of 40-thou square Microstrip and a 60-thou square lip forward, and a footplate level bunker floor in 20thou Plastikard, drilled for a small self-tapping screw, aft. To give this screw something to 'bite' into, three layers of 40thou Plastikard were laminated to the top side of the bunker floor.

Footplate
Replace moulded-on footplate-edge overhang (nowhere near prominent enough). Dress mould part lines on front footplating. Make and fit fore-end footplate lamp-irons and add front sandbox fillers. Make overlay for valve chest inspection flap in front of smokebox (easier than filling in the locating holes for the original Hornby chassis). Make and fit steam-heat supply pipe beneath nearside footplate valencing. Cut off treads of footsteps and install new thinner-but-deeper step treads in .015in Plastikard, with angle detail from Microstrip.

Plenty to chew on here, but not all easy to illustrate. As can be seen from picture 18, Hornby represent the edge of the footplating with a much underfed moulded ridge. Given my intention to use overlays on the side tanks, these would end up being wider than the footplating, which would have looked most odd. My solution was to carve off Hornby's feeble ridge and replace it with edge-mounted .030in x .010in Microstrip, with .060in x .010in inserts

at the cab doorways where the prototype 'steps out' slightly to make a foothold. The new footplate edge was firmly welded on with MEK but is, inevitably, a bit fragile. Using .015in thickness rather than .010in would make a stronger job. Photo 19 shows this new edging, together with the steam-heat pipework below the valence.

Bufferbeams

Retain Hornby buffers and heads but cut off Hornby 'hook' and drill the centre of beam for the draw-hook. Fit coupler loop to front beam. Make and fit scale screw couplings. Make and fit vacuum standards and steam-heat connections at both ends.

All pretty straightforward, and very much as described in Chapter 7. Hornby's buffers may not be sprung, but they are nicely modelled and look the part, so I opted to leave them be. Photo 20 shows the completed front bufferbeam, together with the melted-in front lamp-irons and the cover plate for the valve chest, overlaid in shim brass. Note also the front sandbox filler lid by the base of the tank-front handrail. This is made from a 2mm diameter brass track rivet.

Boiler/smokebox

Remove and stow away safely the vacuum ejector moulding. Remove boiler and smokebox handrails, plug all handrail mounting holes except the foremost one each side of the smokebox. Remove turned safety valves and whistle. Open up in-filled 'daylight' area below boiler, make and fit boiler bottom. Cut off the chimney, dome, safety valve seating and mud-hole door covers from firebox shoulders and remove all boiler bands except the one immediately aft of the smokebox. Smooth all surfaces and eliminate the seam line from the smokebox top. Scribe the join line along boiler top centreline. Fit new boiler bands (paper) in correct locations. Drill holes in the firebox shoulders and fit Alan Gibson's turned-brass washout plugs. Make and fit smokebox top lamp-iron. Fit new cast-brass chimney, dome, twin pop valves on seating and whistle. Drill new holes as needed and fit new handrails to the smokebox front and smokebox/boiler sides. Find and refit vacuum ejector moulding.

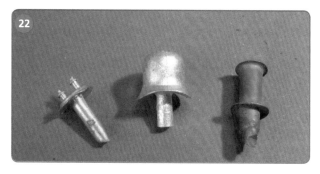

The boiler is, unsurprisingly, one of the main areas of operation in the body rework, calling for a lot of carving-away and smoothing before all the shiny new boiler fittings and other detail can be installed. Picture 21 shows the body at 'low ebb', with all the carving completed but before even the new footplate edging had been applied. The removal of the unwanted fittings and detail is described and illustrated in Chapter 6, as is the 'daylighting' of the boiler and fabrication of the boiler bottom segment. The new lost-wax cast boiler fittings – London Road chimney and safety valves, Gibson 'Deeley' dome – are illustrated in their raw state in photo 22.

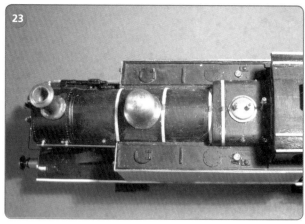

Photo 23 gives an overhead view of the reworked boiler, showing not only the reinstated boiler fittings, but also the scribed boiler-top seam and the new paper boiler-bands, complete with the clamps, represented by tiny slivers of Microrod. Note also the unwanted handrail-knob holes, plugged with plastic rod, and the replacement countersunk wash-out plugs. The lids of the tank-top sandbox fillers (the reason why this 'Jinty' has no tank-side 'keyholes') can also be seen, once again represented with 2mm diameter track rivets. The lost-wax brass whistle is another London Road Models casting.

Side tanks

Remove moulded tank-side top beading, file tank-sides flat. Cut and fit 10thou sheet brass or nickel-silver side-tank overlays with 0.45mm wire top beading soldered on, extended both ends to form mounts for cab doorway handrail pillars at the rear and returns around tank-fronts forward. Make and fit tank-front handrails, steps and lubricators. Add rear sandbox fillers to tank tops.

All pretty plain sailing, with the fitting of the tank-front detailing being the trickiest part, as can be seen in photo 20 opposite. The tank-side overlays, illustrated in photos 24 and 25, are quite straightforward to make – simple rectangles of metal 58mm x 17mm, with a straight length of 0.45mm brass wire soldered along the top edge and bent through 90° at one end to form the tank-front returns. I stuck mine in place with gel cyano, but a thin smear of epoxy would work as well and allow a bit more adjustment time to get everything 'just so'.

Bunker

Remove the moulded-on coal rails and coal load. Cut off moulded bunker lamp-irons, plug chassis locating hole in bunker rear. Build Plastikard bunker front (lower rear of cab) with shovelling plate detail. Cut bunker-side overlays from 10thou metal with 0.45mm beadings to match side tank overlays. Make Plastikard false bunker top with handbrake detail. Overlay bunker top in thin PCB and install etched coal-rails and coal deflector plate. Make and fit new bunker lamp-irons.

The work on the bunker is pretty bound up with that on the cab, especially the all-important cab doorways with their new slim-line handrail pillars, which are supported off the extended beadings of the tank and bunker-side overlays. The all-important overlays were made by the simple expedient of cutting two rectangular blanks of the right height, but over-long. These were then tack-soldered together to give a double thickness, and the required outline of the bunker rear transferred by laying the moulded body on top of the blank and drawing around it.

The blanks were cut roughly to shape with a piercing saw and finished with fine-cut files and plenty of trial-fitting. They were then separated, cleaned up and the wire top beading added as for the side tanks. I extended the rear of my beadings sufficiently to allow me to bend them through 90° to form a bunker-rear top beading in two halves that met in the middle of the bunker back. This was a nice idea, but proved a real pig to get aligned. It would be much simpler to add the bunker-rear beading as a separate piece of wire fixed with cyano.

The other main bunker task was the replacement of the moulded coal load and coal rails. The originals were hacked off with a razor saw, and a small rectangle of thin PCB sheet cut to overlay the plastic bunker top, to which it was attached with gel cyano. I used a set of Crownline etched coal rails with integral coal deflector as replacements. Suitable etchings come in the Brassmasters detailing pack, and historically have been obtainable from a number of sources. I used fine brass strip to extend the uprights of the rails and give nice long 'tails' which could be bent to sit nicely on top of the bunker

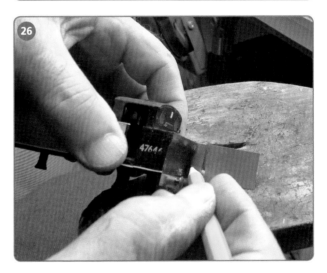

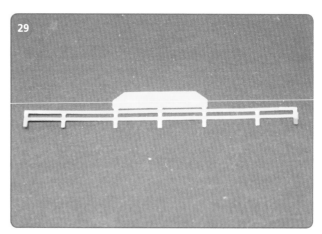

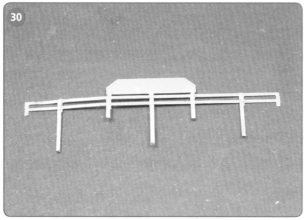

and soldered to the PCB bunker top, as in photos 29–31.

The remaining work on the bunker is the fitment of the bunker-rear detail: lamp-irons, bent to shape from brass strip and melted-in as described in Chapter 7, and the solitary offset step on the upper offside – plus the vacuum standard that properly

forms part of the bufferbeam detail. All this is illustrated in photo 32; the step is made from Plastikard Microstrip.

Cab

Remove the lower part of the fold-up cab interior, cut out the 'slab' handrails from the cab doorways. Carve off existing cab roof rain strips and smooth the cab roof, add new rain strips in correct location from Microstrip. Build up the height of the cab roof ventilator and add an overhanging 'lid', all in Plastikard. Remove the cab rear, cut off lower part to bunker top height. Build the cab floor side sections and supports along each side bridging the cab doorways. Make removable centre section of cab floor. Block in cab front around the motor and build false backhead to enclose/ conceal the gearbox. Make a detailed cosmetic backhead as an overlay to this. (This will end up too far back in cab, but that can be disguised by artfully positioning the loco crew). Paint all internal cab parts before installing.

Much of the trickiest work came in this area. The main problem is that, as with almost any moulded plastic tank loco

in transparent plastic, which is then mask-painted to leave the cab spectacles clear, may be a great production expedient – but makes it the devil of a job to alter the cab interior to make room for a gearbox or fit a proper cab floor.

My solution to this was to cut through the 'folds' of the Hornby moulding to reduce it to three parts, then I could discard the floor and trim off the cab-front and rear at tank-top and bunker-top levels. While I was in carving mode I also cut away the 'slab' handrail pillars from the cab doorways using a piercing saw as illustrated in the little sequence in photos 33–35. Care is needed here as the little strip of footplate left spanning the cab doorways is structurally vital!

The reconstruction of the cab started with the upper cab front being cemented in place and the lower part reinstated in Plastikard, accommodating the rear part of the High Level gearbox within a false boiler back – to which a cosmetic backhead would later be fitted. The footplate-level floor was installed beneath the bunker to provide the rear chassis mounting 'land' and extended far enough forward to support the rear part of the cab floor. This was made as a strip projecting some 8mm into the cab and suitably packed to get it to the right height, on which could then be mounted the bunker front (the lower section of the cab rear moulding).

The cab floor supports spanning the cab doorway, which on No 47306 have horizontal D-shaped cut-outs, were then cut from .020in Plastikard and cemented in place, followed by a narrow (5mm wide) section of floor down each side of the cab. That left a U-shaped area of floor missing, immediately behind and down either side of the boiler back. This floor section was made as a removable 'hatch', located by a lip at either side, which gave me access to the cab interior for painting and to install the cosmetic boiler back-plate. It will also serve as a mounting for the crew (when they book on!) and once I have finished the cab interior I will hold it in place with a couple of small strips of adhesive tape.

body, the cab structure of the 'Jinty' is inherently weak – which is why Bachmann's model has closed cab doors and you cannot take the roof off a Hornby one. Hornby's ingenious arrangement of combining the fixed roof with a cab front, cab floor and cab rear made as a single 'fold-up' clip-in moulding

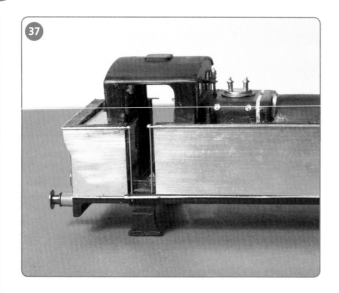

The new wire cabside handrail pillars could, at long last, now be installed, as in pictures 36 and 37. I melted the foot of each pillar into the footplating and touch-soldered the top to the extended beading on the tank and bunker-side overlays. If you don't fancy the melt-in location for the pillar bases, you can drill locating holes from beneath the footplate and secure the 0.5mm nickel-silver wire pillars with cyano.

The last job in the cab doorway area was to reinstate the cab steps in .015in Plastikard strip 2.5mm wide, with the step

flanges represented in .010in x .040in as illustrated in photo 38 – which also shows the D-shaped cut-out in the cab floor support and the step-out in the footplate at the cab doorway. The front footplate steps were similarly dealt with. This left the cab roof to re-detail with new twin rain-strips in the 'low-brow' position characteristic of early 'Jinties', together with a Plastikard cab ventilator modelled in the raised, open position seen in many photos. A 'Jinty' cab is very cramped and could easily get uncomfortably warm (photo 39–40).

Finishing

This completed the basic modelling work; all that remains to do before No 47306 can enter service is to hide the accumulated multitude of sins evident in my final picture with a coat of paint, some transfers and a spot of patination. I also need to add some final details: driving wheel balance weights (which I will cut from stiff paper and attached with cyano), the pre-painted cab backhead, and the all-important crew.

At the time of writing, this work remains to be completed. The paint job will be carried out with aerosols, using red oxide fine surface primer and Holt's satin black, which gives a reasonable livery black for an engine in good shape. No 47306 was not long out of shops in 1958. Transfers will be Methfix, and an etched smokebox door numberplate is on order. The final job will be to coal-up the bunker and add fire-irons to the nearside tank-top. In service, No 47306 will carry removable lamps displayed, of course, as appropriate to her duties. And that is very much what this model is – an appropriate engine for the job in hand, a true 'layout loco' if ever there was one.

Conclusion

Within the context of this book I only have space to explore these two basic examples. But if the foregoing has whetted your appetite for the business of loco-modelling with a moulded-plastic RTR superstructure as a basis, you can do no better than get hold of a copy of Tim Shackleton's inspiring work *Plastic Bodied Locos* (details in the Bibliography). This very much starts where the current essay leaves off, and includes truly heroic reworkings of everyday ingredients into highly realistic portrait models of true distinction and character. Apart from the practical advantages, there is always an additional satisfaction in creating such silken paragons from a comparatively porcine auricle! But whatever your aspirations or starting-point, come on in – the loco-modelling water's lovely!

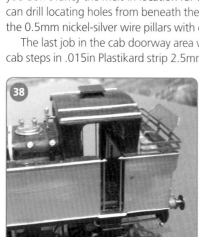

INDEX OF SUPPLIERS

Alan Gibson: Principal source of components including loco wheels and detail parts. Also wide range of etched/composite loco kits available to order. Downloadable catalogue in pdf form. Very good mail order service.
Alan Gibson, PO Box 597, OLDHAM, Lancashire, OL1 9FQ. 0161 678 1607.
http://www.alangibsonworkshop.com
e-mail: sales@alangibsonworkshop.com

Branchlines: Etched chassis kits, some detail parts, and the 'Multi-box' range of etched fold-up gearboxes and motor mounts. Supplier of Mashima motors.
Branchlines, PO Box 4293, WESTBURY, Wiltshire, BA13 9AA. 01373 822231.

Brassmasters: Locomotive details and detailing kits, also ingenious fold-up etched 'Easichas' chassis overlay/conversion kits (EM/P4) for RTR locos.
Brassmasters, PO Box 1137, SUTTON COLDFIELD, West Midlands, B76 1FU.
http://www.brassmasters.co.uk
e-mail: sales@brassmasters.co.uk

Charvo: Precision clear-cast acrylic glazing sheet in thicknesses from 0.3mm upwards.
Snaygill Industrial Estatee, Keighley Road, SKIPTON, North Yorkshire, BD23 2QR.
01756 795028.
http://www.charvo.co.uk

Comet Models: Etched loco chassis kits, gearboxes, detail parts, Supplier of Mashima motors. A primary source for the RTR loco-reworker. Good website.
Comet Models, 'Charnwood', Firs Road, ROSS-ON-WYE, Herefordshire, HR9 5BH.
05602 602188.
http://www.cometmodels.co.uk
e-mail: sales@cometmodels.co.uk

Craftsman: Straightforward etched-brass locomotive kits with pre-formed parts. Good website with downloadable pdf catalogue.
149 Landor Road, Whitnash, LEAMINGTON SPA, Warwickshire, CV31 2LF.
01926 428530 (10.00 – 16.00 hrs)
http://www.craftsmanmodels.co.uk

Dart Castings/ Monty's Model Railways:
Very good loco crew figures. Also supply MJT hornblock assemblies. Good website with secure online store.
Dart Castings, 17 Hurst Close, STAPLEHURST, Kent, TN12 0BX. 01580 892917
http://www.dartcastings.co.uk
e-mail: Enquiries@dartcastings.co.uk

Dave Bradwell: Sophisticated sprung etched RTR-replacement chassis kits biased towards EM/P4, some hi-end complete etched loco kits. Very good instructions.
South Muirnich Cottage, Gorthleck, INVERNESS, Highlands, IV1 2YP. 01456 486377.
Online listing hosted by the Scalefour Society:
http://www.scalefour.org/DaveBradwell

Eileen's Emporium: Prime source for tools and modelling materials, nuts and bolts chemical blackening fluids. Comprehensive website with secure online store.
Unit 19.12 Highnam Business Center, Newent Road, GLOUCESTER, GL2 8DN.
01531 828009.
https://www.eileensemporium.com
E-mail: sales@eileensemporium.com

DJH: Range of cast whitemetal and composite cast/etched loco kits including some useful prototypes. Good website with secure online store.
DJH Model Loco, Project House, Consett Business Park, Villa Real, CONSETT, Co. Durham DH8 6BP. 01207 500050
http://www.djhmodelloco.co.uk

East Kent Models: Comprehensive source of RTR spares including Hornby/Dapol and some Bachmann loco bodies. No site but stocklist available on request by e-mail.
East Kent Models, 89 High Street, WHITSTABLE, Kent CT5 1AY.
01227 770777 (Mon-Sat 09.30 – 17.30hrs.)
E-mail: ekmodels@hotmail.com

Fox Transfers: Wide range of decals covering locomotive lettering, lining and insignia for the 'grouped' era and BR steam. Website includes secure online store.
Fox Transfers, 4 Hill Lane Close, Markfield Industrial Estate, MARKFIELD, Leicestershire LE67 9PN.
0844 815 9711.
(09.00 – 18.00hrs Mon-Fri)
http://www.fox-transfers.co.uk
E-mail: sales@fox-transfers.co.uk

High Level: Wide range of gearboxes, ratios from 30:1 to 108:1, many configurations. hornblock system, etched chassis kits 00/EM/P4 for some RTR locos, small range of very high quality etched loco kits mostly for industrial subjects Supplier of Mashima motors.
14 Tudor Road, CHESTER-le-STREET, Co. Durham DH3 3RY.
01913 882112 (09.00 – 17.00 hrs).
http://www.highlevelkits.co.uk

HMRS Transfers: Methfix and Pressfix numbering/lettering and lining transfers. Printable order form, mail order by post only. Cards accepted.
HMRS Transfers, 8 Gilpin Green, HARPENDEN, Herts, AL5 5NR
http://www.hmrs.org.uk/transfers/list.php

Just Like the Real thing: Aerosol cellulose livery paints. Now being replaced by the new LifeColor sprayable acrylic paints, which include dedicated weathering shades.
JLTRT, 24-26 Whittle Place, South Newmoor Industrial Estate, IRVINE, Ayrshire KA11 4HR.
01224 222988.
http://www.justliketherealthing.co.uk

London Road Models: Extensive range of etched kits for mostly older prototypes; detail parts, suspension components, gearboxes and gears. Old-fashioned mail order only! E-mail contact available via website.
London Road Models, PO Box 643, WATFORD, Herts,WD24 5ZJ
Website (hosted by the Scalefour Society):
http://www.scalefour.org/LondonRoadModels

Mainly Trains: Etched chassis for RTR locos and tender bodies, materials, sundries and detail parts! Swift mail order, secure online store.
Mainly Trains, PO Box 50, WATCHET, Somerset TA23 0WQ.
01278 741333 (Mon-Thurs otherwise answerphone).
http://www.mainlytrains.co.uk

Markits/Romford: 00/EM driving wheels and accessories. Also etched balance weights and other detail parts, sprung buffers, handrail stanchions and smokebox door handles. Only a basic website but includes a downloadable catalogue/price.
P.O.Box 40, WATFORD, Herts, WD24 6TN.
01923 249711. http://www.markits.com

00Works: Batch-built RTR locomotives in 00 gauge only. Very limited availability. 00 Works/ Roderick Bruce, 'Brendon', Langham Road, ROBERTSBRIDGE, East Sussex TN32 5DT.
01580 882183.

PDK Models: Range of straightforward mostly LNER- and Southern-prototype etched locomotive kits, including some very useful subjects.
PDK Models, 8 Rame Terrace, Rame Cross, PENRYN, Cornwall TR10 9DZ.
01209 861130.
http://www.pdkmodels.co.uk
E-mail: pdkmodels@hotmail.co.uk

Index of suppliers (continued)

Phoenix Precision Paints: Very extensive range of dedicated authentic railway colours in sprayable oil-base enamel. Available in tinlets and aerosols. Secure online store.
Phoenix Precision Paints Ltd, PO Box 8238, CHELMSFORD, Essex CM1 7WY.
01268 730594.
http://www.phoenix-paints.co.uk

Roxey Mouldings: Detail parts including etched screw couplings and SR headcode discs. Albion Models range of etched loco kits. Supplier of Mashima motors and gears/mounts.
Roxey Mouldings, 58 Dudley Road, WALTON ON THAMES, Surrey KT12 2JU.
01932 245439.
http://www.roxeymouldings.co.uk
E-mail: dave@roxeymouldings.co.uk

Shawplan Model Products: Mostly cater for the diesel-era modeller but now have laser-cut glazing for a few RTR steam locos.
2 Upper Dunstead Road, Langley Mill, NOTTINGHAM, NG16 4GR. 01773 718468
http://www.shawplan.com
E-mail: brian@shawplan.com

South Eastern Finecast: Comprehensive range of cast-whitemetal locomotive kits with etched chassis, based on the old Wills range but now updated and extended.
South-Eastern Finecast, Glenn House, Hartfield Road, FOREST ROW, West Sussex RH18 5DZ.
01342 824711.
http://www.sefinecast.co.uk

Springside Models: 4mm loco details including etched balance weights, screw and link couplings and (very good) GWR boiler mountings. Jewelled locomotive lamps.
Springside Models, 2 Springside Cottages, Dornafield Road, Ipplepen, NEWTON ABBOT, Devon TQ12 5SJ. 01803 813749
http://www.springsidemodels.com

Ultrascale: Fine scale (fine 00/EM or P4) locomotive driving wheels and drop-in wheel/gear conversions for RTR locos. High quality gears,
Gear Services (Letchworth) Ltd., Unit 25, Such Close 2 Industrial Estate, LETCHWORTH, Herts SG6 1JF. 01462 681007.
http://www.ultrascale.com

247 Developments: Extensive range of etched brass locomotive name, number, works and shed allocation plates. Non-listed plates produced to special order. Also detail parts.
247 Developments, Seven Acres, Meltham Road, MARSDEN, West Yorkshire HD7 6JZ.
01484 840996.
http://www.247developments.co.uk

UK Model Shop Directory: Useful portal site listing wide range of UK-based model railway suppliers and manufacturers.
http://www.ukmodelshops.co.uk

Please note: *Unless specifically advised to the contrary on a website please don't call on suppliers, particularly at private addresses, without making prior arrangements. Listings current to November 2012. Errors and omissions excepted.*

BIBLIOGRAPHY

General prototype information

Books

The British Steam Locomotive 1825–1925, E.L. Ahrons (Loco Publishing Co, 1927).
The Locomotive of Today (8th edn), ed. W.J. Bell (Loco Publishing Co, 1927).
British Locomotives, C.J. Bowen-Cooke (Whittaker & Co, 1893).
British Locomotive Practice 1900–1908, Proceedings of the Institution of Mechanical Engineers (I.M.E., 1908).
Our Home Railways, Vols 1 and 2, W.J. Gordon (Warnes, 1910).
The Railways of England, W.M. Acworth (John Murray, 1900).
Locomotive Management (8th edn), Hodgson and Lake (St Margarets Technical Press, 1942).
Locomotive Manufacturers Association Handbook (Locomotive Manufacturers Association, 1949).
British Steam Railways, O.S. Nock (A & C Black, 1961).
British Locomotives of the 20th Century, Vols 1 and 2, O.S. Nock (Patrick Stephens Limited, 1984).
Locomotive and Train Working in the Latter Part of the Nineteenth Century, Vols 1, 2, 4 & 5, E.L. Ahrons (Heffer and Sons, 1952), (extracted from *The Railway Magazine* 1900–1928).
British Steam Since 1900, Dr W.A. Tuplin (David and Charles, 1969).
Scottish Locomotive History 1831–1923, Campbell Highet (George, Allen and Unwin, 1970).

Other

The Locomotive Magazine, various editions, 1897–1930.
The Railway Magazine, various editions 1901–1967.
British Railways Rule Book (1951).
Various working timetables and traffic notices covering train working and locomotive usage.
Great Western Locomotive Allocations 1921 and 1934, Harrison and Pocock (Wild Swan Publications).
'Shed by Shed' BR loco allocation series, parts 1 (LMR), 2 (ER), 3 (NER), 4 (Scottish), 5 (SR) and 6 (WR), Tony Walmsley (St. Petrock InfoPublishing).

Modelling titles

Miniature Locomotive Construction, John Ahern (Percival, Marshall, 1948).
Model Locomotive Construction in 4mm Scale, R Guy Williams (Ian Allan, 1979).
Locomotive Kit Chassis Construction in 4mm, Iain Rice (Wild Swan Publications, 1993).
Plastic Bodied Locos, Tim Shackleton (Wild Swan Publications, 1999).
Whitemetal Locos: a Kitbuilder's Guide, Iain Rice (Wild Swan Publications, 1989).
A Modeller's Handbook of Painting and Lining, Ian Rathbone (Wild Swan Publications, 2008).
Aspects of Modelling – Weathering Locomotives, Tim Shackleton (Ian Allan, 2010).

INDEX